EXILED

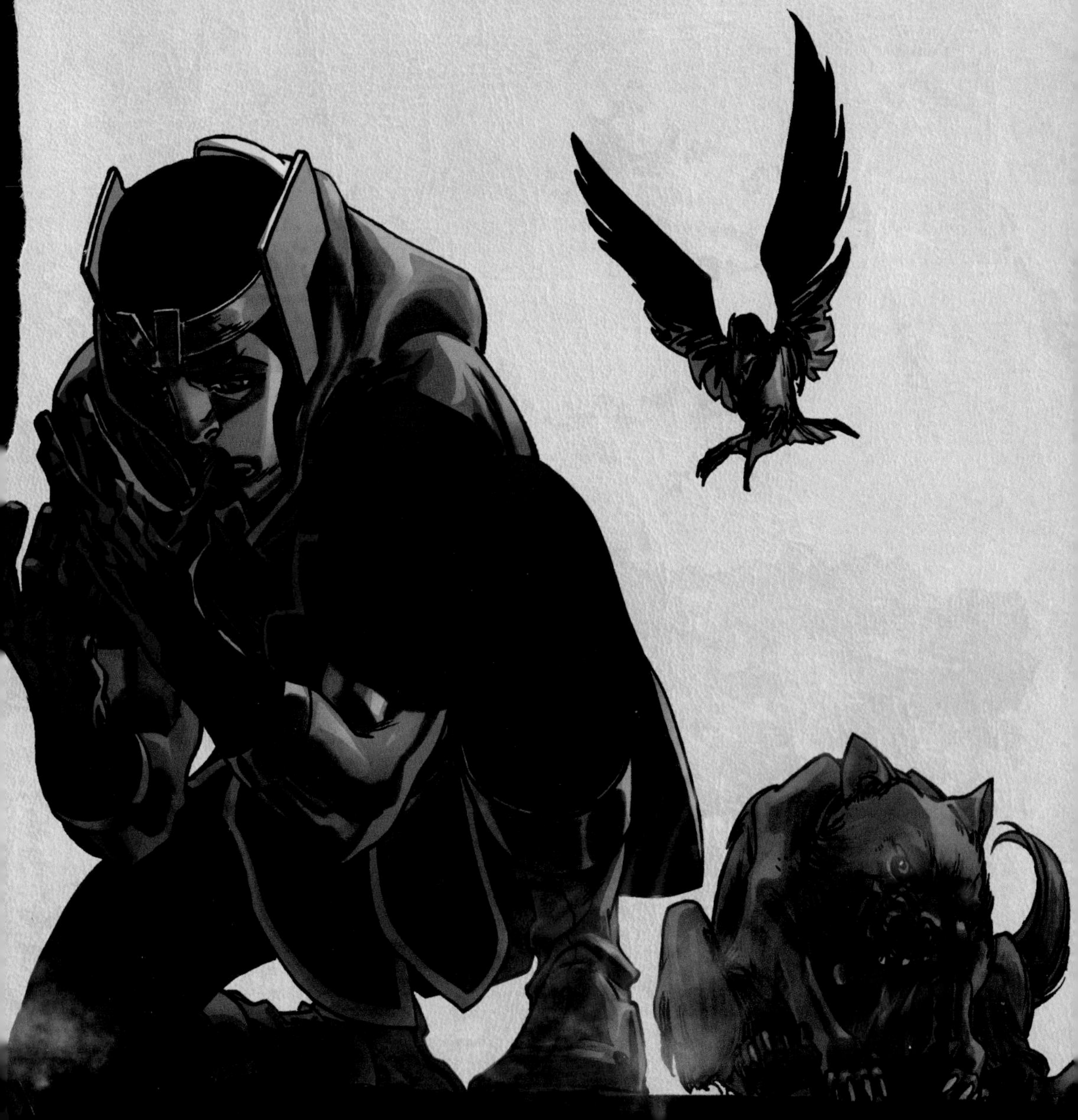

Writers
Kieron Gillen, Dan Abnett & Andy Lanning

Artist
Carmine Di Giandomenico

Color Artist:
Andy Troy
with SOTOCOLOR (Journey Into Mystery #638)

Letterer
VC's Clayton Cowles

Cover Artist
Stephanie Hans

Assistant Editors
John Denning & Jake Thomas

Editors
Lauren Sankovitch & Bill Rosemann

Special Thanks to SEBASTIAN GIRNER

JOURNEY INTO MYSTERY/NEW MUTANTS: EXILED. Contains material originally published in magazine form as EXILED #1, NEW MUTANTS #42-43 and JOURNEY INTO MYSTERY #637-638. First printing 2012. ISBN# 978-0-7851-6540-8. Published by MARVEL WORLDWIDE, INC., a subsidiary of MARVEL ENTERTAINMENT, LLC. OFFICE OF PUBLICATION: 135 West 50th Street, New York, NY 10020. Copyright © 2012 Marvel Characters, Inc. All rights reserved. $16.99 per copy in the U.S. and $18.99 in Canada (GST #R127032852); Canadian Agreement #40668537. All characters featured in this issue and the distinctive names and likenesses thereof, and all related indicia are trademarks of Marvel Characters, Inc. No similarity between any of the names, characters, persons, and/or institutions in this magazine with those of any living or dead person or institution is intended, and any such similarity which may exist is purely coincidental. **Printed in the U.S.A.** ALAN FINE, EVP - Office of the President, Marvel Worldwide, Inc. and EVP & CMO Marvel Characters B.V.; DAN BUCKLEY, Publisher & President - Print, Animation & Digital Divisions; JOE QUESADA, Chief Creative Officer; TOM BREVOORT, SVP of Publishing; DAVID BOGART, SVP of Operations & Procurement, Publishing; RUWAN JAYATILLEKE, SVP & Associate Publisher, Publishing; C.B. CEBULSKI, SVP of Creator & Content Development; DAVID GABRIEL, SVP of Publishing Sales & Circulation; MICHAEL PASCIULLO, SVP of Brand Planning & Communications; JIM O'KEEFE, VP of Operations & Logistics; DAN CARR, Executive Director of Publishing Technology; SUSAN CRESPI, Editorial Operations Manager; ALEX MORALES, Publishing Operations Manager; STAN LEE, Chairman Emeritus. For information regarding advertising in Marvel Comics or on Marvel.com, please contact Niza Disla, Director of Marvel Partnerships, at ndisla@marvel.com. For Marvel subscription inquiries, please call 800-217-9158. **Manufactured between 9/13/2012 and 10/16/2012 by QUAD/GRAPHICS, DUBUQUE, IA, USA.**

10 9 8 7 6 5 4 3 2 1

Collection Editor: Cory Levine
Assistant Editors: Alex Starbuck & Nelson Ribeiro
Editors, Special Projects: Jennifer Grünwald & Mark D. Beazley
Senior Editor, Special Projects: Jeff Youngquist
Senior Vice President of Sales: David Gabriel
SVP of Brand Planning & Communications: Michael Pasciullo
Book Design: Jeff Powell

Editor In Chief: Axel Alonso
Chief Creative Officer: Joe Quesada
Publisher: Dan Buckley
Executive Producer: Alan Fine

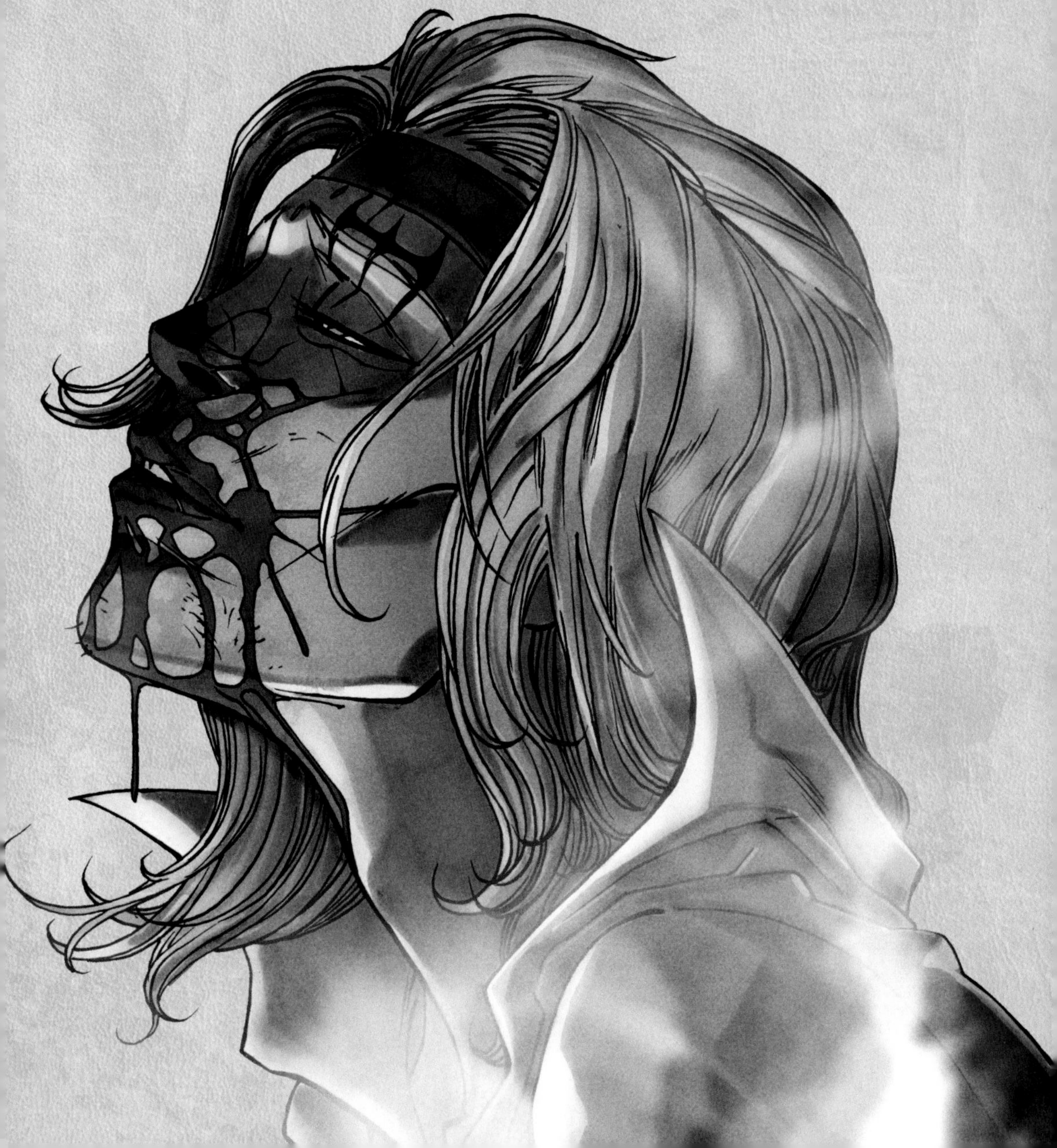

EXILED

NEW MUTANTS

AS AN ELITE MUTANT STRIKE FORCE, THE NEW MUTAN
WALK A NARROW ROAD, SEEKING COMMON GROUND W
HUMANS BY TRYING TO LIVE A NORMAL LIFE AMONG THEM

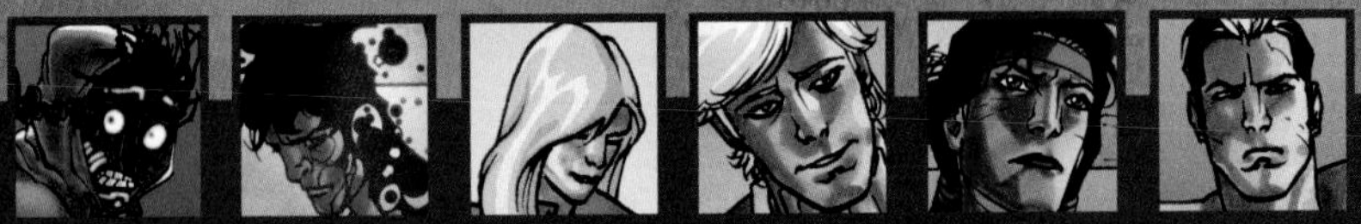

WARLOCK SUNSPOT MAGMA CYPHER DANI X-MAN

JOURNEY INTO MYSTERY

IN A FLOATING CITY HIGH ABOVE THE EARTH'S SURFACE, T
ASGARDIANS ARE LIVING GODS WHO SEEK TO INSPIRE THE VE
BEST IN HUMANITY.

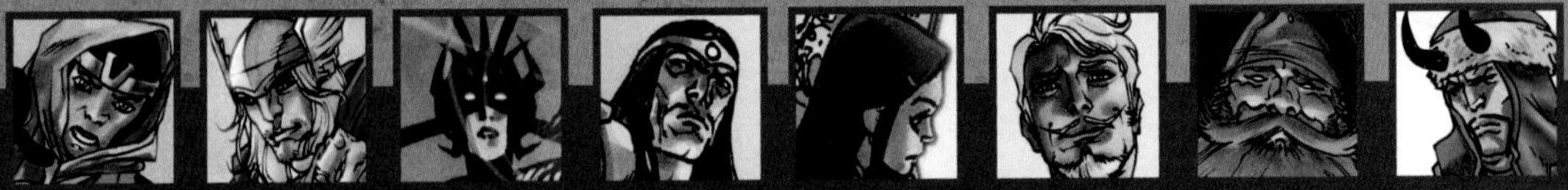

LOKI THOR HELA TYR LEAH FANDRAL VOLSTAGG HOGUN

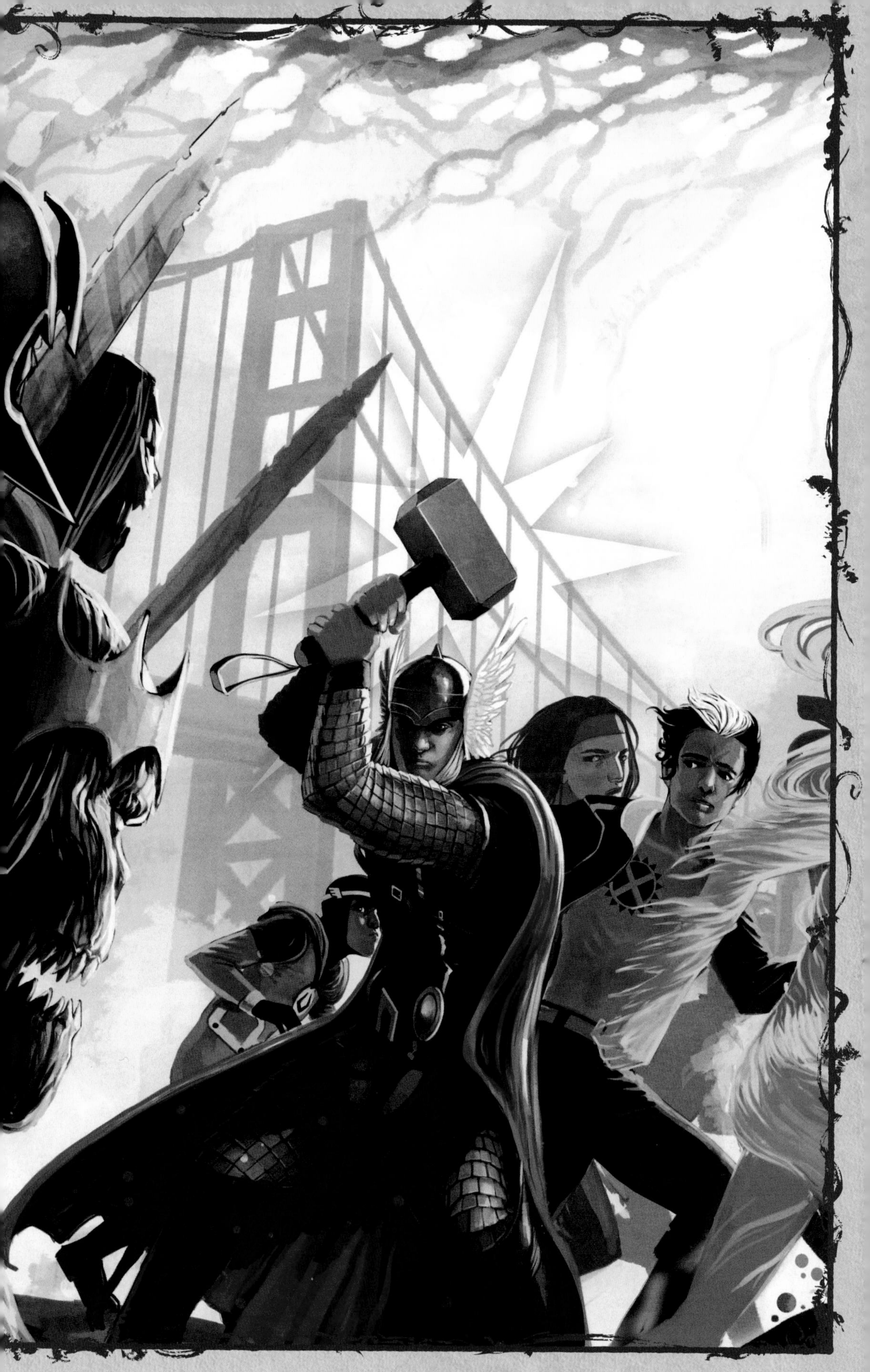

EXILED #1: "OF GODS AND X-MEN"

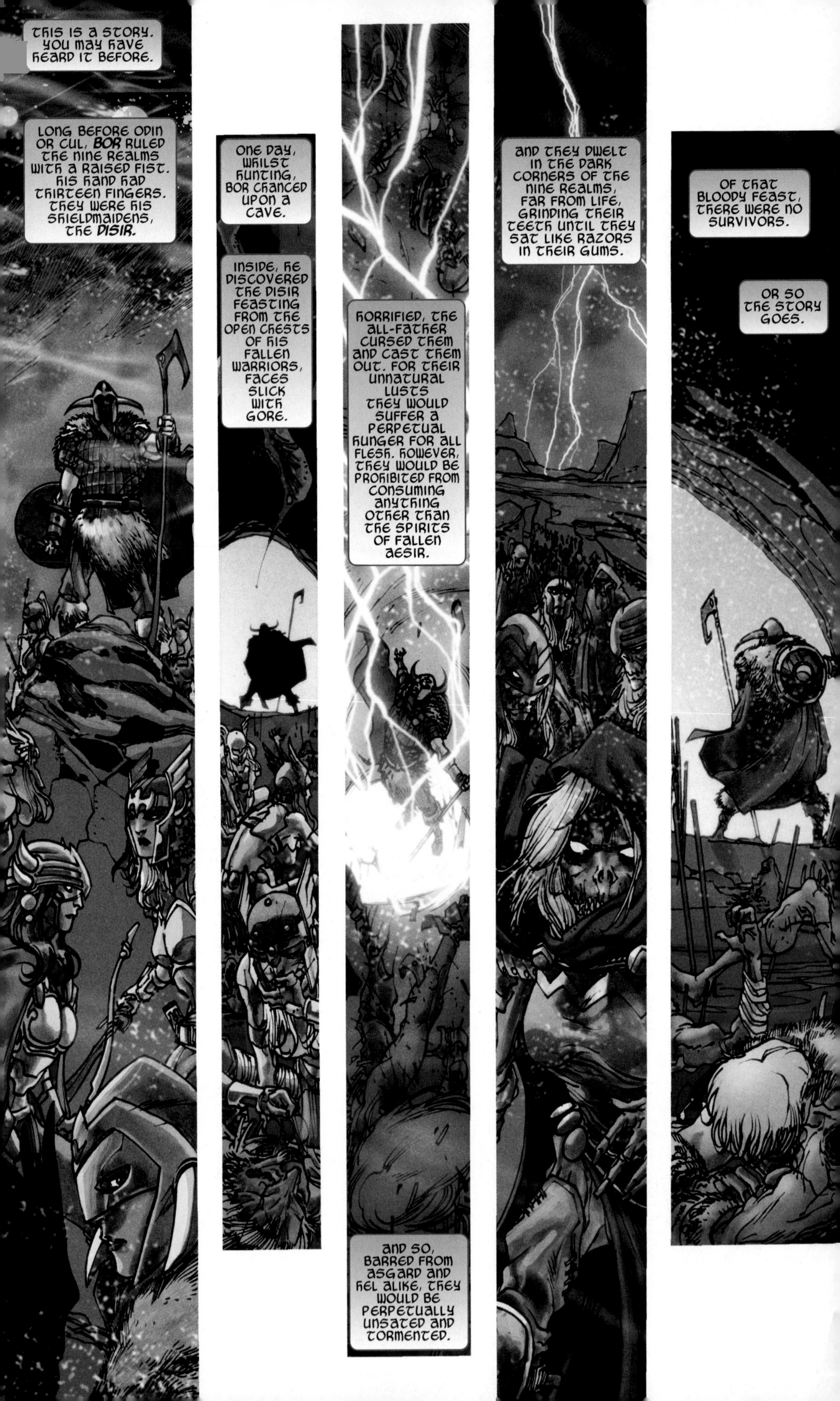

THIS IS A STORY. YOU MAY HAVE HEARD IT BEFORE.
LONG BEFORE ODIN OR CUL, BOR RULED THE NINE REALMS WITH A RAISED FIST. HIS HAND HAD THIRTEEN FINGERS. THEY WERE HIS SHIELDMAIDENS, THE DISIR.
ONE DAY, WHILST HUNTING, BOR CHANCED UPON A CAVE.
INSIDE, HE DISCOVERED THE DISIR FEASTING FROM THE OPEN CHESTS OF HIS FALLEN WARRIORS, FACES SLICK WITH GORE.
HORRIFIED, THE ALL-FATHER CURSED THEM AND CAST THEM OUT. FOR THEIR UNNATURAL LUSTS THEY WOULD SUFFER A PERPETUAL HUNGER FOR ALL FLESH. HOWEVER, THEY WOULD BE PROHIBITED FROM CONSUMING ANYTHING OTHER THAN THE SPIRITS OF FALLEN AESIR.
AND SO, BARRED FROM ASGARD AND HEL ALIKE, THEY WOULD BE PERPETUALLY UNSATED AND TORMENTED.
AND THEY DWELT IN THE DARK CORNERS OF THE NINE REALMS, FAR FROM LIFE, GRINDING THEIR TEETH UNTIL THEY SAT LIKE RAZORS IN THEIR GUMS.
OF THAT BLOODY FEAST, THERE WERE NO SURVIVORS.
OR SO THE STORY GOES.

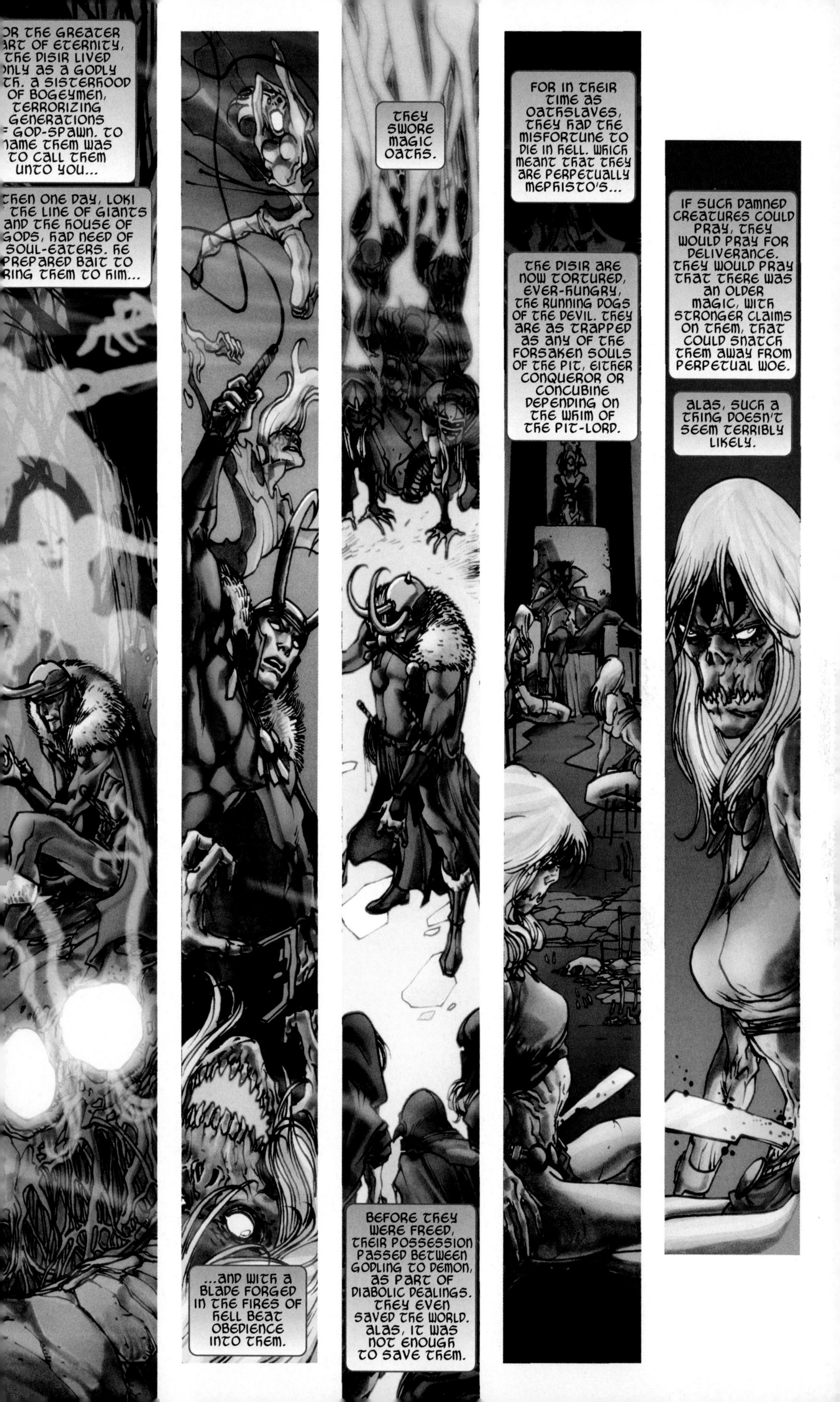

OR THE GREATER ART OF ETERNITY, THE DISIR LIVED ONLY AS A GODLY TH. A SISTERHOOD OF BOGEYMEN, TERRORIZING GENERATIONS F GOD-SPAWN. TO NAME THEM WAS TO CALL THEM UNTO YOU...
THEN ONE DAY, LOKI THE LINE OF GIANTS AND THE HOUSE OF GODS, HAD NEED OF SOUL-EATERS. HE PREPARED BAIT TO RING THEM TO HIM...
...AND WITH A BLADE FORGED IN THE FIRES OF HELL BEAT OBEDIENCE INTO THEM.
THEY SWORE MAGIC OATHS.
BEFORE THEY WERE FREED, THEIR POSSESSION PASSED BETWEEN GODLING TO DEMON, AS PART OF DIABOLIC DEALINGS. THEY EVEN SAVED THE WORLD. ALAS, IT WAS NOT ENOUGH TO SAVE THEM.
FOR IN THEIR TIME AS OATHSLAVES, THEY HAD THE MISFORTUNE TO DIE IN HELL. WHICH MEANT THAT THEY ARE PERPETUALLY MEPHISTO'S...
THE DISIR ARE NOW TORTURED, EVER-HUNGRY, THE RUNNING DOGS OF THE DEVIL. THEY ARE AS TRAPPED AS ANY OF THE FORSAKEN SOULS OF THE PIT, EITHER CONQUEROR OR CONCUBINE DEPENDING ON THE WHIM OF THE PIT-LORD.
IF SUCH DAMNED CREATURES COULD PRAY, THEY WOULD PRAY FOR DELIVERANCE. THEY WOULD PRAY THAT THERE WAS AN OLDER MAGIC, WITH STRONGER CLAIMS ON THEM, THAT COULD SNATCH THEM AWAY FROM PERPETUAL WOE.
ALAS, SUCH A THING DOESN'T SEEM TERRIBLY LIKELY.

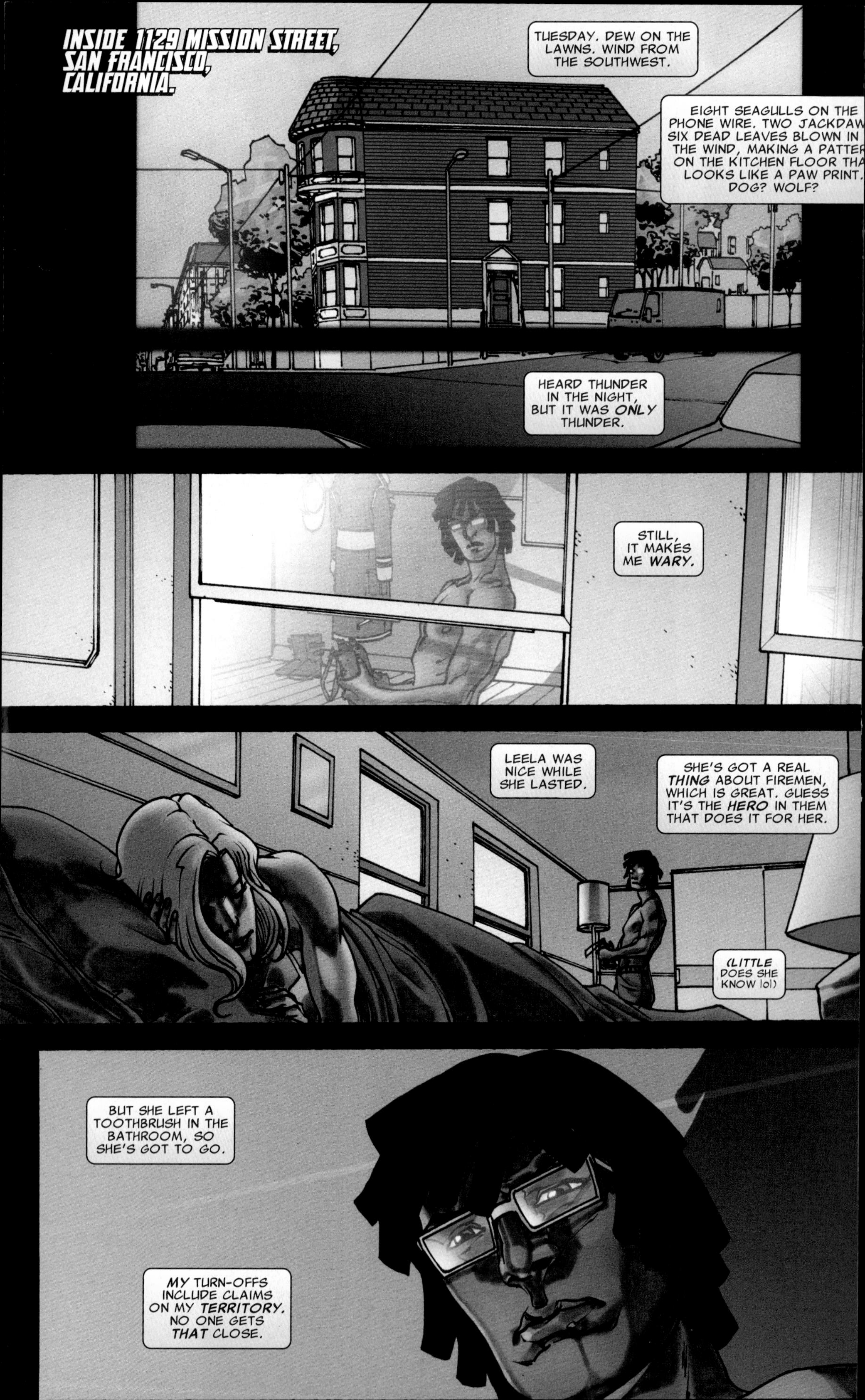
INSIDE 1129 MISSION STREET, SAN FRANCISCO, CALIFORNIA.
TUESDAY. DEW ON THE LAWNS. WIND FROM THE SOUTHWEST.
EIGHT SEAGULLS ON THE PHONE WIRE. TWO JACKDAW SIX DEAD LEAVES BLOWN IN THE WIND, MAKING A PATTER ON THE KITCHEN FLOOR THA LOOKS LIKE A PAW PRINT. DOG? WOLF?
HEARD THUNDER IN THE NIGHT, BUT IT WAS ONLY THUNDER.
STILL, IT MAKES ME WARY.
LEELA WAS NICE WHILE SHE LASTED.
SHE'S GOT A REAL THING ABOUT FIREMEN, WHICH IS GREAT. GUESS IT'S THE HERO IN THEM THAT DOES IT FOR HER.
(LITTLE DOES SHE KNOW lol)
BUT SHE LEFT A TOOTHBRUSH IN THE BATHROOM, SO SHE'S GOT TO GO.
MY TURN-OFFS INCLUDE CLAIMS ON MY TERRITORY. NO ONE GETS THAT CLOSE.

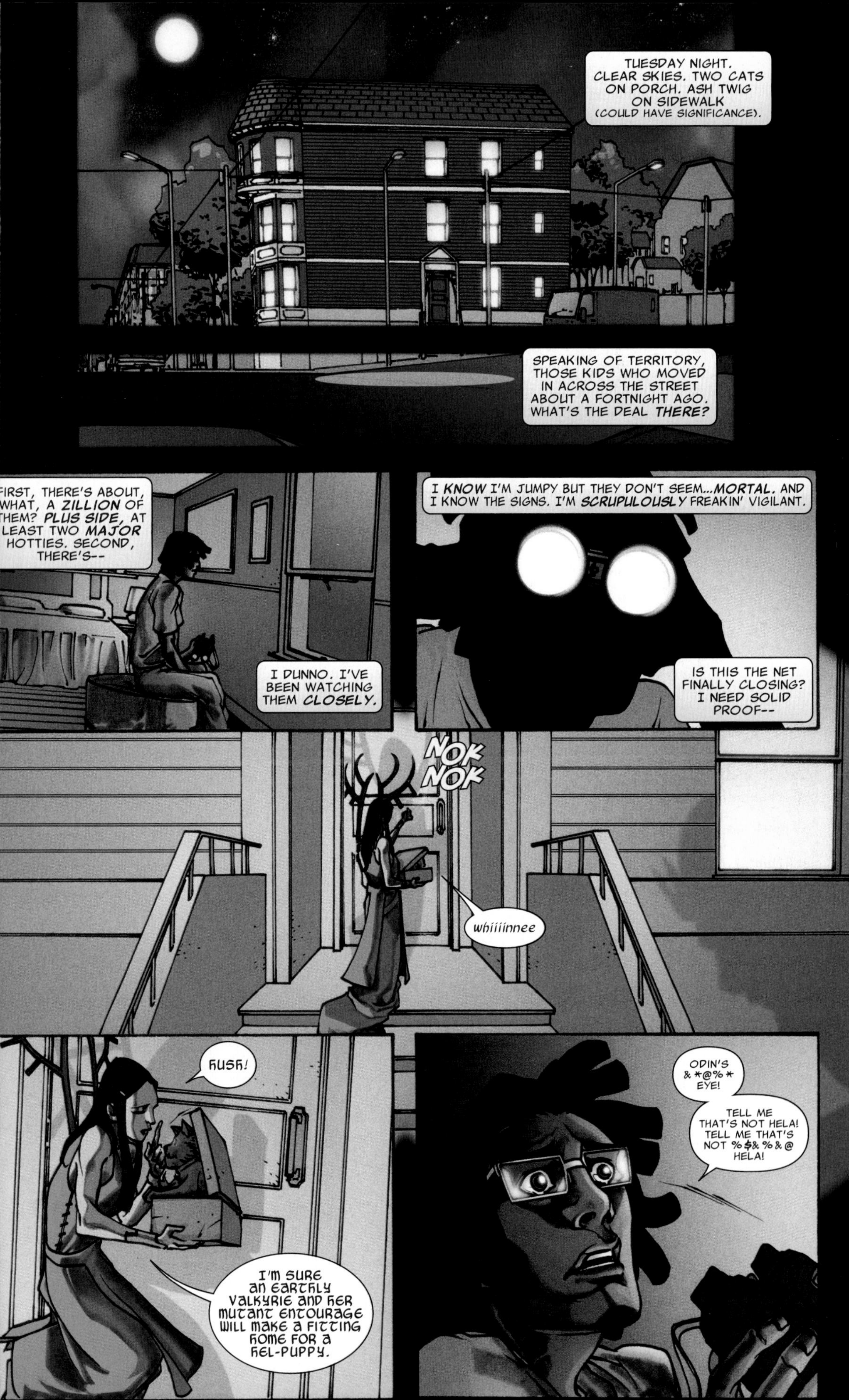
TUESDAY NIGHT. CLEAR SKIES. TWO CATS ON PORCH. ASH TWIG ON SIDEWALK (COULD HAVE SIGNIFICANCE).
SPEAKING OF TERRITORY, THOSE KIDS WHO MOVED IN ACROSS THE STREET ABOUT A FORTNIGHT AGO. WHAT'S THE DEAL THERE?
FIRST, THERE'S ABOUT, WHAT, A ZILLION OF THEM? PLUS SIDE, AT LEAST TWO MAJOR HOTTIES. SECOND, THERE'S--
I DUNNO. I'VE BEEN WATCHING THEM CLOSELY.
I KNOW I'M JUMPY BUT THEY DON'T SEEM...MORTAL. AND I KNOW THE SIGNS. I'M SCRUPULOUSLY FREAKIN' VIGILANT.
IS THIS THE NET FINALLY CLOSING? I NEED SOLID PROOF--
NOK NOK
whiiiinnee
HUSH!
I'M SURE AN EARTHLY VALKYRIE AND HER MUTANT ENTOURAGE WILL MAKE A FITTING HOME FOR A HEL-PUPPY.
ODIN'S &*@%* EYE!
TELL ME THAT'S NOT HELA! TELL ME THAT'S NOT %$&%&@ HELA!

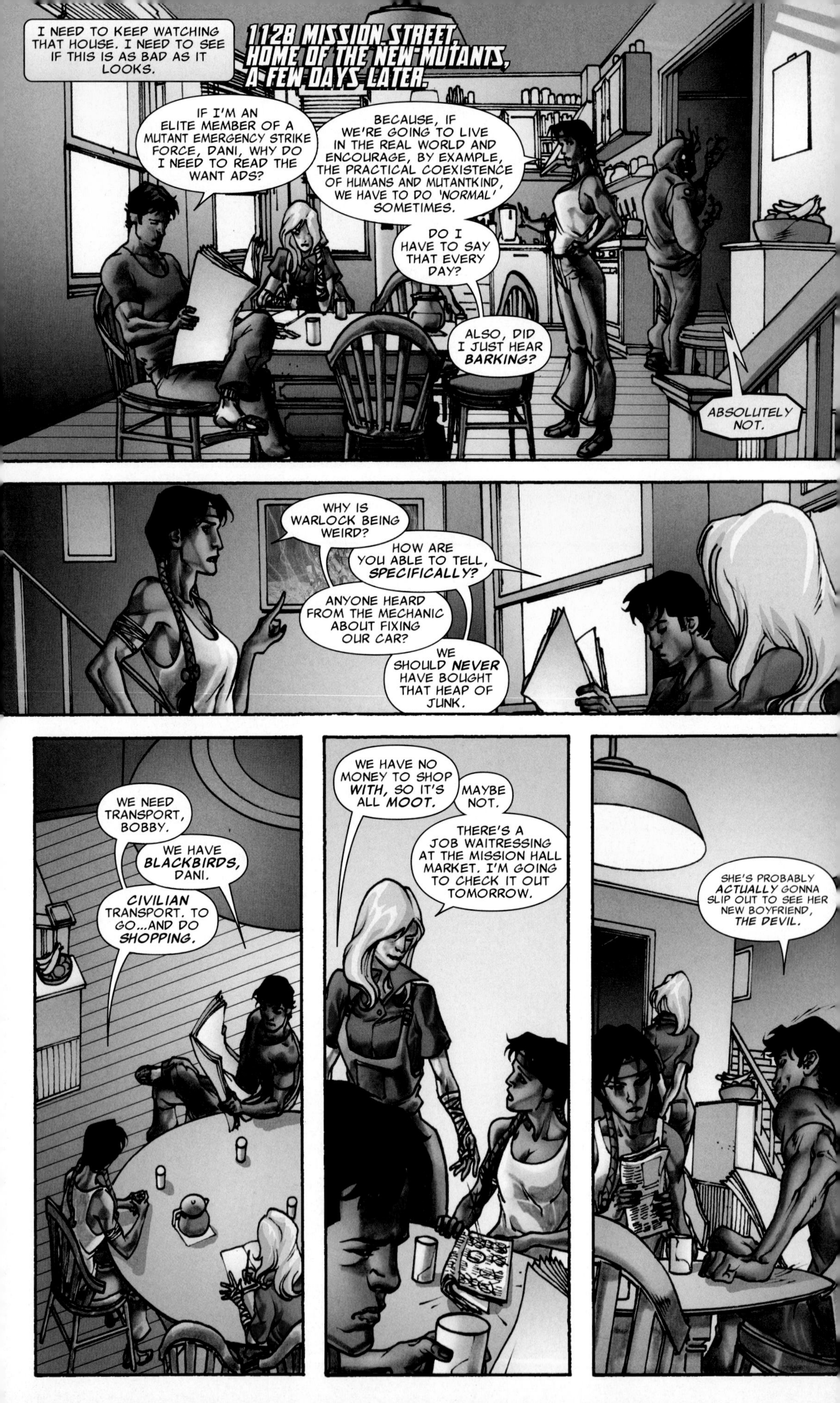
I NEED TO KEEP WATCHING THAT HOUSE. I NEED TO SEE IF THIS IS AS BAD AS IT LOOKS.
1128 MISSION STREET, HOME OF THE NEW MUTANTS, A FEW DAYS LATER.
IF I'M AN ELITE MEMBER OF A MUTANT EMERGENCY STRIKE FORCE, DANI, WHY DO I NEED TO READ THE WANT ADS?
BECAUSE, IF WE'RE GOING TO LIVE IN THE REAL WORLD AND ENCOURAGE, BY EXAMPLE, THE PRACTICAL COEXISTENCE OF HUMANS AND MUTANTKIND, WE HAVE TO DO 'NORMAL' SOMETIMES.
DO I HAVE TO SAY THAT EVERY DAY?
ALSO, DID I JUST HEAR BARKING?
ABSOLUTELY NOT.
WHY IS WARLOCK BEING WEIRD?
HOW ARE YOU ABLE TO TELL, SPECIFICALLY?
ANYONE HEARD FROM THE MECHANIC ABOUT FIXING OUR CAR?
WE SHOULD NEVER HAVE BOUGHT THAT HEAP OF JUNK.
WE NEED TRANSPORT, BOBBY.
WE HAVE BLACKBIRDS, DANI.
CIVILIAN TRANSPORT. TO GO...AND DO SHOPPING.
WE HAVE NO MONEY TO SHOP WITH, SO IT'S ALL MOOT.
MAYBE NOT.
THERE'S A JOB WAITRESSING AT THE MISSION HALL MARKET. I'M GOING TO CHECK IT OUT TOMORROW.
SHE'S PROBABLY ACTUALLY GONNA SLIP OUT TO SEE HER NEW BOYFRIEND, THE DEVIL.

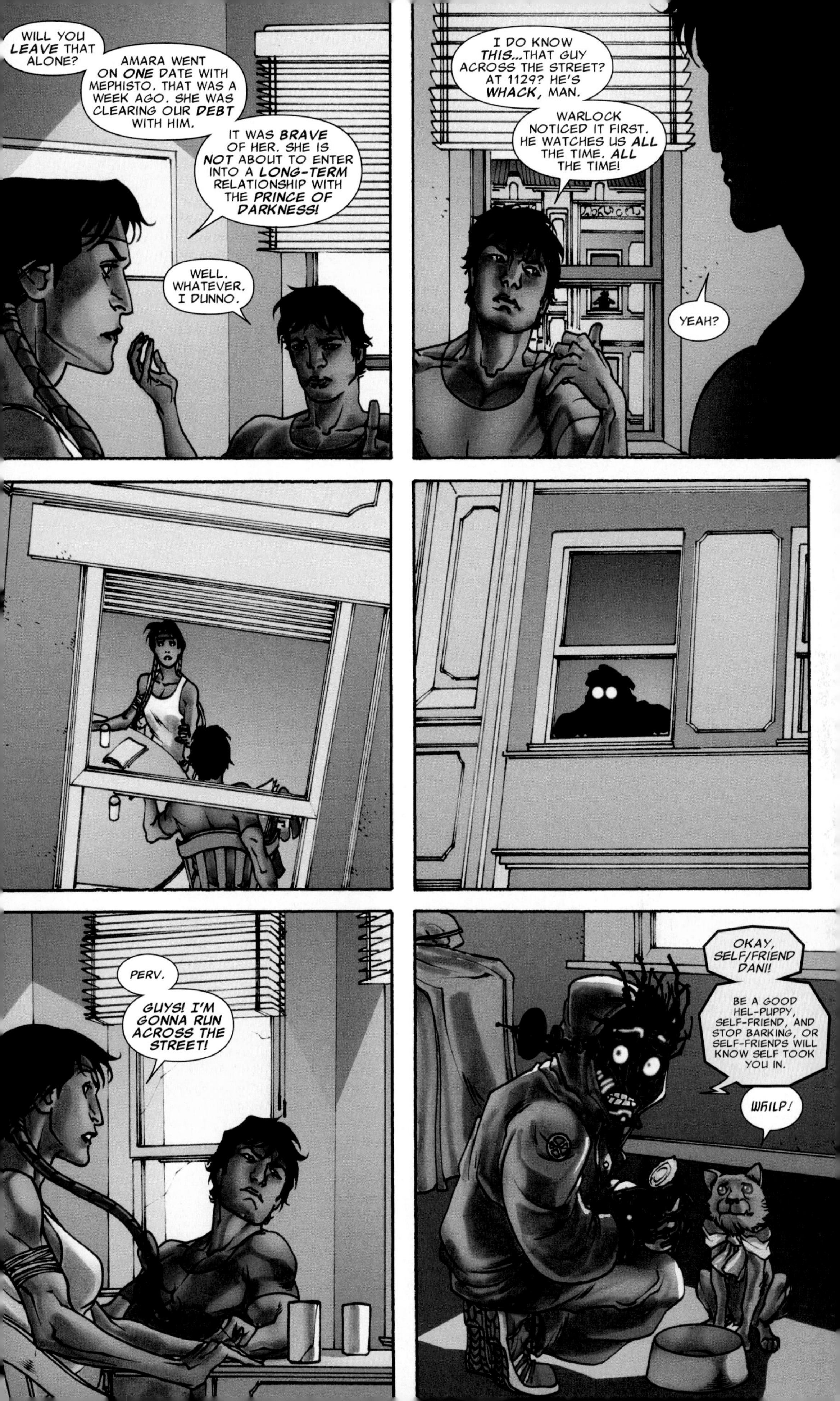
WILL YOU LEAVE THAT ALONE?
AMARA WENT ON ONE DATE WITH MEPHISTO. THAT WAS A WEEK AGO. SHE WAS CLEARING OUR DEBT WITH HIM.
IT WAS BRAVE OF HER. SHE IS NOT ABOUT TO ENTER INTO A LONG-TERM RELATIONSHIP WITH THE PRINCE OF DARKNESS!
WELL. WHATEVER. I DUNNO.
I DO KNOW THIS...THAT GUY ACROSS THE STREET? AT 1129? HE'S WHACK, MAN.
WARLOCK NOTICED IT FIRST. HE WATCHES US ALL THE TIME. ALL THE TIME!
YEAH?
PERV.
GUYS! I'M GONNA RUN ACROSS THE STREET!
OKAY, SELF/FRIEND DANI!
BE A GOOD HEL-PUPPY, SELF-FRIEND, AND STOP BARKING, OR SELF-FRIENDS WILL KNOW SELF TOOK YOU IN.
WHILP!

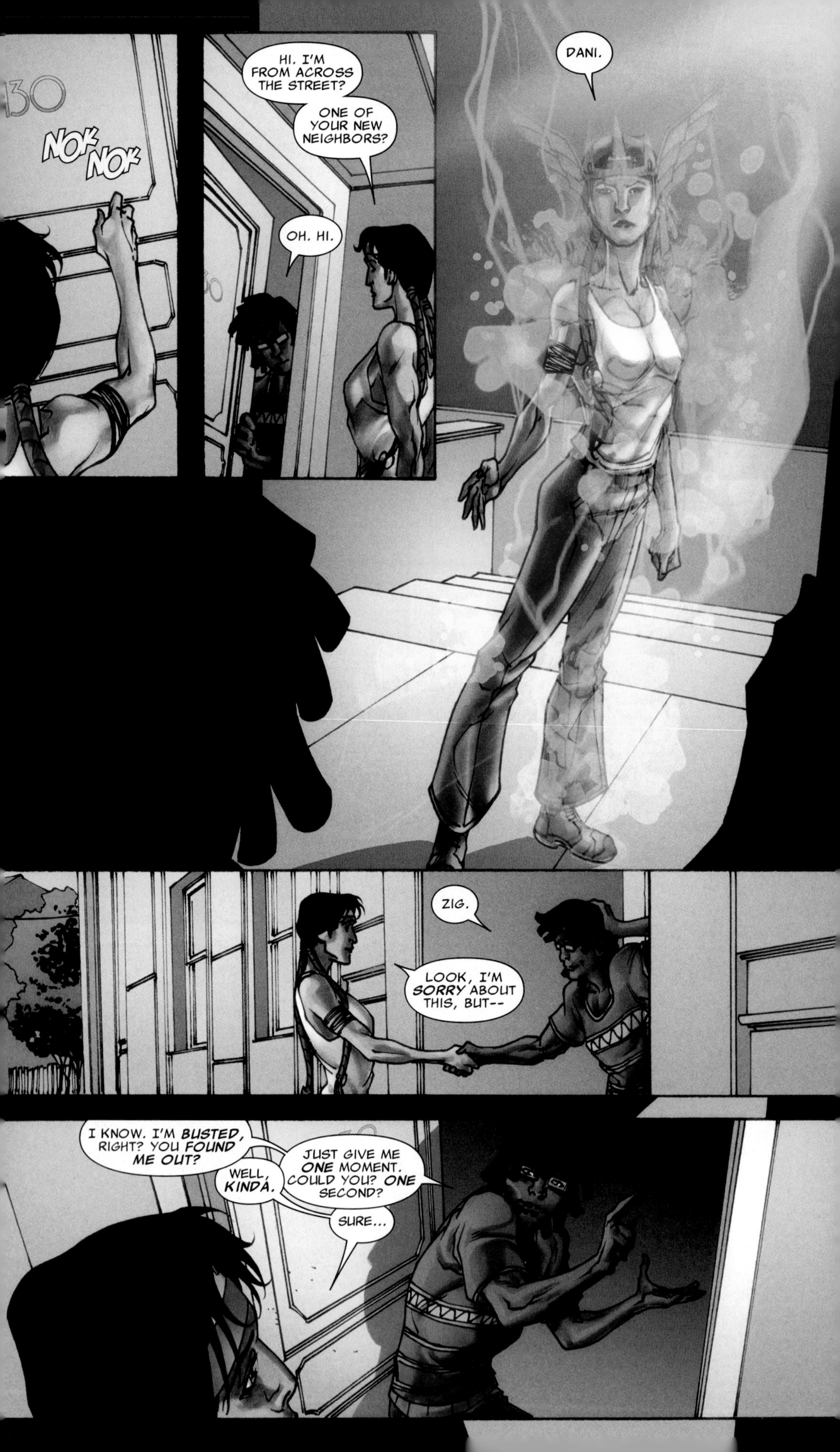

NOK NOK
HI. I'M FROM ACROSS THE STREET?
ONE OF YOUR NEW NEIGHBORS?
OH. HI.
DANI.
ZIG.
LOOK, I'M SORRY ABOUT THIS, BUT--
I KNOW. I'M BUSTED, RIGHT? YOU FOUND ME OUT?
WELL, KINDA.
JUST GIVE ME ONE MOMENT. COULD YOU? ONE SECOND?
SURE...

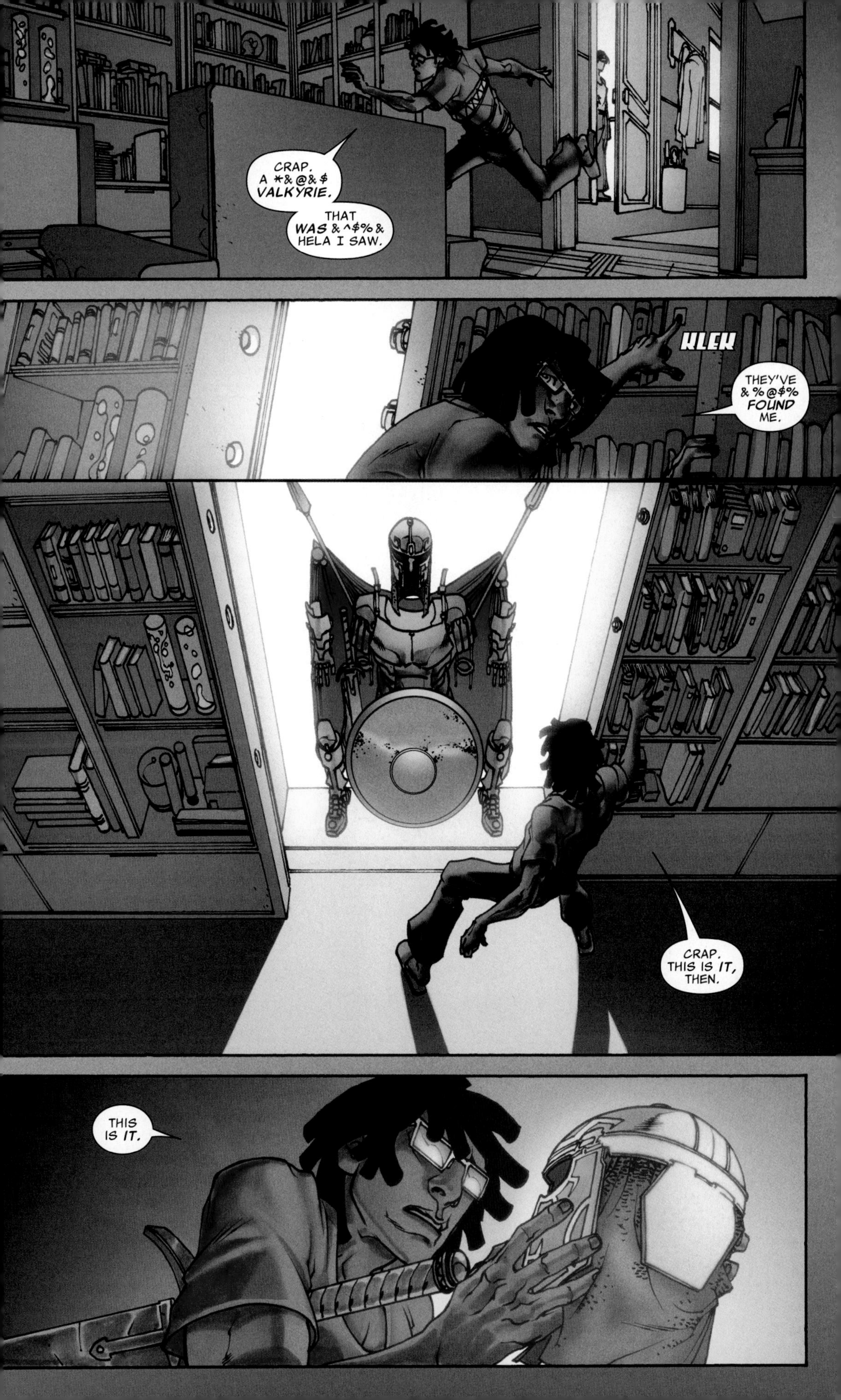
CRAP. A *&@&$ VALKYRIE.
THAT WAS &^$%& HELA I SAW.
KLEK
THEY'VE &%@$% FOUND ME.
CRAP. THIS IS IT, THEN.
THIS IS IT.

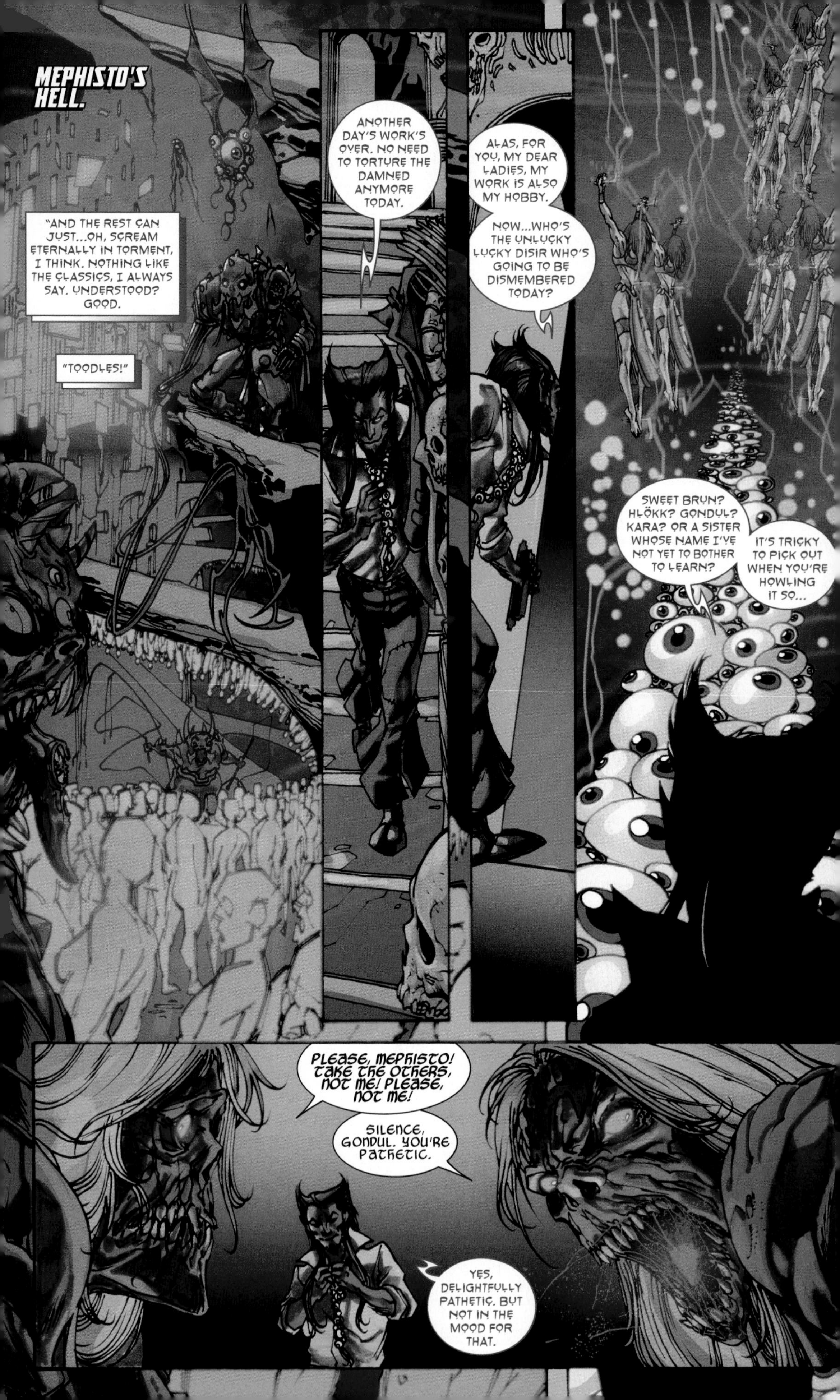
MEPHISTO'S HELL.
"AND THE REST CAN JUST...OH, SCREAM ETERNALLY IN TORMENT, I THINK. NOTHING LIKE THE CLASSICS, I ALWAYS SAY. UNDERSTOOD? GOOD.
"TOODLES!"
ANOTHER DAY'S WORK'S OVER. NO NEED TO TORTURE THE DAMNED ANYMORE TODAY.
ALAS, FOR YOU, MY DEAR LADIES, MY WORK IS ALSO MY HOBBY.
NOW...WHO'S THE UNLUCKY LUCKY DISIR WHO'S GOING TO BE DISMEMBERED TODAY?
SWEET BRUN? HLÖKK? GONDUL? KARA? OR A SISTER WHOSE NAME I'VE NOT YET TO BOTHER TO LEARN?
IT'S TRICKY TO PICK OUT WHEN YOU'RE HOWLING IT SO...
PLEASE, MEPHISTO! TAKE THE OTHERS, NOT ME! PLEASE, NOT ME!
SILENCE, GONDUL. YOU'RE PATHETIC.
YES, DELIGHTFULLY PATHETIC. BUT NOT IN THE MOOD FOR THAT.

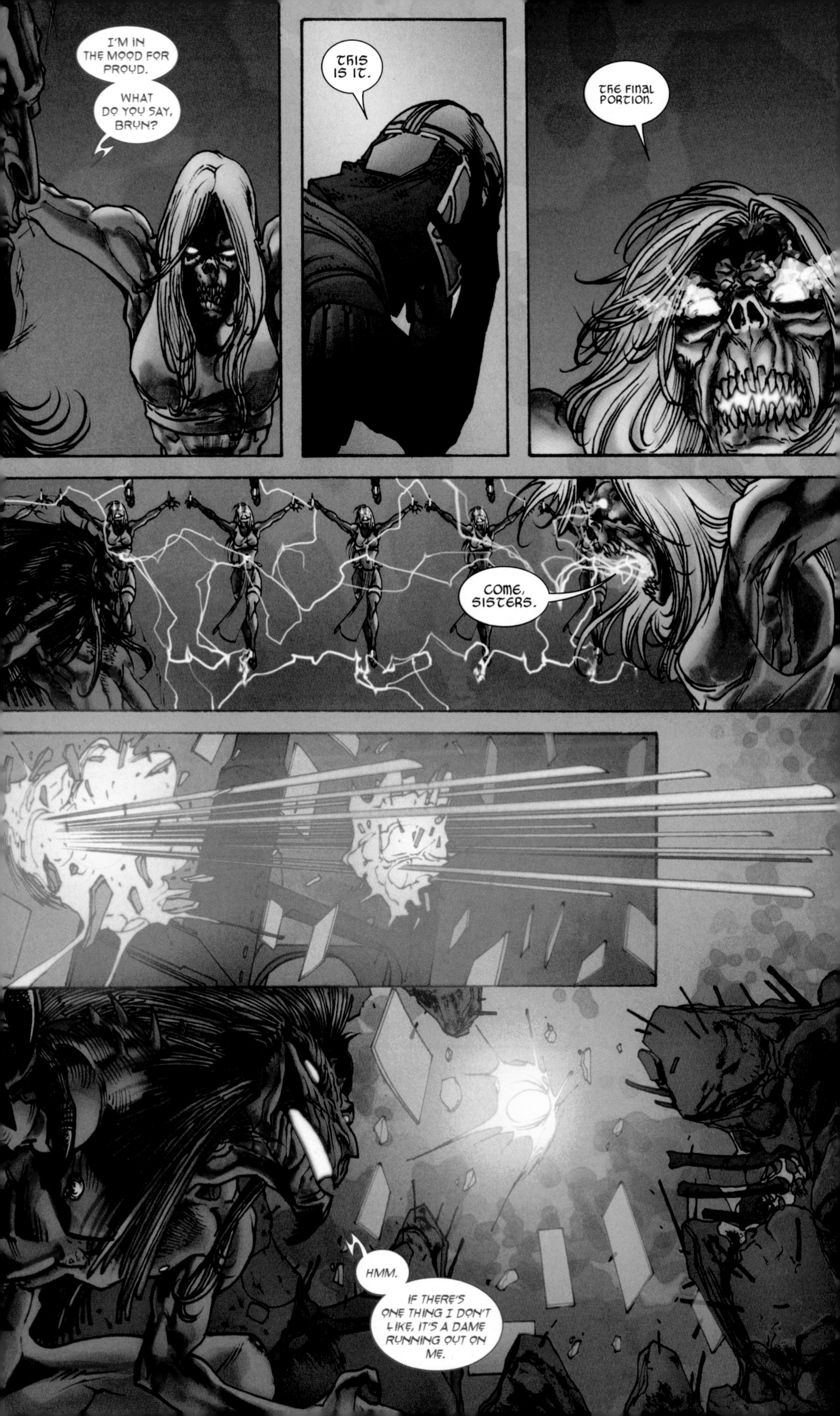
I'M IN THE MOOD FOR PROUD.
WHAT DO YOU SAY, BRUN?
THIS IS IT.
THE FINAL PORTION.
COME, SISTERS.
HMM.
IF THERE'S ONE THING I DON'T LIKE, IT'S A DAME RUNNING OUT ON ME.

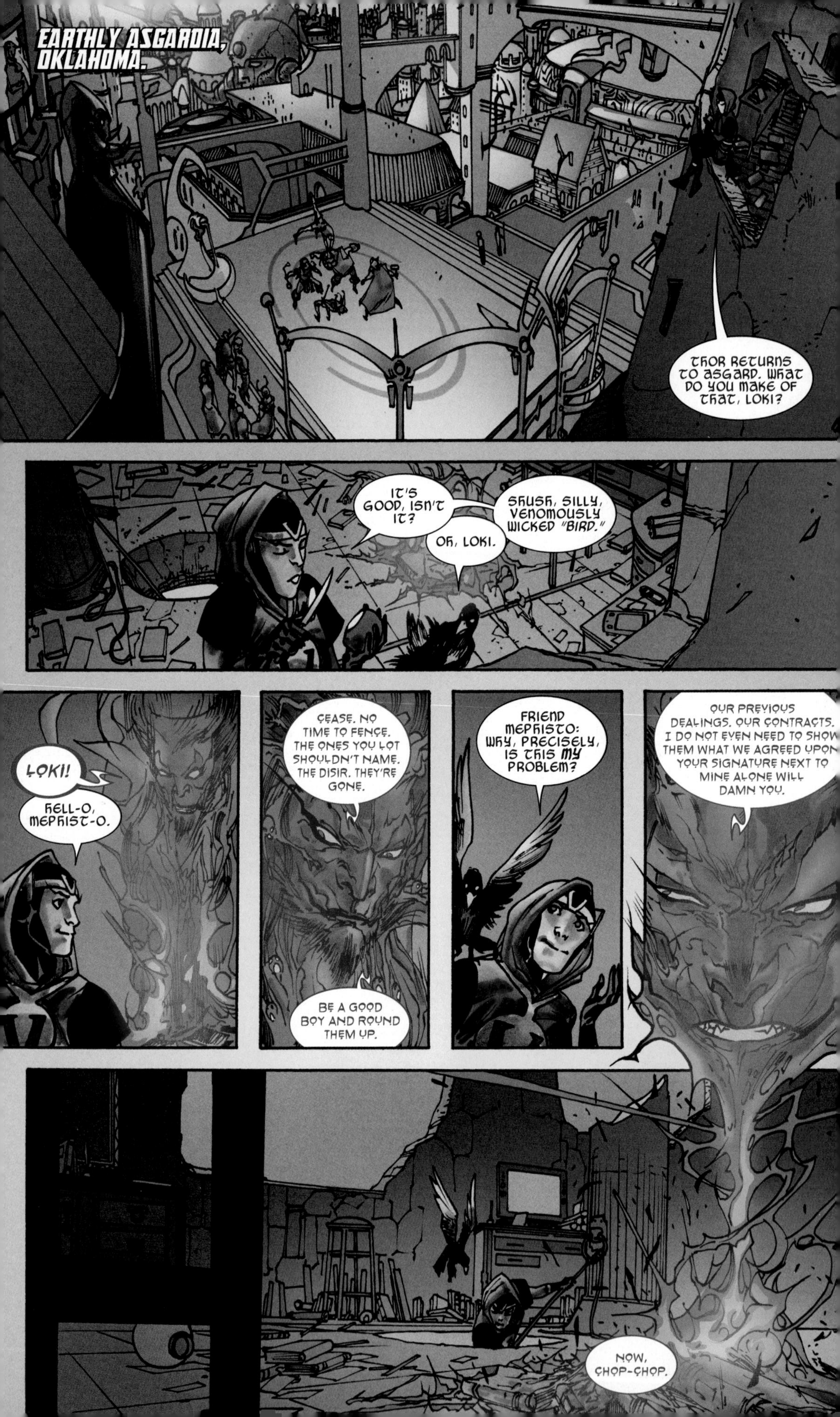
EARTHLY ASGARDIA, OKLAHOMA.
THOR RETURNS TO ASGARD. WHAT DO YOU MAKE OF THAT, LOKI?
IT'S GOOD, ISN'T IT?
SHUSH, SILLY, VENOMOUSLY WICKED "BIRD."
OH, LOKI.
LOKI!
HELL-O, MEPHIST-O.
CEASE. NO TIME TO FENCE. THE ONES YOU LOT SHOULDN'T NAME. THE DISIR. THEY'RE GONE.
BE A GOOD BOY AND ROUND THEM UP.
FRIEND MEPHISTO: WHY, PRECISELY, IS THIS MY PROBLEM?
OUR PREVIOUS DEALINGS. OUR CONTRACTS. I DO NOT EVEN NEED TO SHOW THEM WHAT WE AGREED UPON. YOUR SIGNATURE NEXT TO MINE ALONE WILL DAMN YOU.
NOW, CHOP-CHOP.

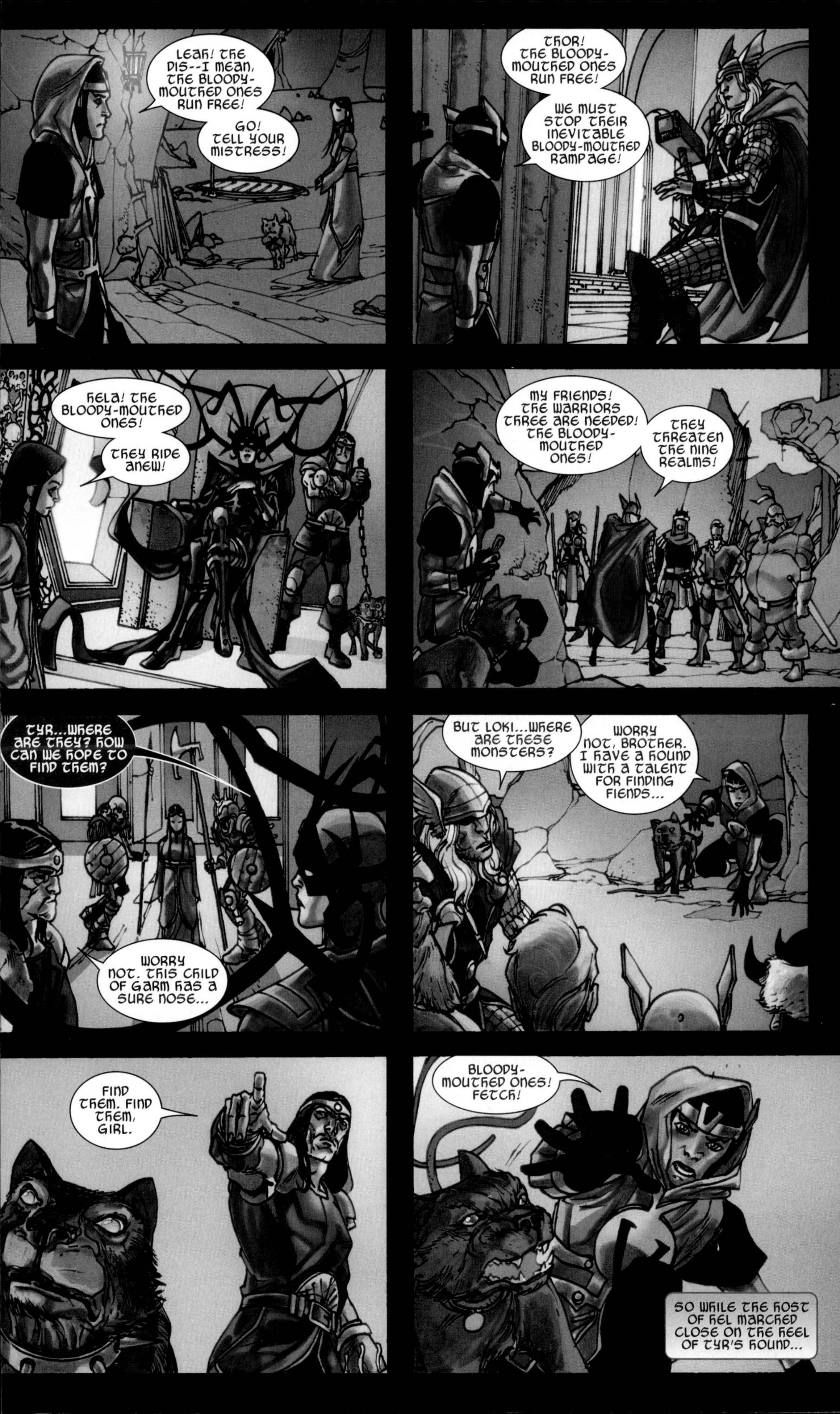
LEAH! THE DIS--I MEAN, THE BLOODY-MOUTHED ONES RUN FREE!
GO! TELL YOUR MISTRESS!
THOR! THE BLOODY-MOUTHED ONES RUN FREE!
WE MUST STOP THEIR INEVITABLE BLOODY-MOUTHED RAMPAGE!
HELA! THE BLOODY-MOUTHED ONES!
THEY RIDE ANEW!
MY FRIENDS! THE WARRIORS THREE ARE NEEDED! THE BLOODY-MOUTHED ONES!
THEY THREATEN THE NINE REALMS!
TYR...WHERE ARE THEY? HOW CAN WE HOPE TO FIND THEM?
WORRY NOT. THIS CHILD OF GARM HAS A SURE NOSE...
BUT LOKI...WHERE ARE THESE MONSTERS?
WORRY NOT, BROTHER. I HAVE A HOUND WITH A TALENT FOR FINDING FIENDS...
FIND THEM. FIND THEM, GIRL.
BLOODY-MOUTHED ONES! FETCH!
SO WHILE THE HOST OF HEL MARCHED CLOSE ON THE HEEL OF TYR'S HOUND...

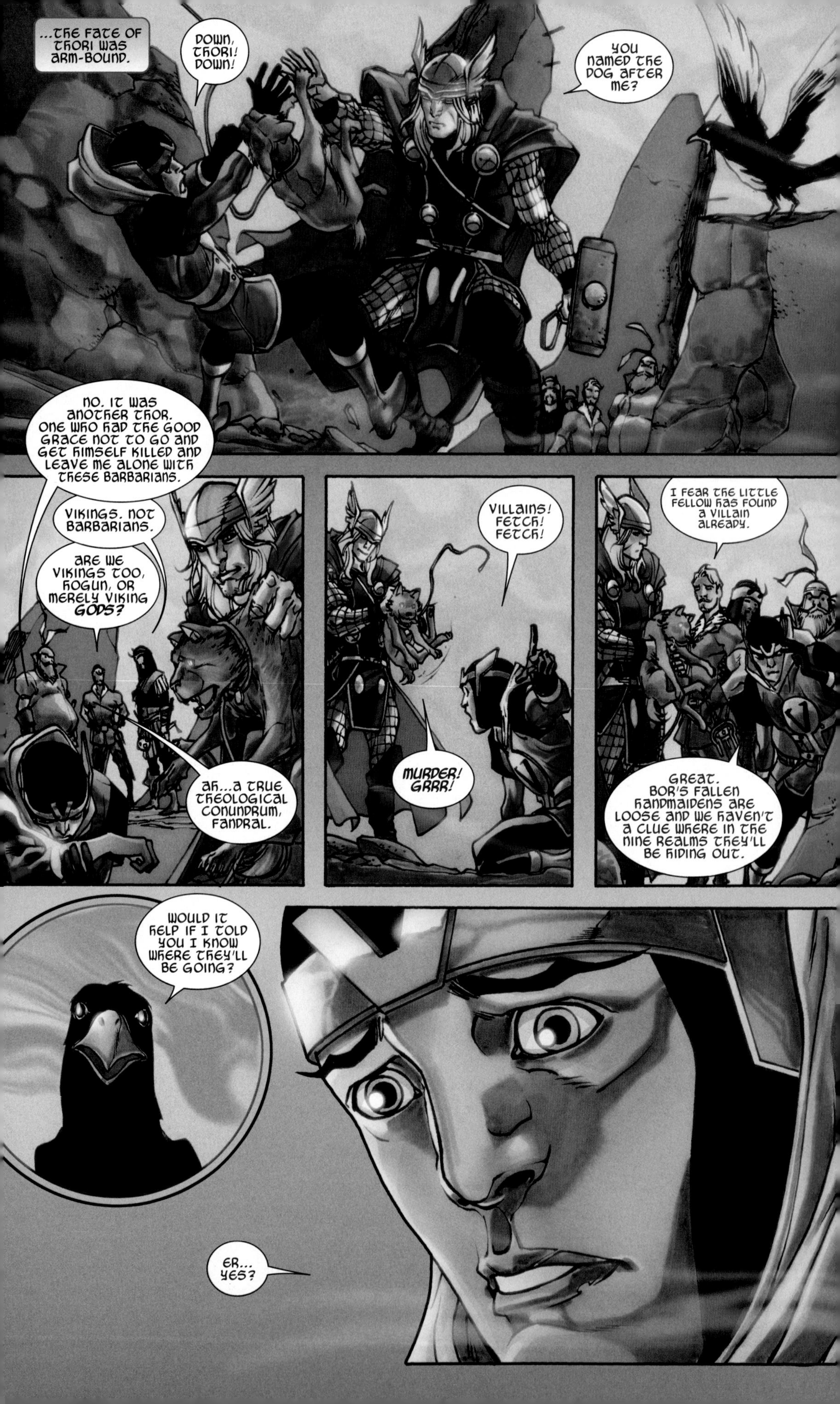
...THE FATE OF THORI WAS ARM-BOUND.
DOWN, THORI! DOWN!
YOU NAMED THE DOG AFTER ME?
NO. IT WAS ANOTHER THOR. ONE WHO HAD THE GOOD GRACE NOT TO GO AND GET HIMSELF KILLED AND LEAVE ME ALONE WITH THESE BARBARIANS.
VIKINGS. NOT BARBARIANS.
ARE WE VIKINGS TOO, HOGUN, OR MERELY VIKING GODS?
AH...A TRUE THEOLOGICAL CONUNDRUM, FANDRAL.
VILLAINS! FETCH! FETCH!
MURDER! GRRR!
I FEAR THE LITTLE FELLOW HAS FOUND A VILLAIN ALREADY.
GREAT. BOR'S FALLEN HANDMAIDENS ARE LOOSE AND WE HAVEN'T A CLUE WHERE IN THE NINE REALMS THEY'LL BE HIDING OUT.
WOULD IT HELP IF I TOLD YOU I KNOW WHERE THEY'LL BE GOING?
ER... YES?

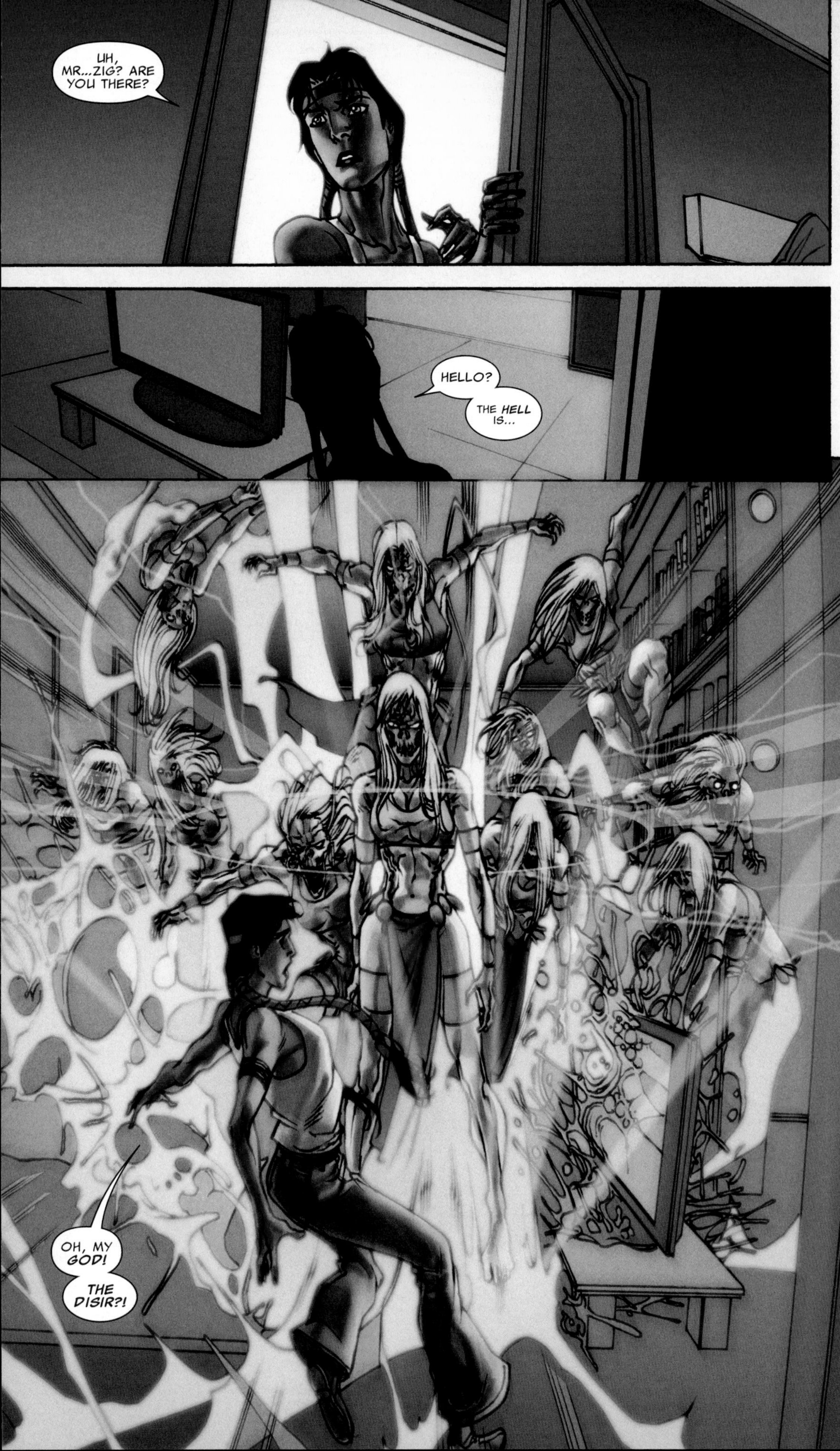
UH, MR...ZIG? ARE YOU THERE?
HELLO?
THE HELL IS...
OH, MY GOD!
THE DISIR?!

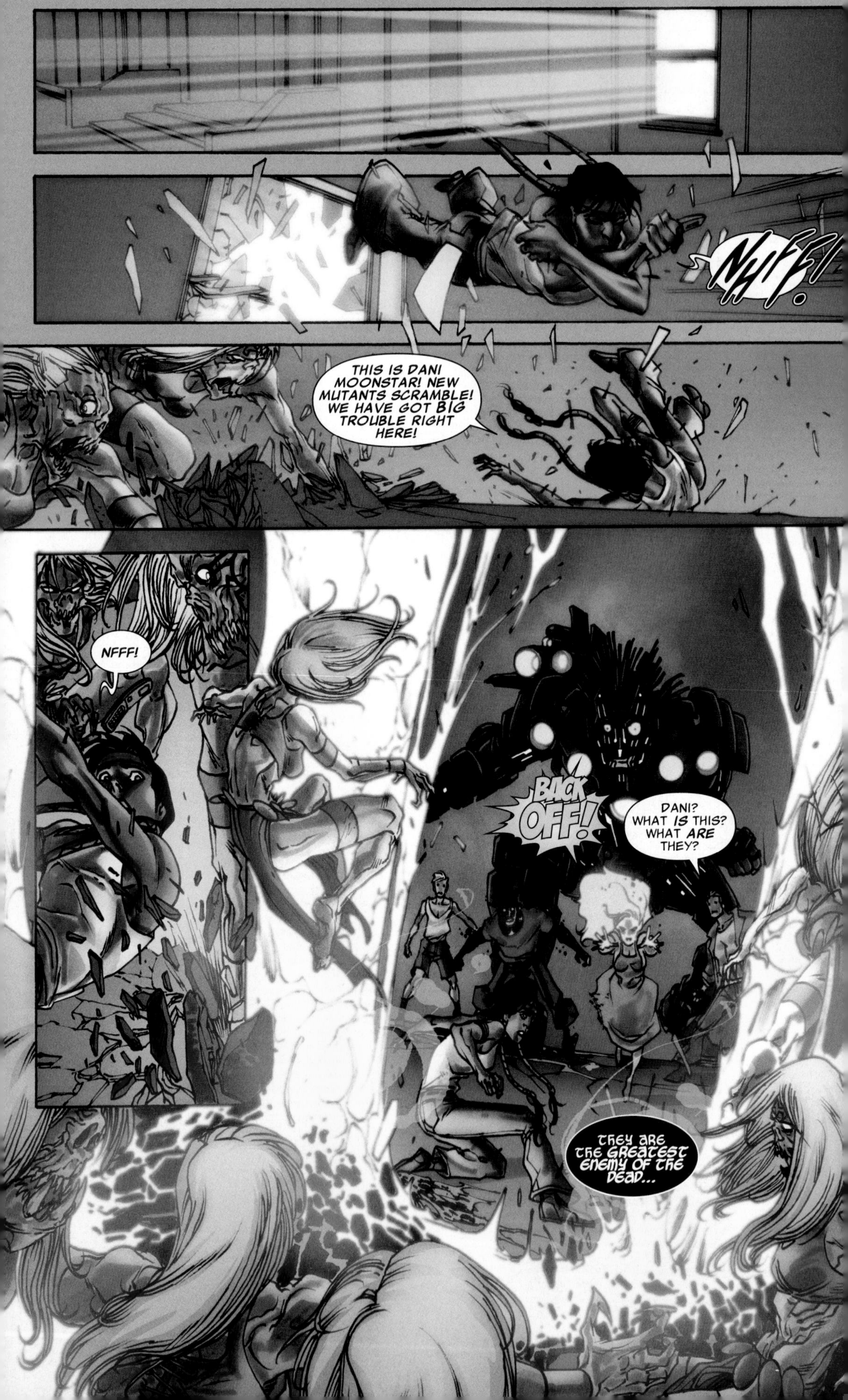
NHFF!
THIS IS DANI MOONSTAR! NEW MUTANTS SCRAMBLE! WE HAVE GOT BIG TROUBLE RIGHT HERE!
NFFF!
BACK OFF!
DANI? WHAT IS THIS? WHAT ARE THEY?
THEY ARE THE GREATEST ENEMY OF THE DEAD...

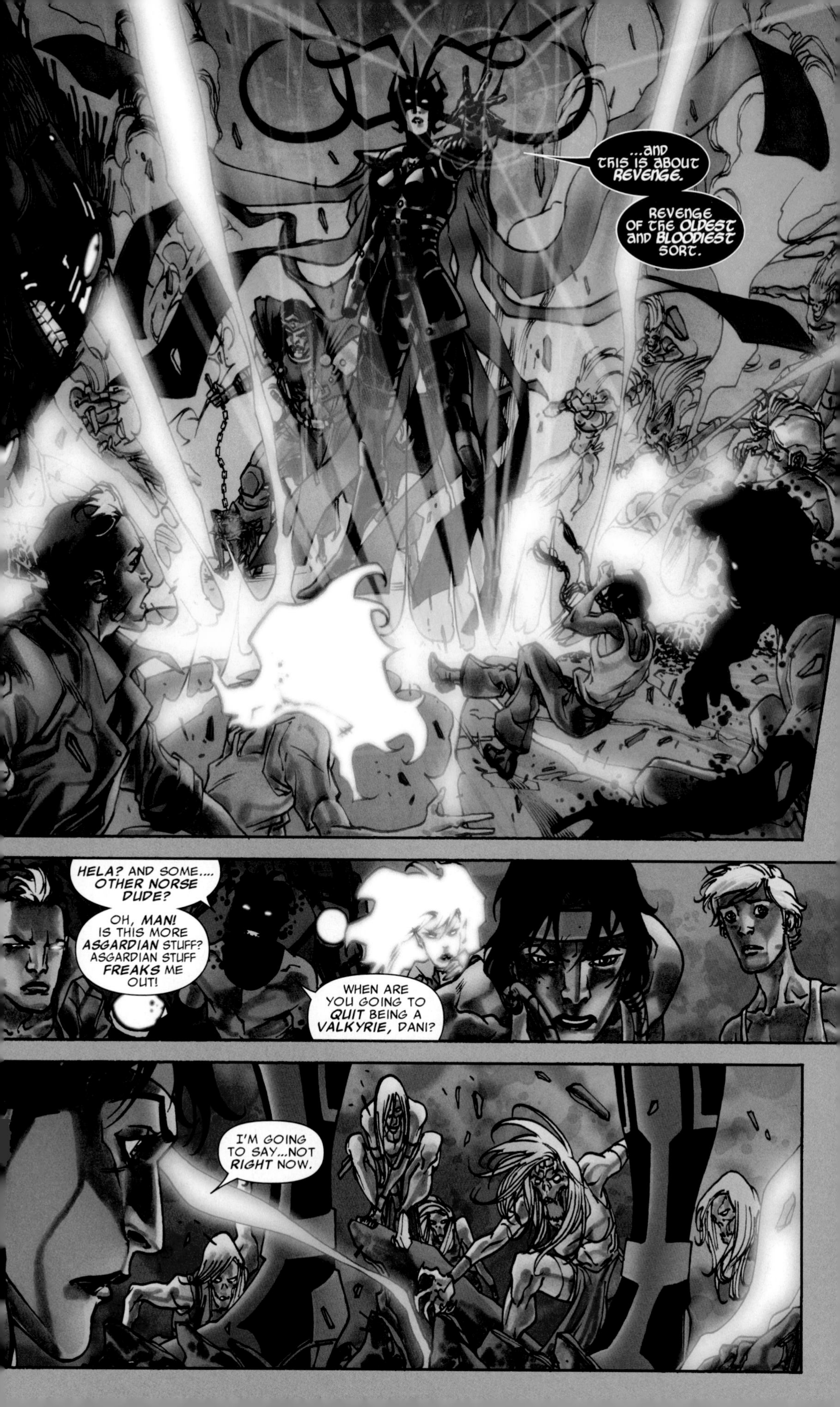
...and this is about revenge.
Revenge of the oldest and bloodiest sort.
HELA? AND SOME.... OTHER NORSE DUDE?
OH, MAN! IS THIS MORE ASGARDIAN STUFF? ASGARDIAN STUFF FREAKS ME OUT!
WHEN ARE YOU GOING TO QUIT BEING A VALKYRIE, DANI?
I'M GOING TO SAY...NOT RIGHT NOW.

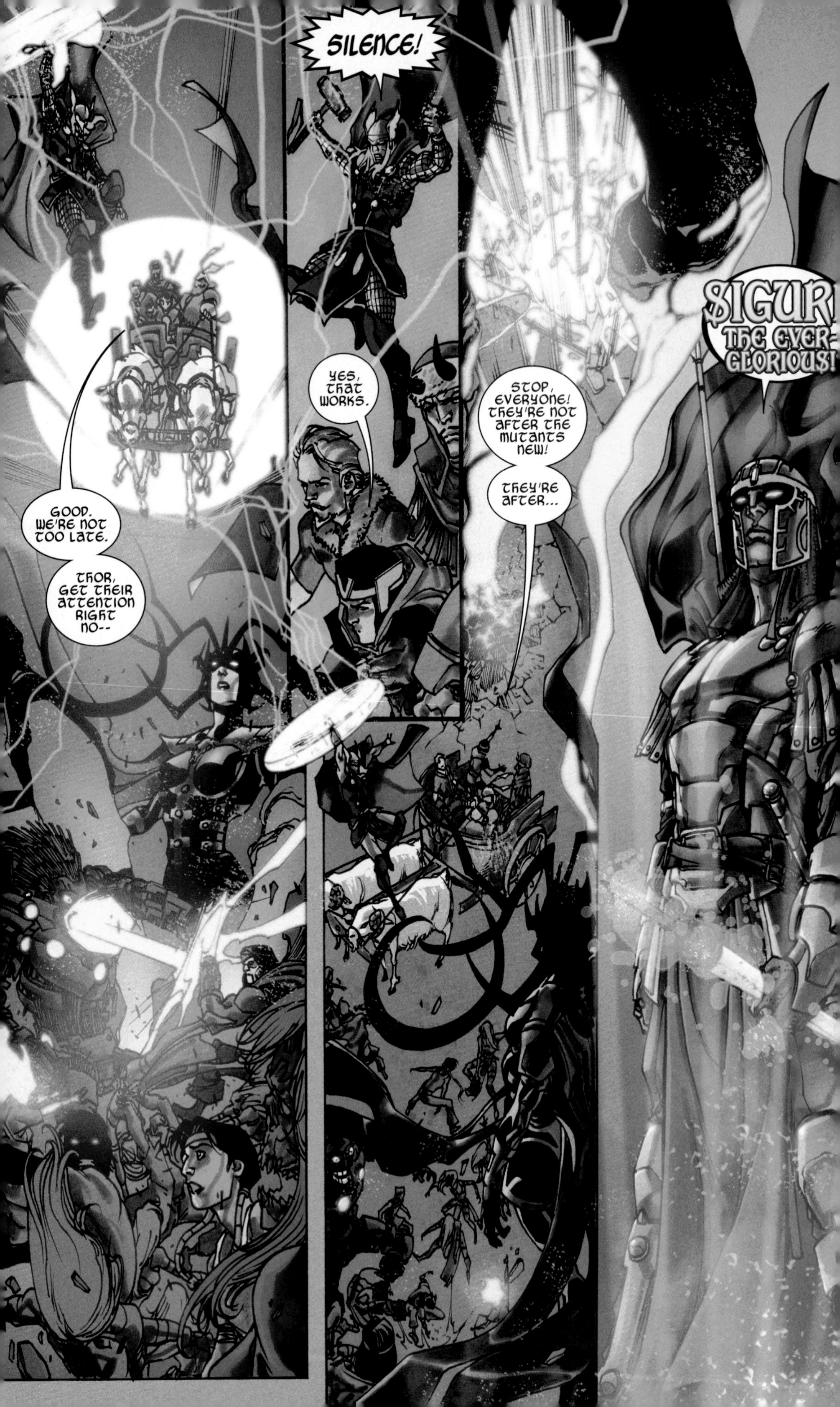

SILENCE!
GOOD. WE'RE NOT TOO LATE.
THOR, GET THEIR ATTENTION RIGHT NO--
YES, THAT WORKS.
STOP, EVERYONE! THEY'RE NOT AFTER THE MUTANTS NOW!
THEY'RE AFTER...
SIGURD THE EVER-GLORIOUS!

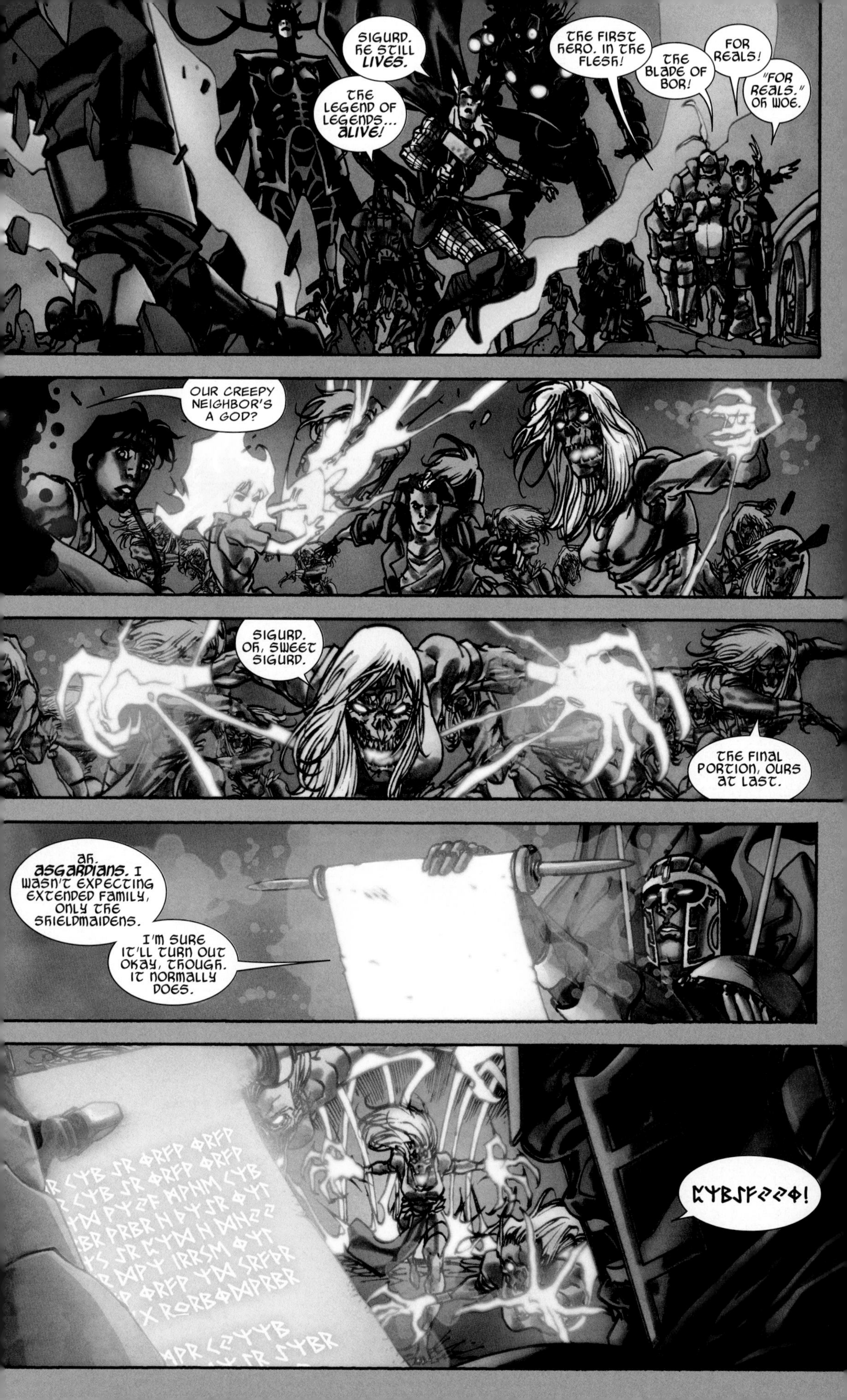
SIGURD. HE STILL LIVES.
THE LEGEND OF LEGENDS... ALIVE!
THE FIRST HERO. IN THE FLESH!
THE BLADE OF BOR!
FOR REALS!
"FOR REALS." OH WOE.
OUR CREEPY NEIGHBOR'S A GOD?
SIGURD. OH, SWEET SIGURD.
THE FINAL PORTION, OURS AT LAST.
AH. ASGARDIANS. I WASN'T EXPECTING EXTENDED FAMILY, ONLY THE SHIELDMAIDENS.
I'M SURE IT'LL TURN OUT OKAY, THOUGH. IT NORMALLY DOES.

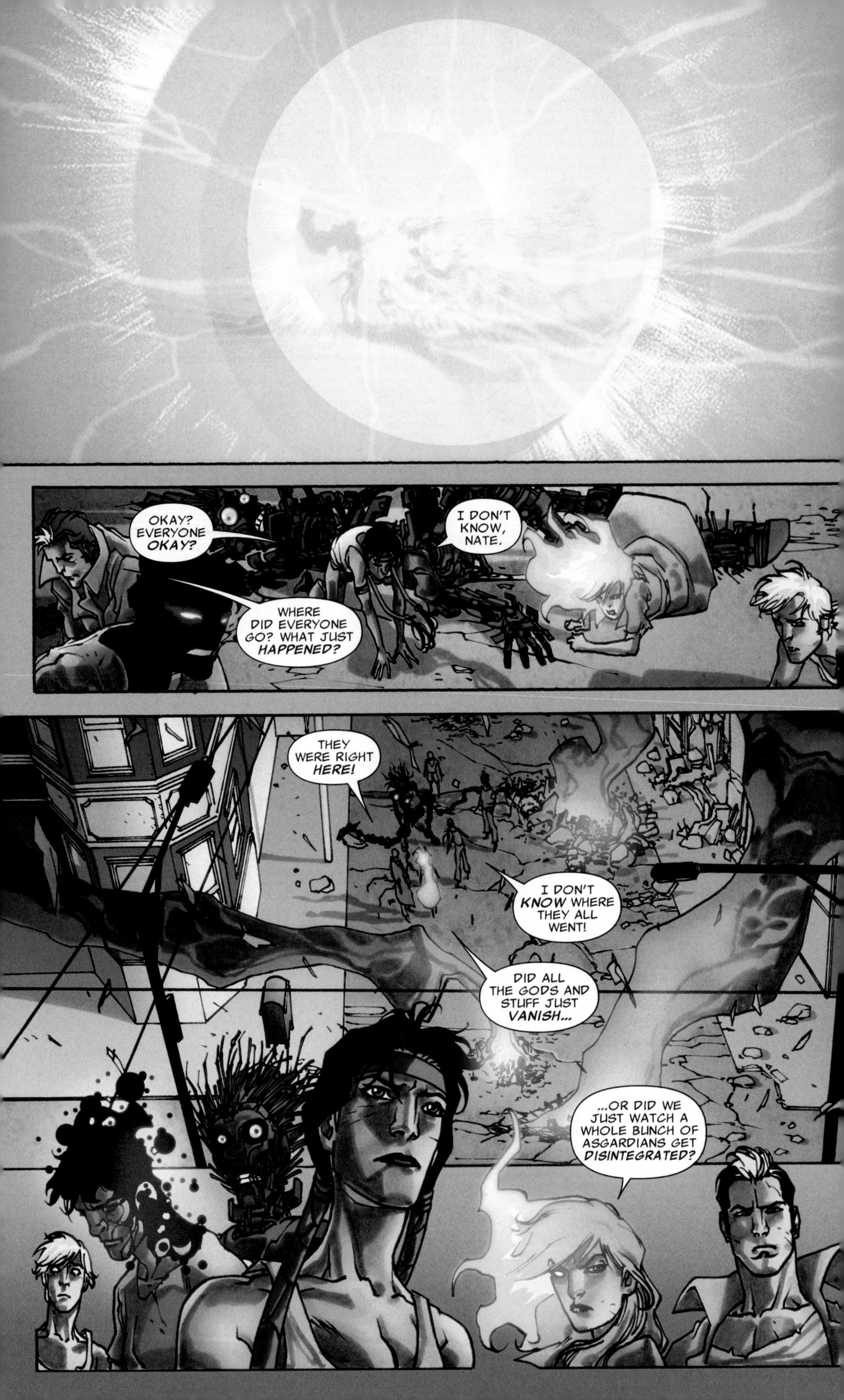
OKAY? EVERYONE OKAY?
I DON'T KNOW, NATE.
WHERE DID EVERYONE GO? WHAT JUST HAPPENED?
THEY WERE RIGHT HERE!
I DON'T KNOW WHERE THEY ALL WENT!
DID ALL THE GODS AND STUFF JUST VANISH...
...OR DID WE JUST WATCH A WHOLE BUNCH OF ASGARDIANS GET DISINTEGRATED?

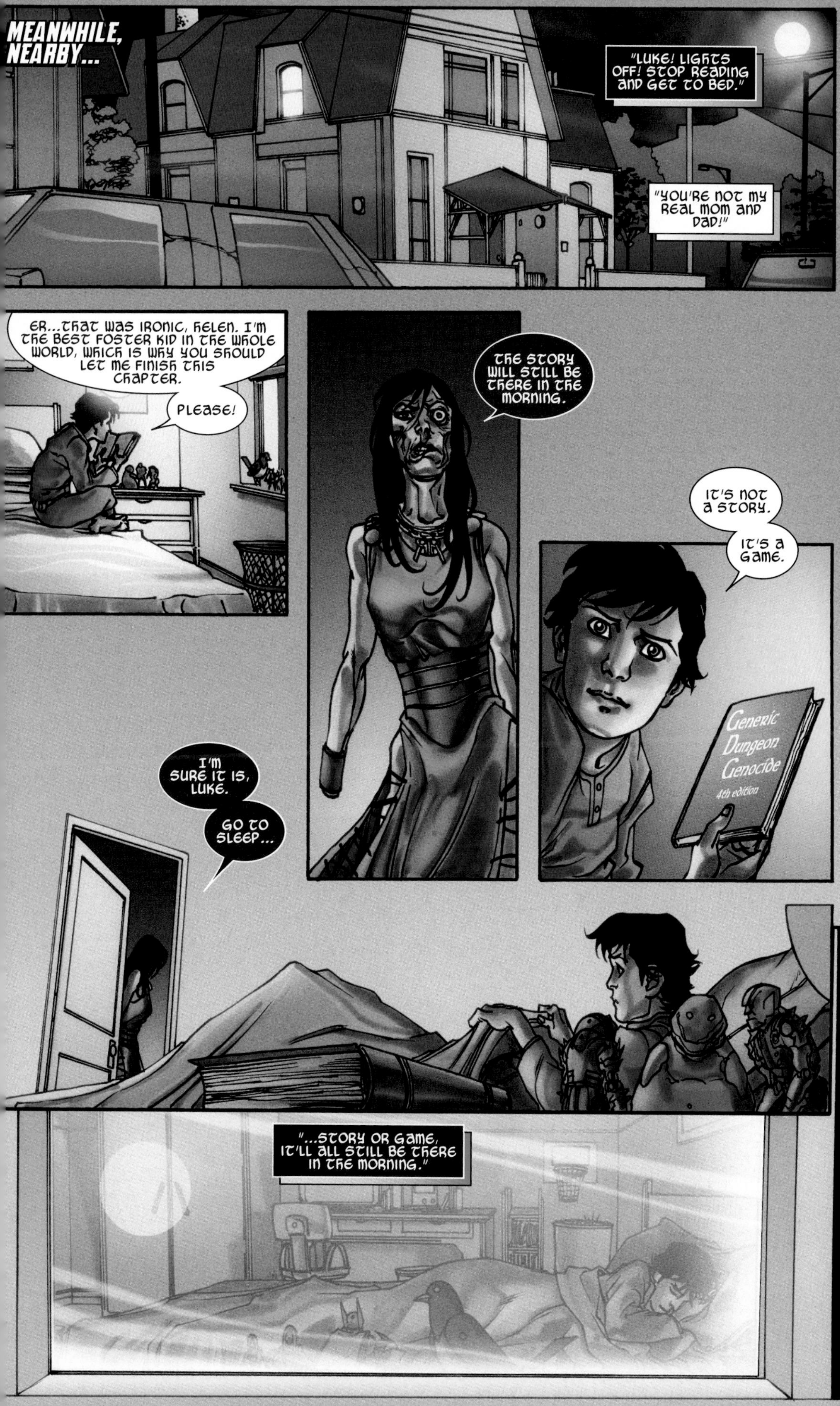
MEANWHILE, NEARBY...
"LUKE! LIGHTS OFF! STOP READING AND GET TO BED."
"YOU'RE NOT MY REAL MOM AND DAD!"
ER...THAT WAS IRONIC, HELEN. I'M THE BEST FOSTER KID IN THE WHOLE WORLD, WHICH IS WHY YOU SHOULD LET ME FINISH THIS CHAPTER.
PLEASE!
THE STORY WILL STILL BE THERE IN THE MORNING.
IT'S NOT A STORY.
IT'S A GAME.
Generic Dungeon Genocide
4th edition
I'M SURE IT IS, LUKE.
GO TO SLEEP...
"...STORY OR GAME, IT'LL ALL STILL BE THERE IN THE MORNING."

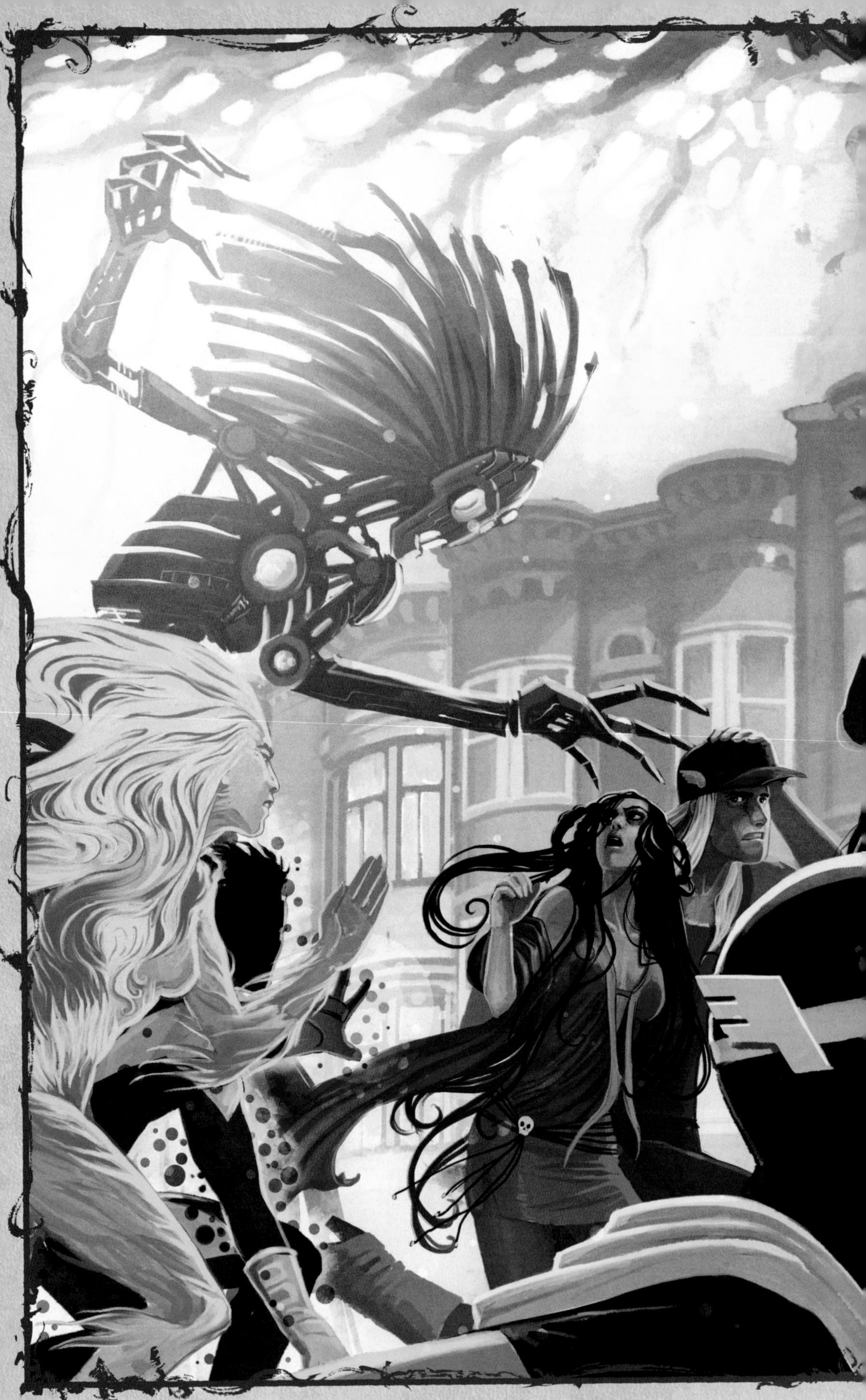

JOURNEY INTO MYSTERY #637: "THERE GOETH THE NEIGHBORHOOD

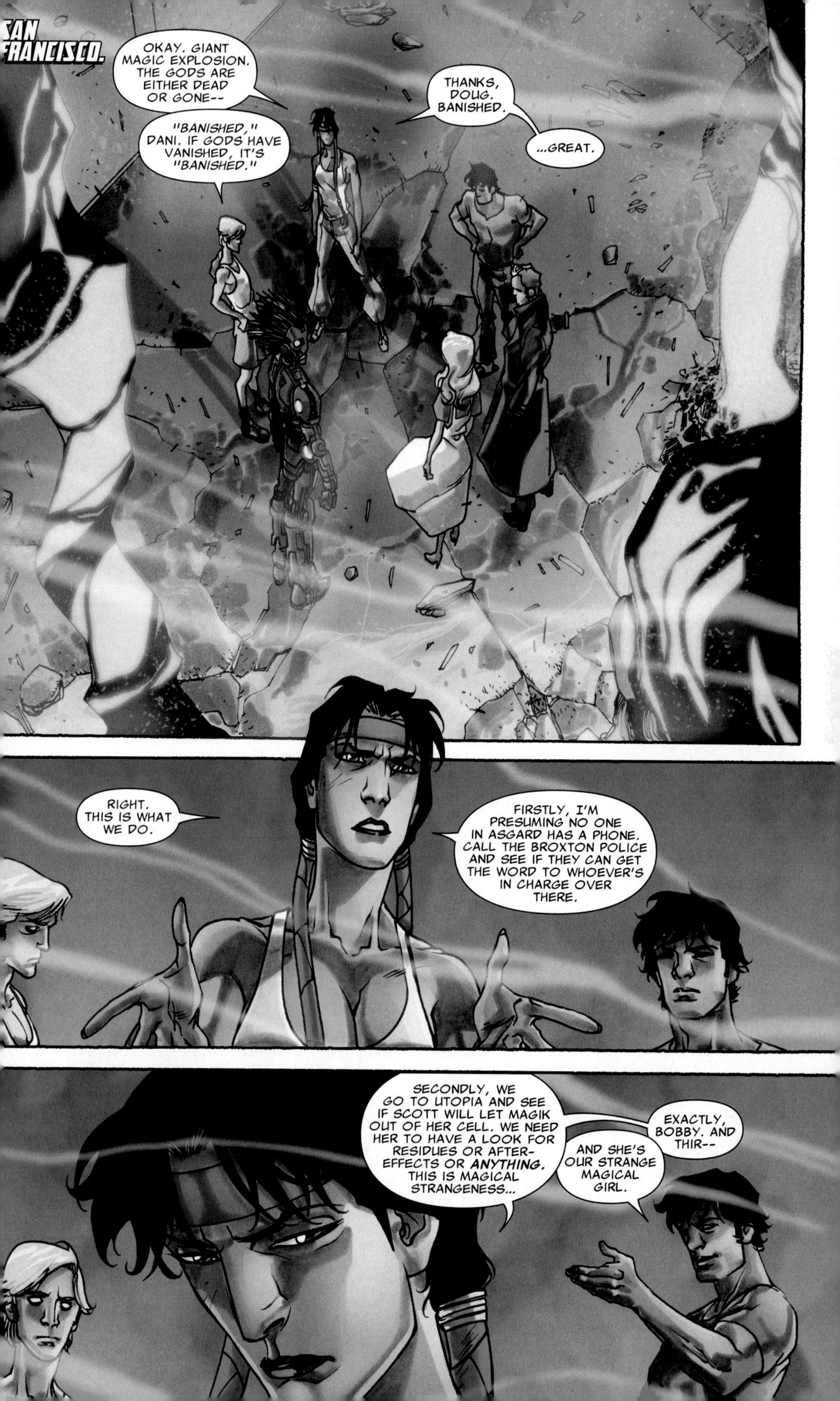
SAN FRANCISCO.
OKAY. GIANT MAGIC EXPLOSION. THE GODS ARE EITHER DEAD OR GONE--
"BANISHED," DANI. IF GODS HAVE VANISHED, IT'S "BANISHED."
THANKS, DOUG. BANISHED.
...GREAT.
RIGHT. THIS IS WHAT WE DO.
FIRSTLY, I'M PRESUMING NO ONE IN ASGARD HAS A PHONE. CALL THE BROXTON POLICE AND SEE IF THEY CAN GET THE WORD TO WHOEVER'S IN CHARGE OVER THERE.
SECONDLY, WE GO TO UTOPIA AND SEE IF SCOTT WILL LET MAGIK OUT OF HER CELL. WE NEED HER TO HAVE A LOOK FOR RESIDUES OR AFTER-EFFECTS OR ANYTHING. THIS IS MAGICAL STRANGENESS...
AND SHE'S OUR STRANGE MAGICAL GIRL.
EXACTLY, BOBBY. AND THIR--

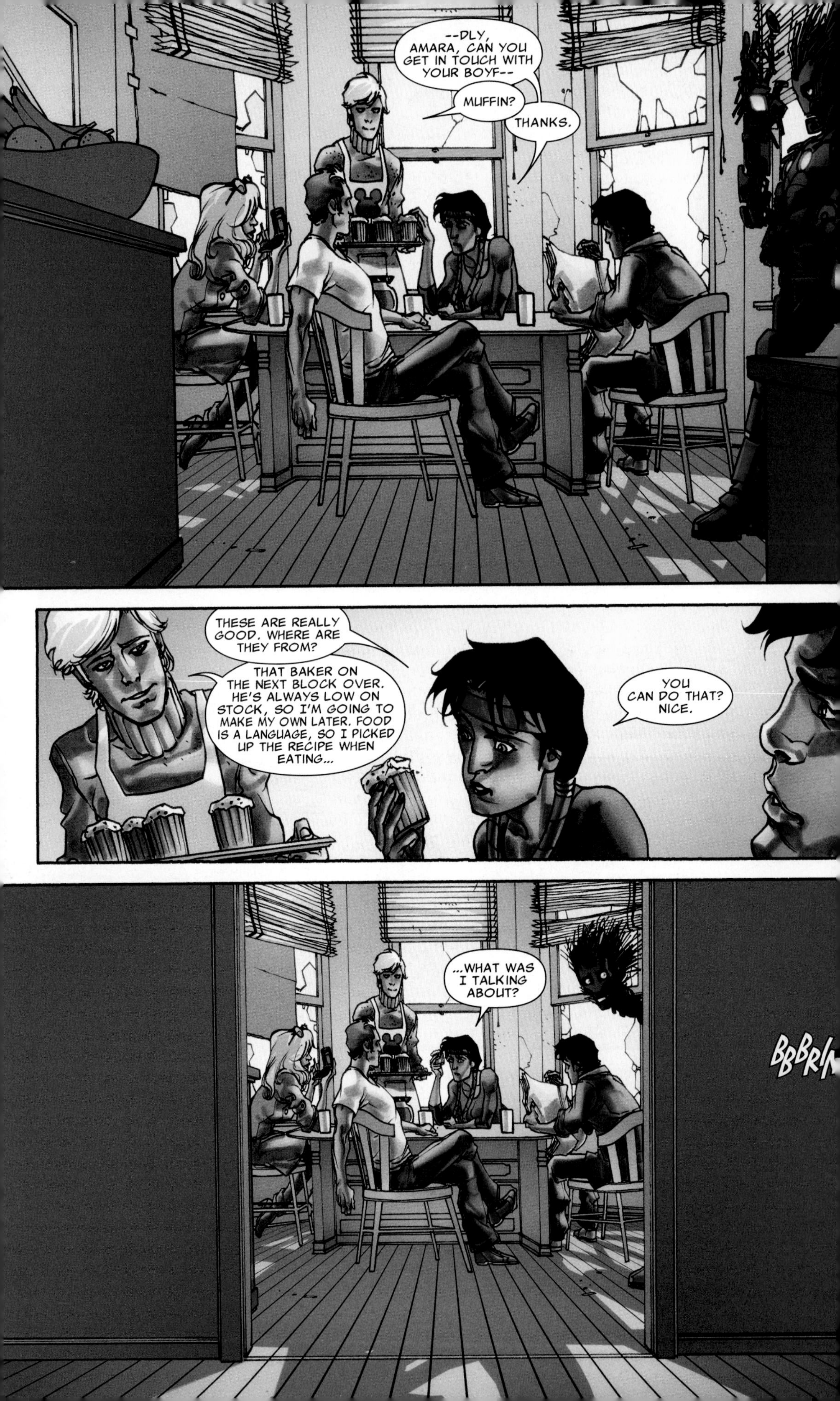
--DLY, AMARA, CAN YOU GET IN TOUCH WITH YOUR BOYF--
MUFFIN?
THANKS.
THESE ARE REALLY GOOD. WHERE ARE THEY FROM?
THAT BAKER ON THE NEXT BLOCK OVER. HE'S ALWAYS LOW ON STOCK, SO I'M GOING TO MAKE MY OWN LATER. FOOD IS A LANGUAGE, SO I PICKED UP THE RECIPE WHEN EATING...
YOU CAN DO THAT? NICE.
...WHAT WAS I TALKING ABOUT?
BBBRIN

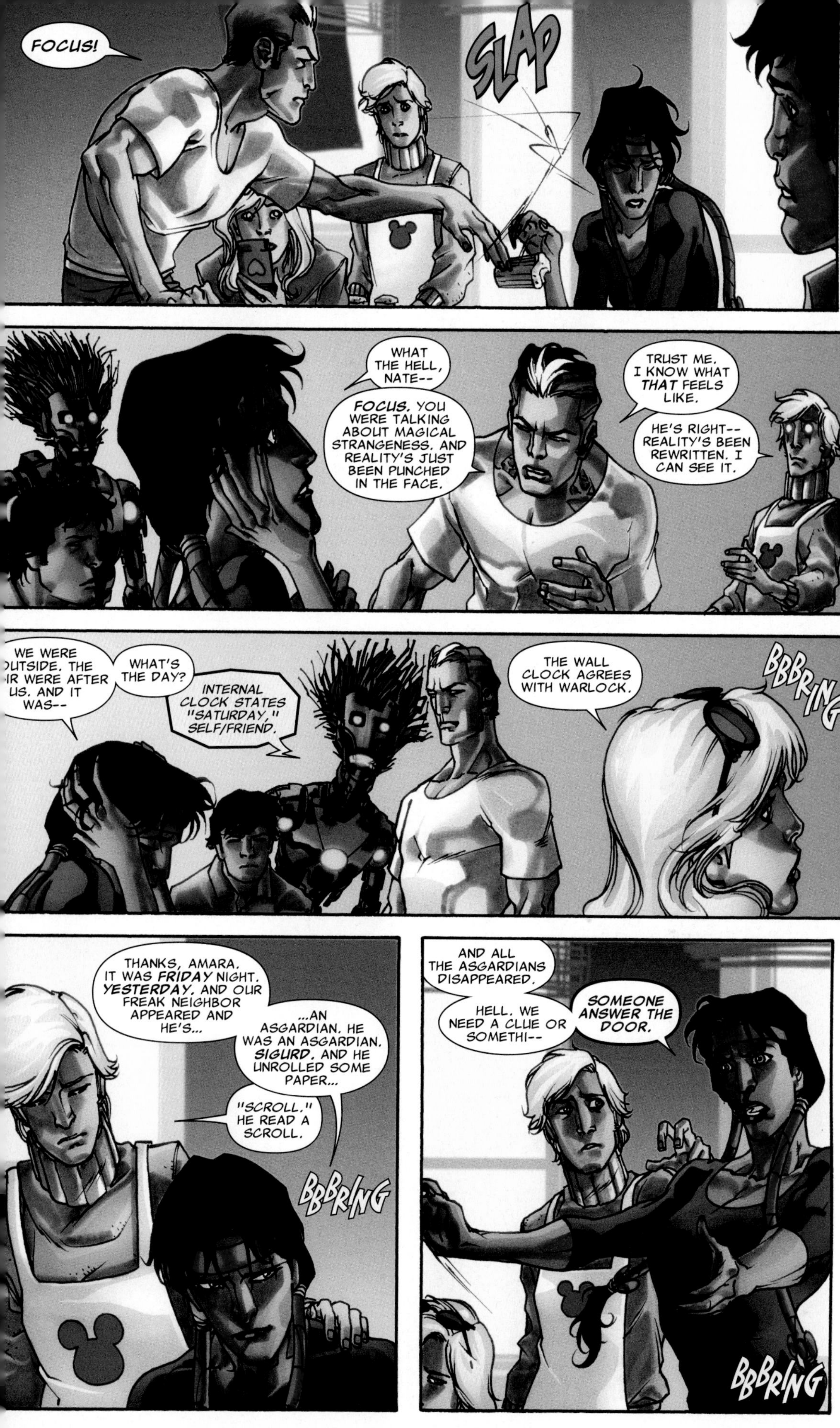
FOCUS!
SLAP
WHAT THE HELL, NATE--
FOCUS. YOU WERE TALKING ABOUT MAGICAL STRANGENESS. AND REALITY'S JUST BEEN PUNCHED IN THE FACE.
TRUST ME. I KNOW WHAT THAT FEELS LIKE.
HE'S RIGHT-- REALITY'S BEEN REWRITTEN. I CAN SEE IT.
WE WERE OUTSIDE. THE IR WERE AFTER US. AND IT WAS--
WHAT'S THE DAY?
INTERNAL CLOCK STATES "SATURDAY," SELF/FRIEND.
THE WALL CLOCK AGREES WITH WARLOCK.
BBBRING
THANKS, AMARA. IT WAS FRIDAY NIGHT. YESTERDAY. AND OUR FREAK NEIGHBOR APPEARED AND HE'S...
...AN ASGARDIAN. HE WAS AN ASGARDIAN. SIGURD. AND HE UNROLLED SOME PAPER...
"SCROLL." HE READ A SCROLL.
BBBRING
AND ALL THE ASGARDIANS DISAPPEARED.
HELL. WE NEED A CLUE OR SOMETHI--
SOMEONE ANSWER THE DOOR.
BBBRING

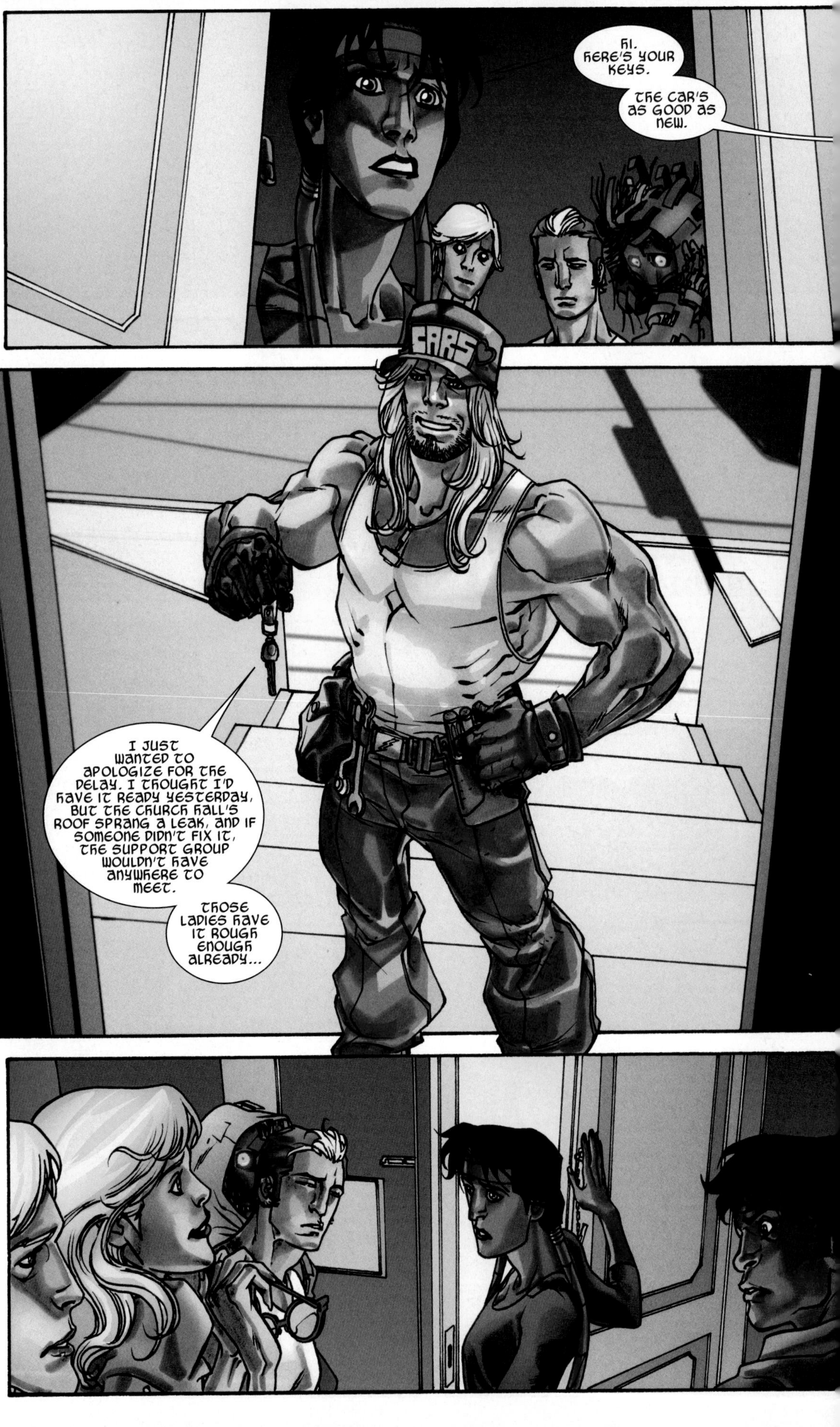
HI. HERE'S YOUR KEYS.
THE CAR'S AS GOOD AS NEW.
CARS
I JUST WANTED TO APOLOGIZE FOR THE DELAY. I THOUGHT I'D HAVE IT READY YESTERDAY, BUT THE CHURCH HALL'S ROOF SPRANG A LEAK, AND IF SOMEONE DIDN'T FIX IT, THE SUPPORT GROUP WOULDN'T HAVE ANYWHERE TO MEET.
THOSE LADIES HAVE IT ROUGH ENOUGH ALREADY...

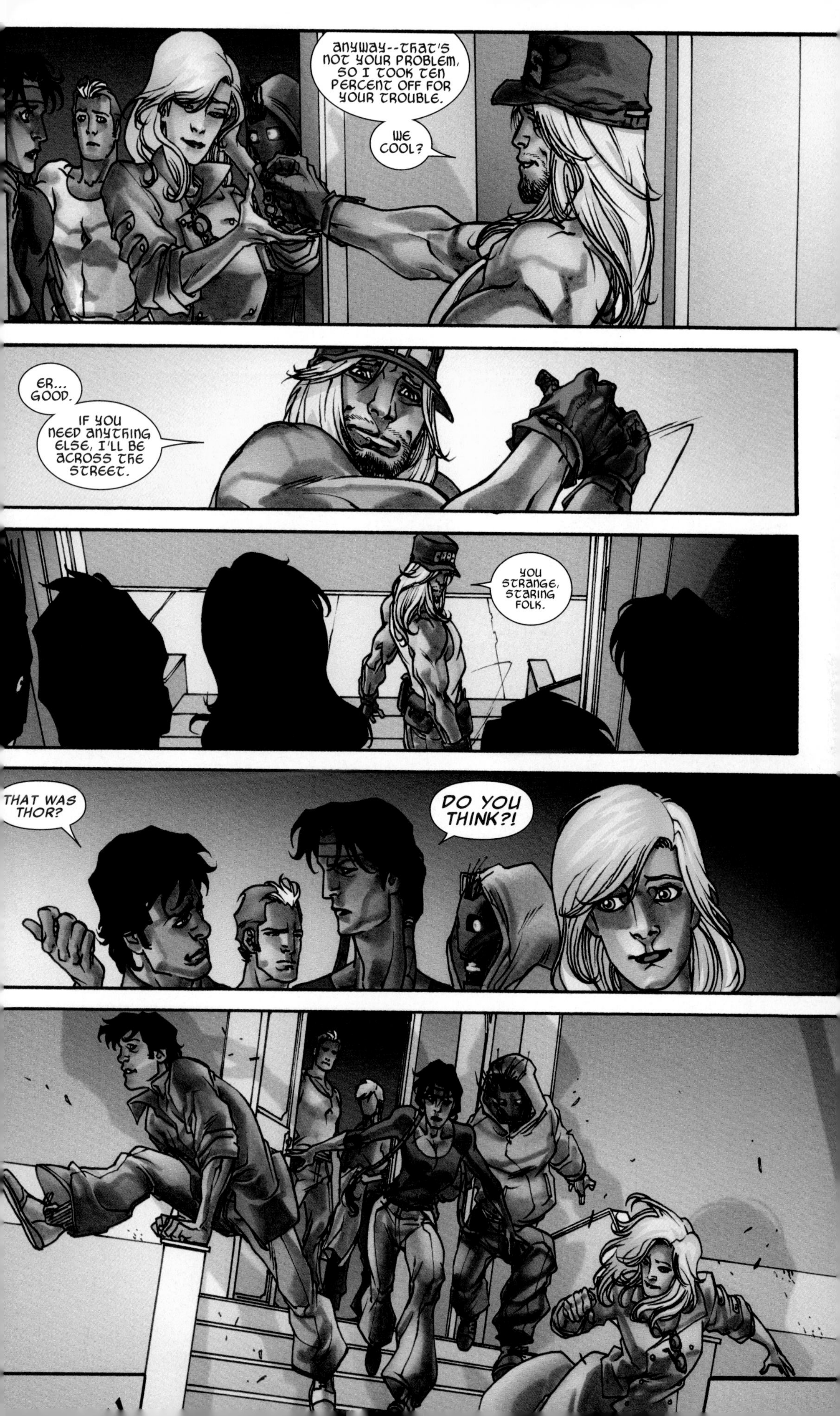
ANYWAY--THAT'S NOT YOUR PROBLEM, SO I TOOK TEN PERCENT OFF FOR YOUR TROUBLE.
WE COOL?
ER... GOOD.
IF YOU NEED ANYTHING ELSE, I'LL BE ACROSS THE STREET.
YOU STRANGE, STARING FOLK.
THAT WAS THOR?
DO YOU THINK?!

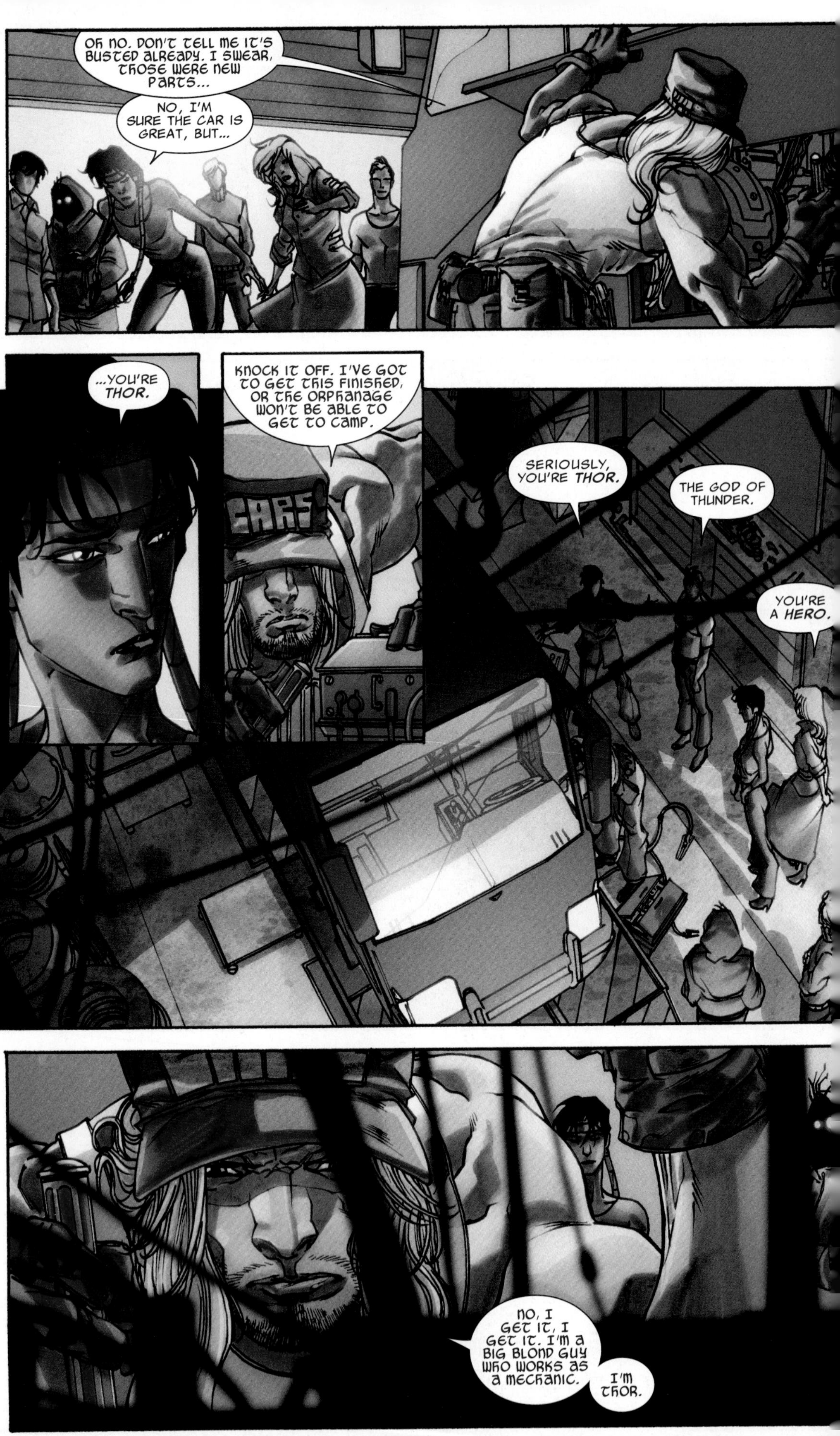

OH NO. DON'T TELL ME IT'S BUSTED ALREADY. I SWEAR, THOSE WERE NEW PARTS...
NO, I'M SURE THE CAR IS GREAT, BUT...
...YOU'RE THOR.
KNOCK IT OFF. I'VE GOT TO GET THIS FINISHED, OR THE ORPHANAGE WON'T BE ABLE TO GET TO CAMP.
CARS
SERIOUSLY, YOU'RE THOR.
THE GOD OF THUNDER.
YOU'RE A HERO.
NO, I GET IT, I GET IT. I'M A BIG BLOND GUY WHO WORKS AS A MECHANIC.
I'M THOR.

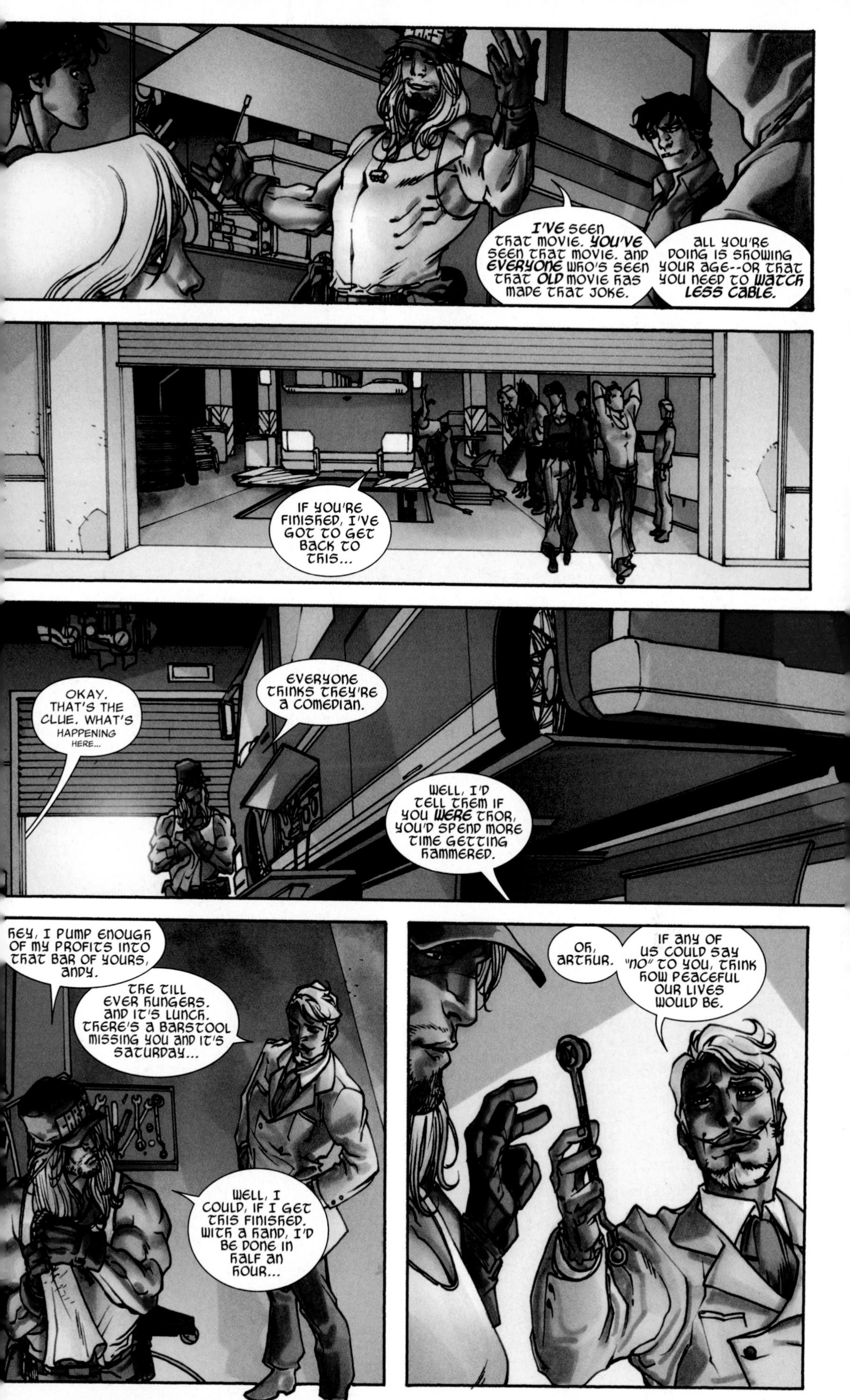
I'VE SEEN THAT MOVIE. YOU'VE SEEN THAT MOVIE. AND EVERYONE WHO'S SEEN THAT OLD MOVIE HAS MADE THAT JOKE.
ALL YOU'RE DOING IS SHOWING YOUR AGE--OR THAT YOU NEED TO WATCH LESS CABLE.
IF YOU'RE FINISHED, I'VE GOT TO GET BACK TO THIS...
OKAY. THAT'S THE CLUE. WHAT'S HAPPENING HERE...
EVERYONE THINKS THEY'RE A COMEDIAN.
WELL, I'D TELL THEM IF YOU WERE THOR, YOU'D SPEND MORE TIME GETTING HAMMERED.
HEY, I PUMP ENOUGH OF MY PROFITS INTO THAT BAR OF YOURS, ANDY.
THE TILL EVER HUNGERS. AND IT'S LUNCH. THERE'S A BARSTOOL MISSING YOU AND IT'S SATURDAY...
WELL, I COULD, IF I GET THIS FINISHED. WITH A HAND, I'D BE DONE IN HALF AN HOUR...
OH, ARTHUR.
IF ANY OF US COULD SAY "NO" TO YOU, THINK HOW PEACEFUL OUR LIVES WOULD BE.

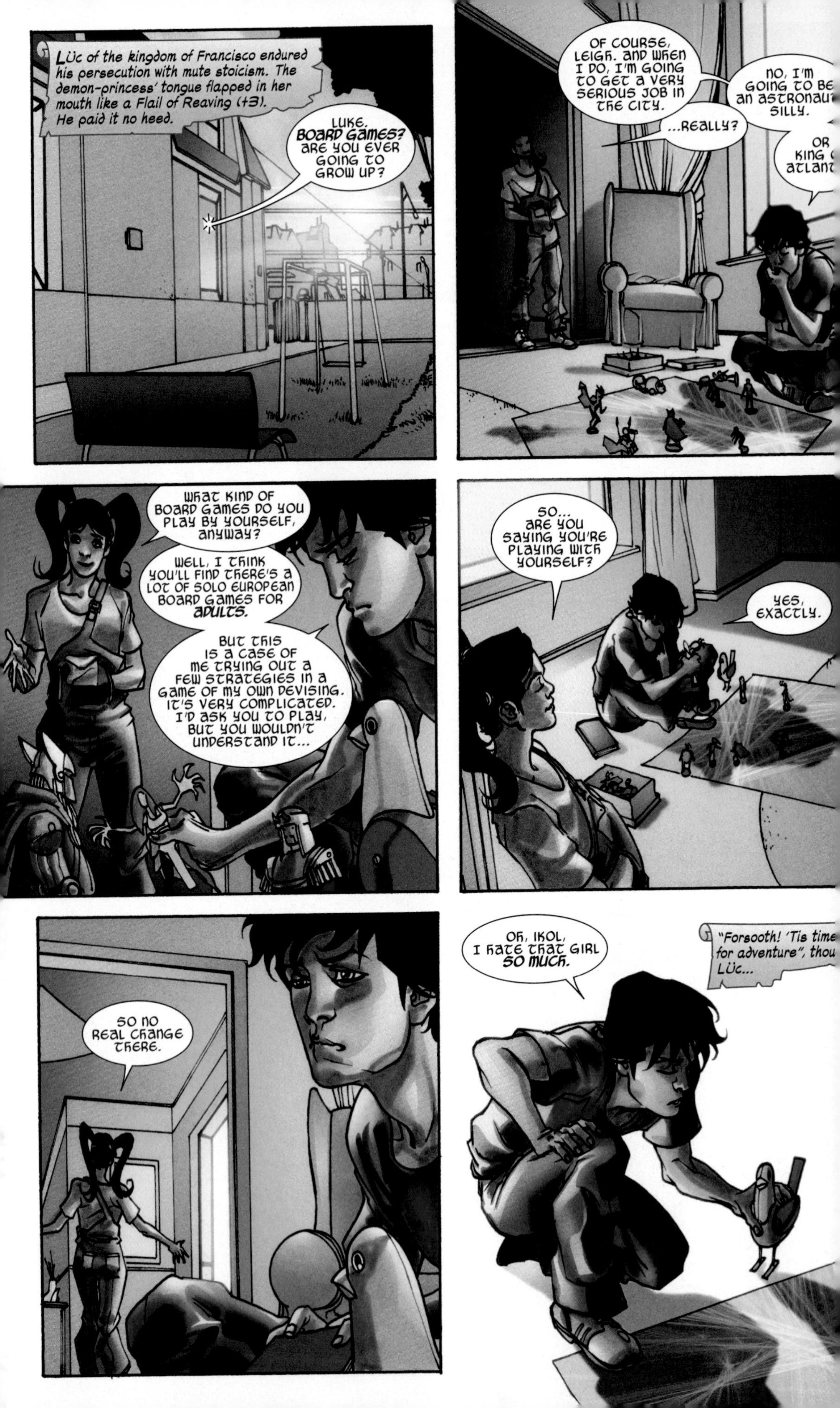
Lüc of the kingdom of Francisco endured his persecution with mute stoicism. The demon-princess' tongue flapped in her mouth like a Flail of Reaving (+3). He paid it no heed.
LUKE. BOARD GAMES? ARE YOU EVER GOING TO GROW UP?
OF COURSE, LEIGH. AND WHEN I DO, I'M GOING TO GET A VERY SERIOUS JOB IN THE CITY.
...REALLY?
NO, I'M GOING TO BE AN ASTRONAUT SILLY.
OR KING
WHAT KIND OF BOARD GAMES DO YOU PLAY BY YOURSELF, ANYWAY?
WELL, I THINK YOU'LL FIND THERE'S A LOT OF SOLO EUROPEAN BOARD GAMES FOR ADULTS.
BUT THIS IS A CASE OF ME TRYING OUT A FEW STRATEGIES IN A GAME OF MY OWN DEVISING. IT'S VERY COMPLICATED. I'D ASK YOU TO PLAY, BUT YOU WOULDN'T UNDERSTAND IT...
SO... ARE YOU SAYING YOU'RE PLAYING WITH YOURSELF?
YES, EXACTLY.
SO NO REAL CHANGE THERE.
OH, IKOL, I HATE THAT GIRL SO MUCH.
"Forsooth! 'Tis time for adventure", thou
Lüc...

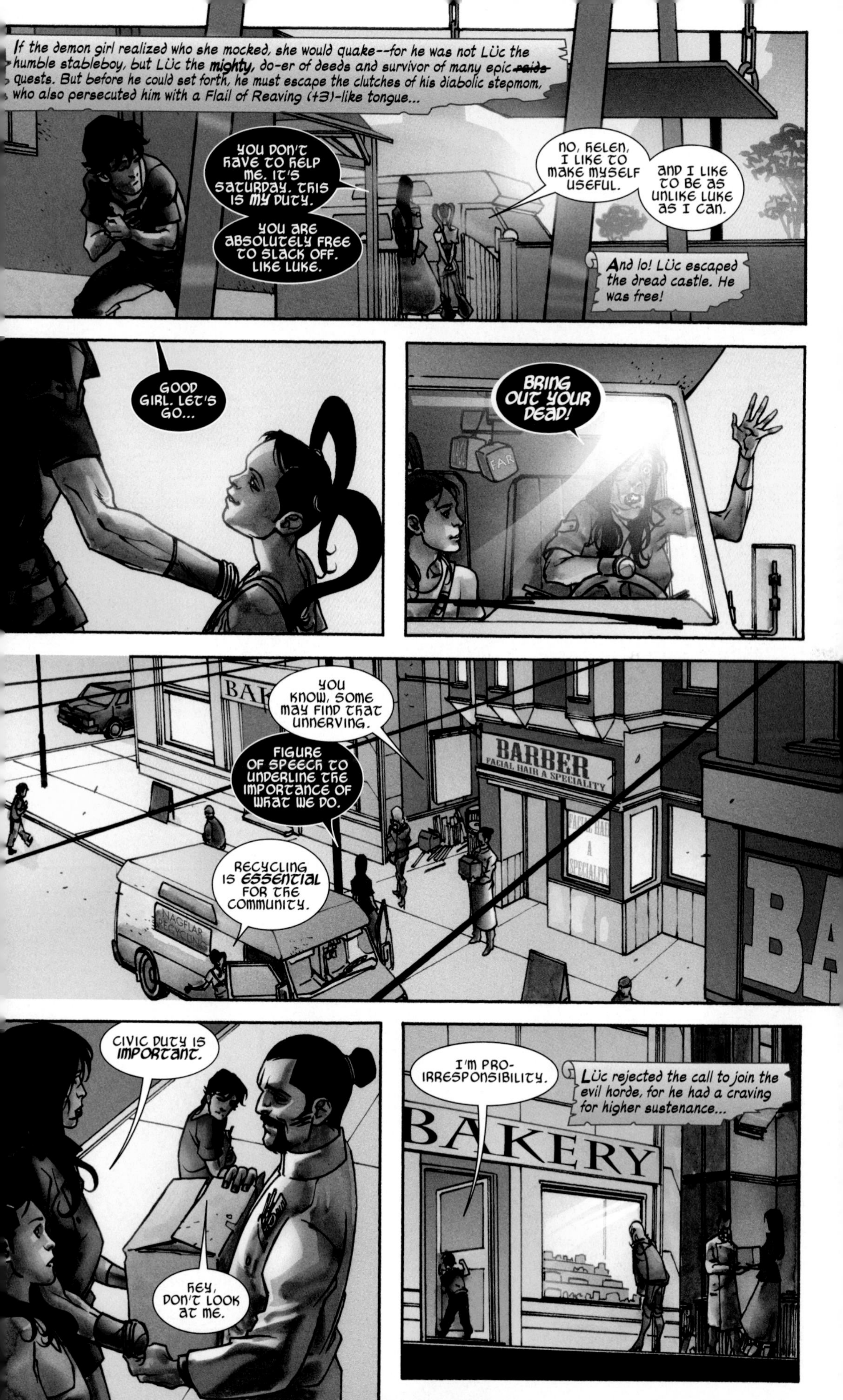
If the demon girl realized who she mocked, she would quake--for he was not Lüc the humble stableboy, but Lüc the mighty, do-er of deeds and survivor of many epic raids quests. But before he could set forth, he must escape the clutches of his diabolic stepmom, who also persecuted him with a Flail of Reaving (+3)-like tongue...
You don't have to help me. It's Saturday. This is my duty.
You are absolutely free to slack off. Like Luke.
No, Helen, I like to make myself useful.
And I like to be as unlike Luke as I can.
And lo! Lüc escaped the dread castle. He was free!
Good girl. Let's go...
Bring out your dead!
FAR
You know, some may find that unnerving.
Figure of speech to underline the importance of what we do.
Recycling is essential for the community.
BAK
BARBER
FACIAL HAIR A SPECIALITY
FACIAL HAIR A SPECIALITY
NAGFLAR RECYCLING
BA
Civic duty is important.
Hey, don't look at me.
I'm pro-irresponsibility.
Lüc rejected the call to join the evil horde, for he had a craving for higher sustenance...
BAKERY

WHAT DO YOU MEAN YOU DON'T HAVE ANY GLAZED DOUGHNUTS?

SOLD OUT.

MAN!

HAVE YOU GOT THE GLUTEN-FREE, UNSEEDED, NON-DAIRY, UNSUGARED UNLEAVENED BUNS?

YOU'RE IN LUCK, LADY. THEY'RE THE ONES I HAVEN'T EATEN--I MEAN, SOLD.

YOU DO KNOW THEY'RE TOTALLY INEDIBLE, THOUGH?

THE INEDIBLE IS ALL THE SISTERS OF THE DISORDERED EATERS IN RECOVERY CAN MANAGE. OUR APPETITES ARE VERY DELICATE WITH OUR FOOD INTOLERANCES AND ALLERGIES.

I DOUBT ANYONE WILL TOUCH THEM, BUT IT'S GOOD TO HAVE SOMETHING FOR EVERYONE TO STARE AT.

AND YOU DO LOOK SO DELICIOUS.

WHAT?

THEY LOOK SO DELICIOUS. I MEAN, THEY.

The only succor in th hard, oh-so-hard wor had been denied to l

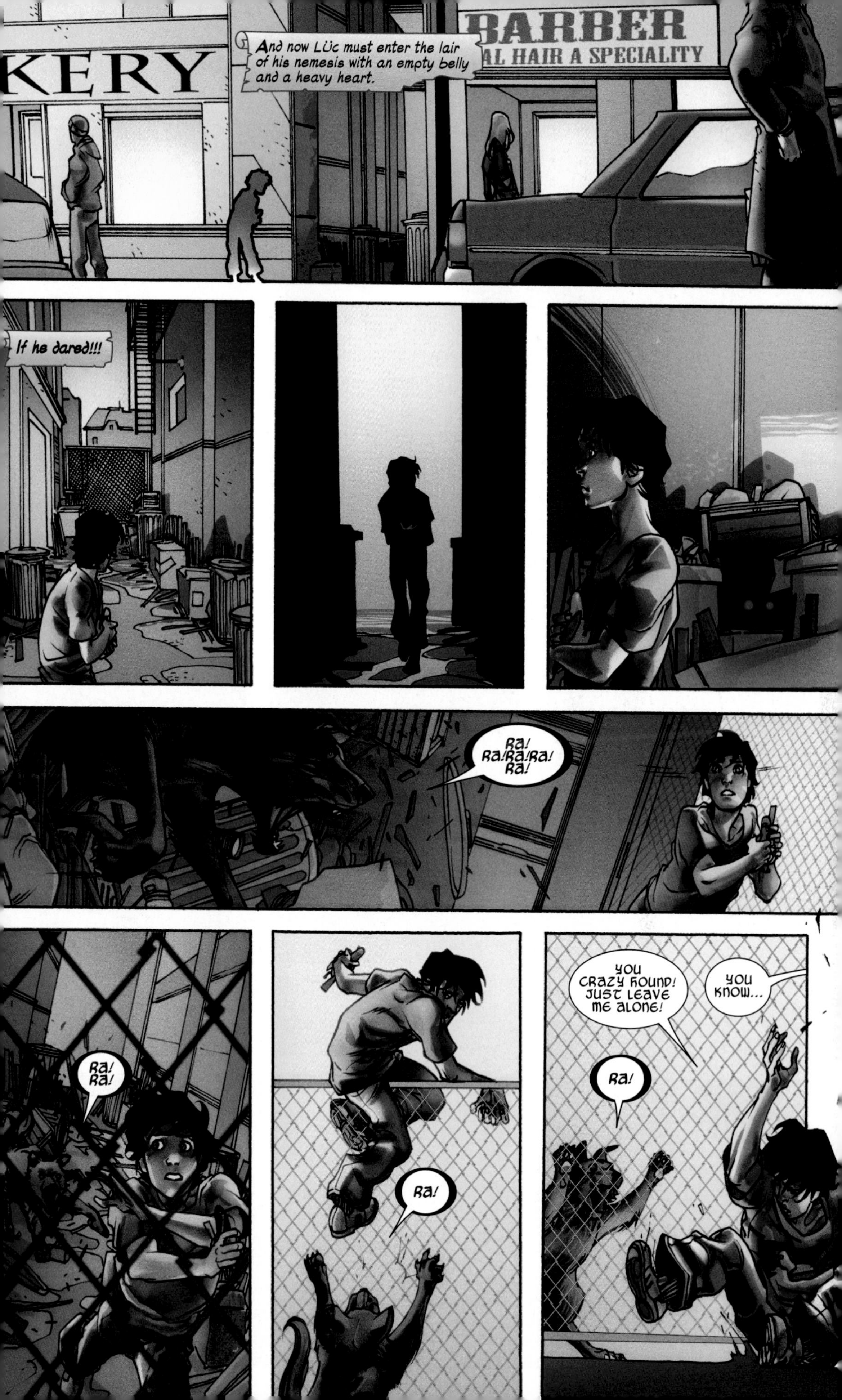
KERY
BARBER
AL HAIR A SPECIALITY
And now Lüc must enter the lair of his nemesis with an empty belly and a heavy heart.
If he dared!!!
RA! RA! RA! RA! RA!
RA! RA!
RA!
YOU CRAZY HOUND! JUST LEAVE ME ALONE!
YOU KNOW...
RA!

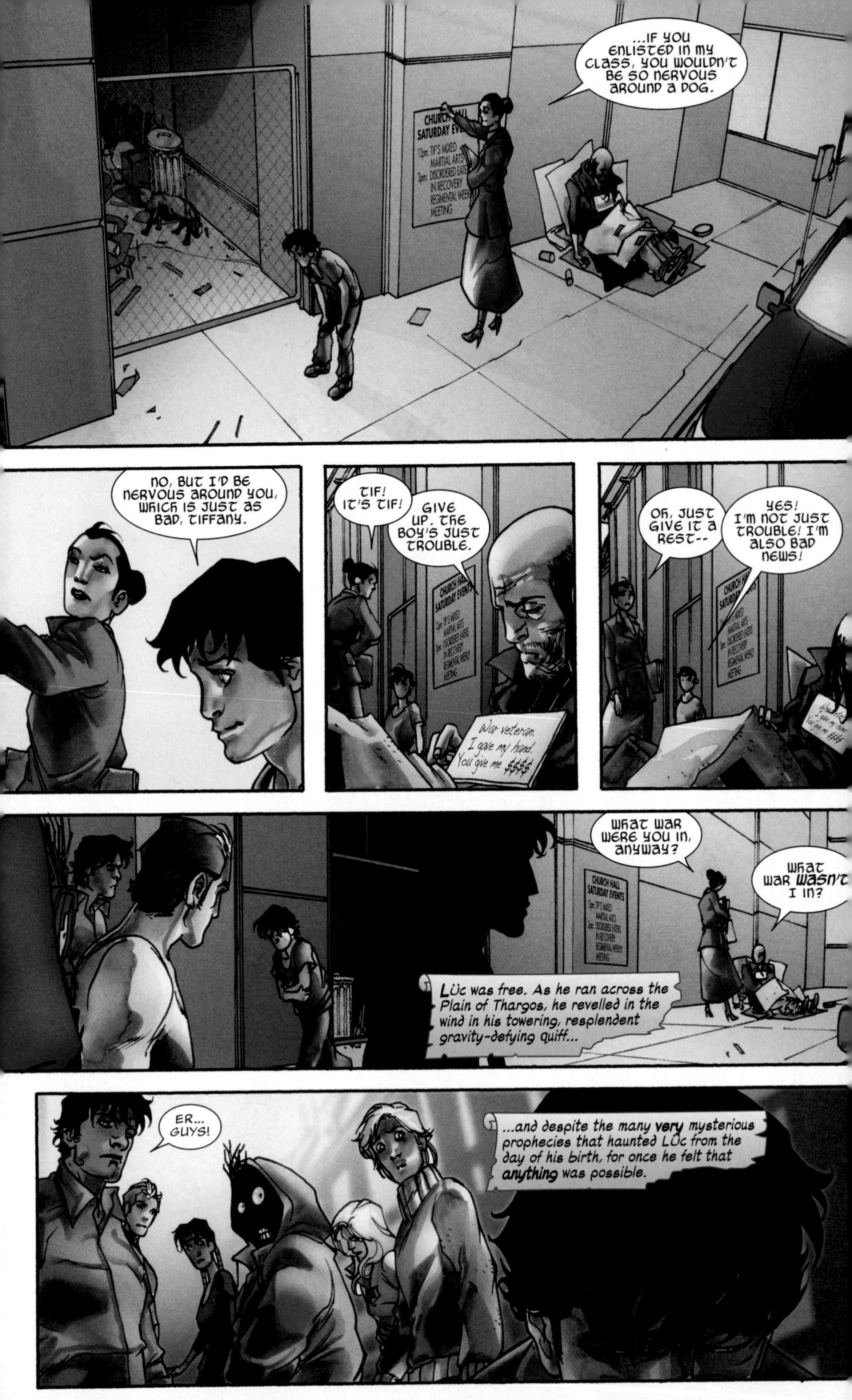

...IF YOU ENLISTED IN MY CLASS, YOU WOULDN'T BE SO NERVOUS AROUND A DOG.
CHURCH HALL SATURDAY EVENTS 12pm: TIF'S MIXED MARTIAL ARTS 3pm: DISORDERED EATERS IN RECOVERY REGIMENTAL WEEKLY MEETING
NO, BUT I'D BE NERVOUS AROUND YOU, WHICH IS JUST AS BAD, TIFFANY.
TIF! IT'S TIF!
GIVE UP. THE BOY'S JUST TROUBLE.
War veteran. I gave my hand. You give me $$$$
OH, JUST GIVE IT A REST--
YES! I'M NOT JUST TROUBLE! I'M ALSO BAD NEWS!
WHAT WAR WERE YOU IN, ANYWAY?
WHAT WAR WASN'T I IN?
LÜC was free. As he ran across the Plain of Thargos, he revelled in the wind in his towering, resplendent gravity-defying quiff...
ER... GUYS!
...and despite the many very mysterious prophecies that haunted LÜC from the day of his birth, for once he felt that anything was possible.

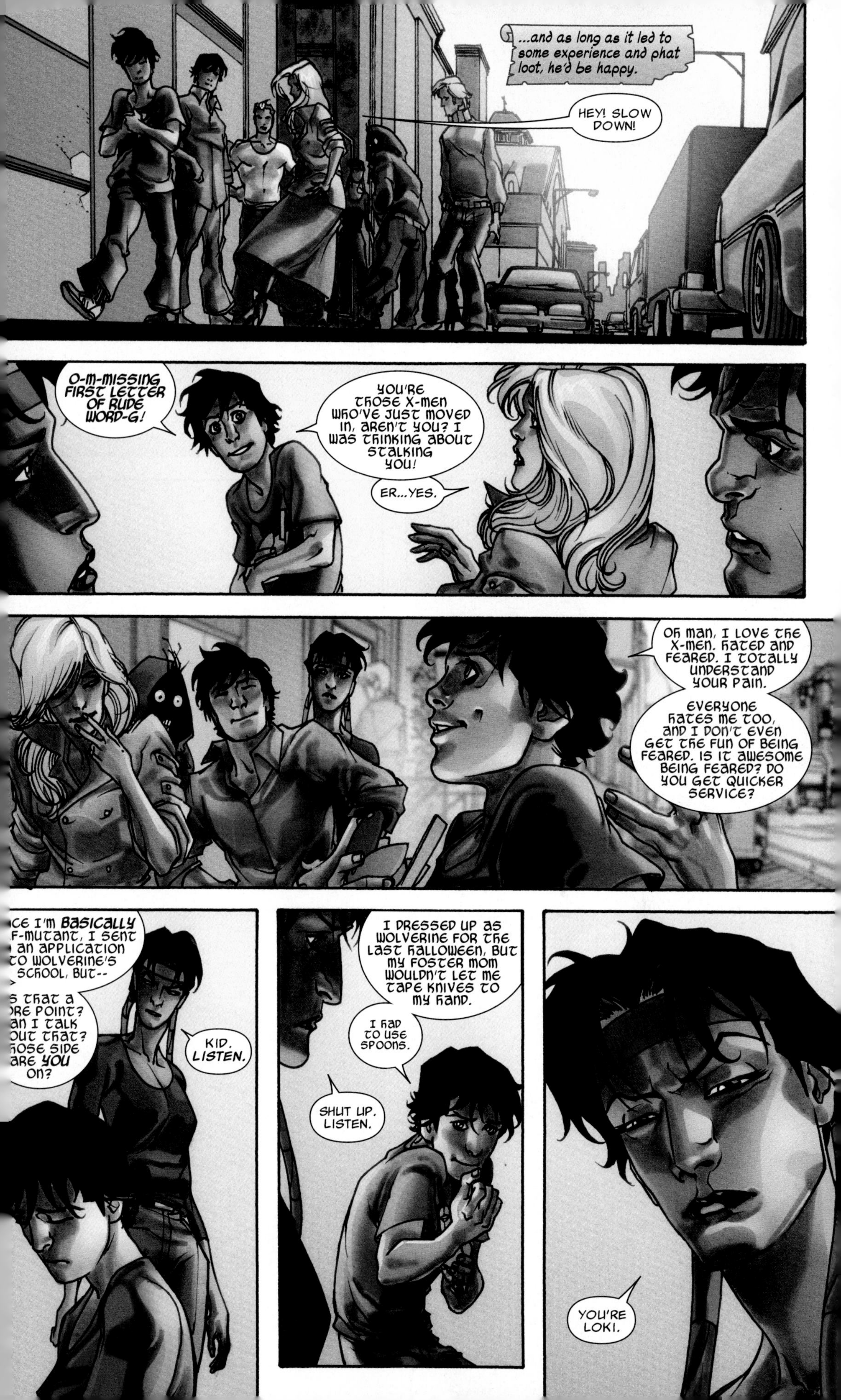
...and as long as it led to some experience and phat loot, he'd be happy.
HEY! SLOW DOWN!
O-M-MISSING FIRST LETTER OF RUDE WORD-G!
YOU'RE THOSE X-MEN WHO'VE JUST MOVED IN, AREN'T YOU? I WAS THINKING ABOUT STALKING YOU!
ER...YES.
OH MAN, I LOVE THE X-MEN. HATED AND FEARED. I TOTALLY UNDERSTAND YOUR PAIN.
EVERYONE HATES ME TOO, AND I DON'T EVEN GET THE FUN OF BEING FEARED. IS IT AWESOME BEING FEARED? DO YOU GET QUICKER SERVICE?
CE I'M BASICALLY F-MUTANT, I SENT AN APPLICATION TO WOLVERINE'S SCHOOL, BUT--
S THAT A ORE POINT? AN I TALK OUT THAT? HOSE SIDE ARE YOU ON?
KID. LISTEN.
I DRESSED UP AS WOLVERINE FOR THE LAST HALLOWEEN, BUT MY FOSTER MOM WOULDN'T LET ME TAPE KNIVES TO MY HAND.
I HAD TO USE SPOONS.
SHUT UP. LISTEN.
YOU'RE LOKI.

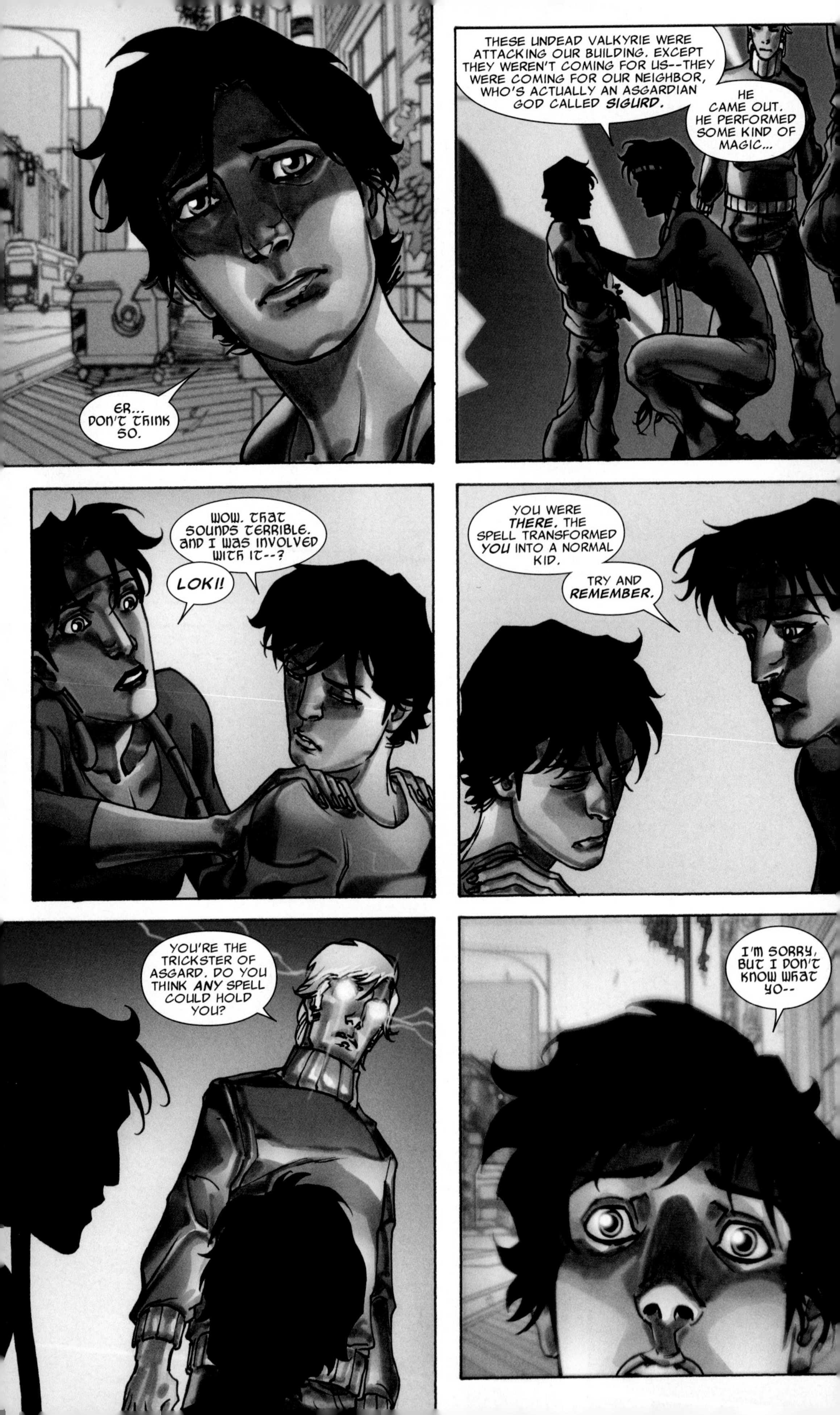
ER... DON'T THINK SO.
THESE UNDEAD VALKYRIE WERE ATTACKING OUR BUILDING. EXCEPT THEY WEREN'T COMING FOR US--THEY WERE COMING FOR OUR NEIGHBOR, WHO'S ACTUALLY AN ASGARDIAN GOD CALLED SIGURD.
HE CAME OUT. HE PERFORMED SOME KIND OF MAGIC...
WOW. THAT SOUNDS TERRIBLE. AND I WAS INVOLVED WITH IT--?
LOKI!
YOU WERE THERE. THE SPELL TRANSFORMED YOU INTO A NORMAL KID.
TRY AND REMEMBER.
YOU'RE THE TRICKSTER OF ASGARD. DO YOU THINK ANY SPELL COULD HOLD YOU?
I'M SORRY, BUT I DON'T KNOW WHAT YO--

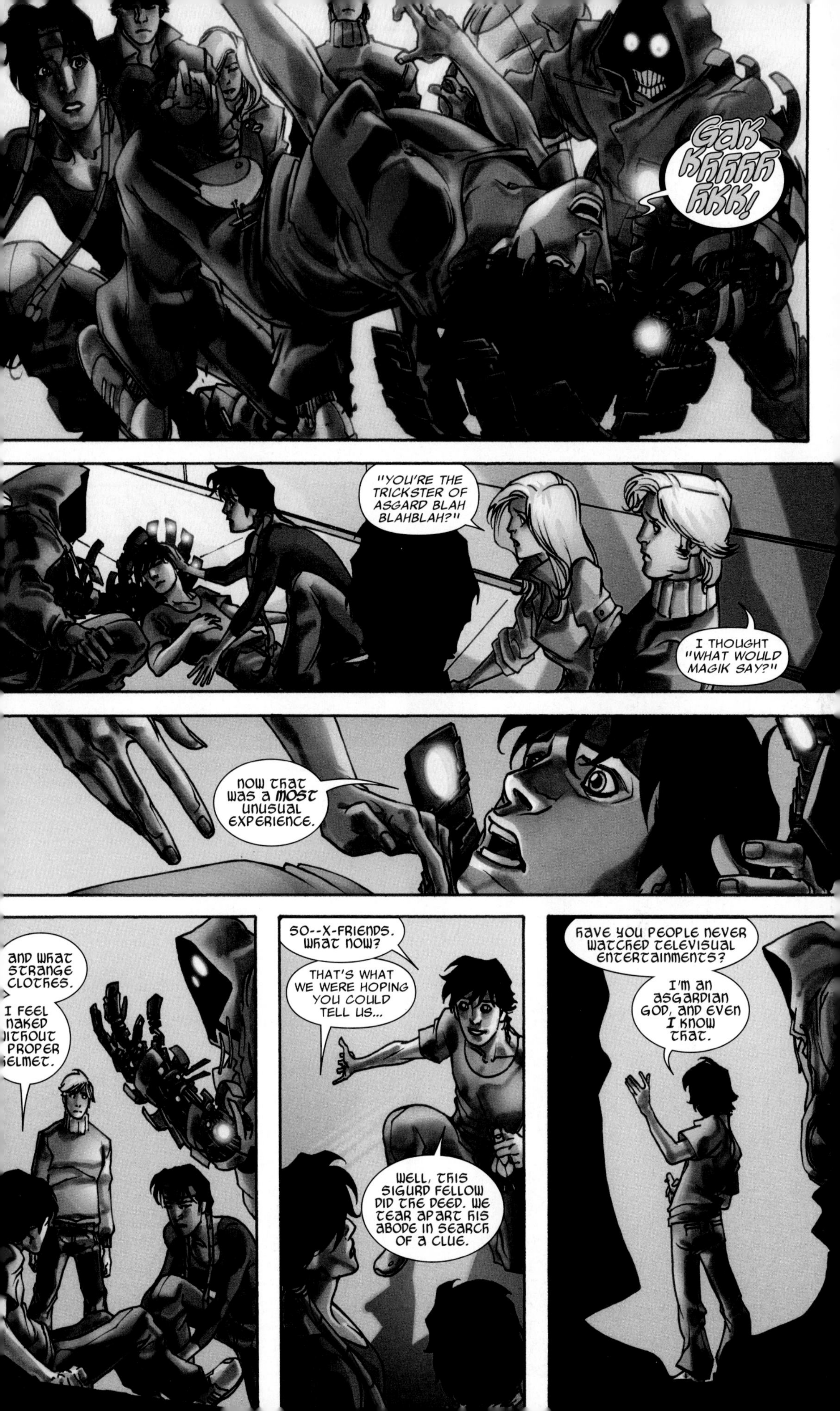
GAK KHHHH HKK!
"YOU'RE THE TRICKSTER OF ASGARD BLAH BLAHBLAH?"
I THOUGHT "WHAT WOULD MAGIK SAY?"
NOW THAT WAS A MOST UNUSUAL EXPERIENCE.
AND WHAT STRANGE CLOTHES.
I FEEL NAKED WITHOUT PROPER HELMET.
SO--X-FRIENDS. WHAT NOW?
THAT'S WHAT WE WERE HOPING YOU COULD TELL US...
WELL, THIS SIGURD FELLOW DID THE DEED. WE TEAR APART HIS ABODE IN SEARCH OF A CLUE.
HAVE YOU PEOPLE NEVER WATCHED TELEVISUAL ENTERTAINMENTS?
I'M AN ASGARDIAN GOD, AND EVEN I KNOW THAT.

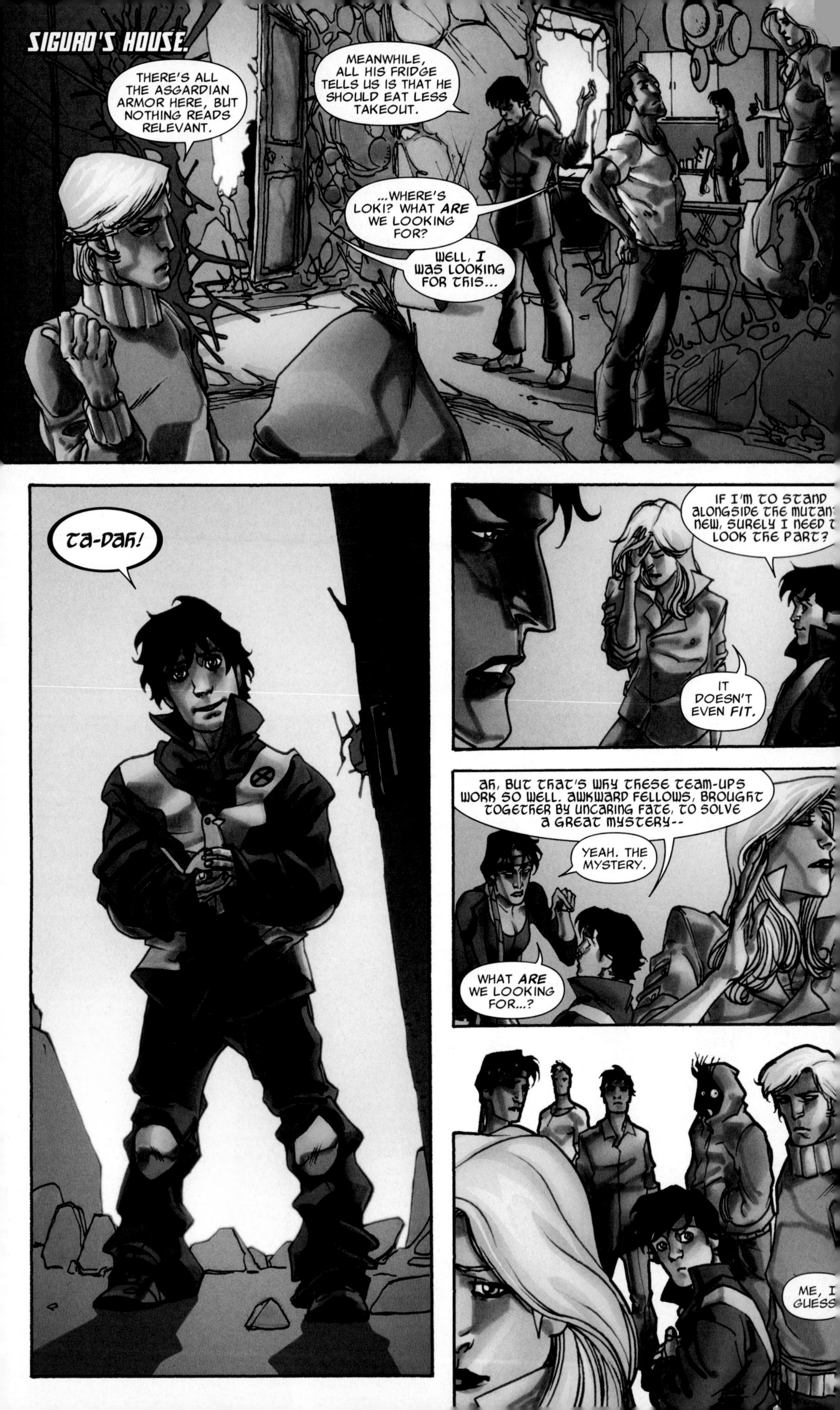
SIGURD'S HOUSE.
THERE'S ALL THE ASGARDIAN ARMOR HERE, BUT NOTHING READS RELEVANT.
MEANWHILE, ALL HIS FRIDGE TELLS US IS THAT HE SHOULD EAT LESS TAKEOUT.
...WHERE'S LOKI? WHAT ARE WE LOOKING FOR?
WELL, I WAS LOOKING FOR THIS...
TA-DAH!
IF I'M TO STAND ALONGSIDE THE MUTAN NEW, SURELY I NEED T LOOK THE PART?
IT DOESN'T EVEN FIT.
AH, BUT THAT'S WHY THESE TEAM-UPS WORK SO WELL. AWKWARD FELLOWS, BROUGHT TOGETHER BY UNCARING FATE, TO SOLVE A GREAT MYSTERY--
YEAH. THE MYSTERY.
WHAT ARE WE LOOKING FOR...?
ME, I GUESS

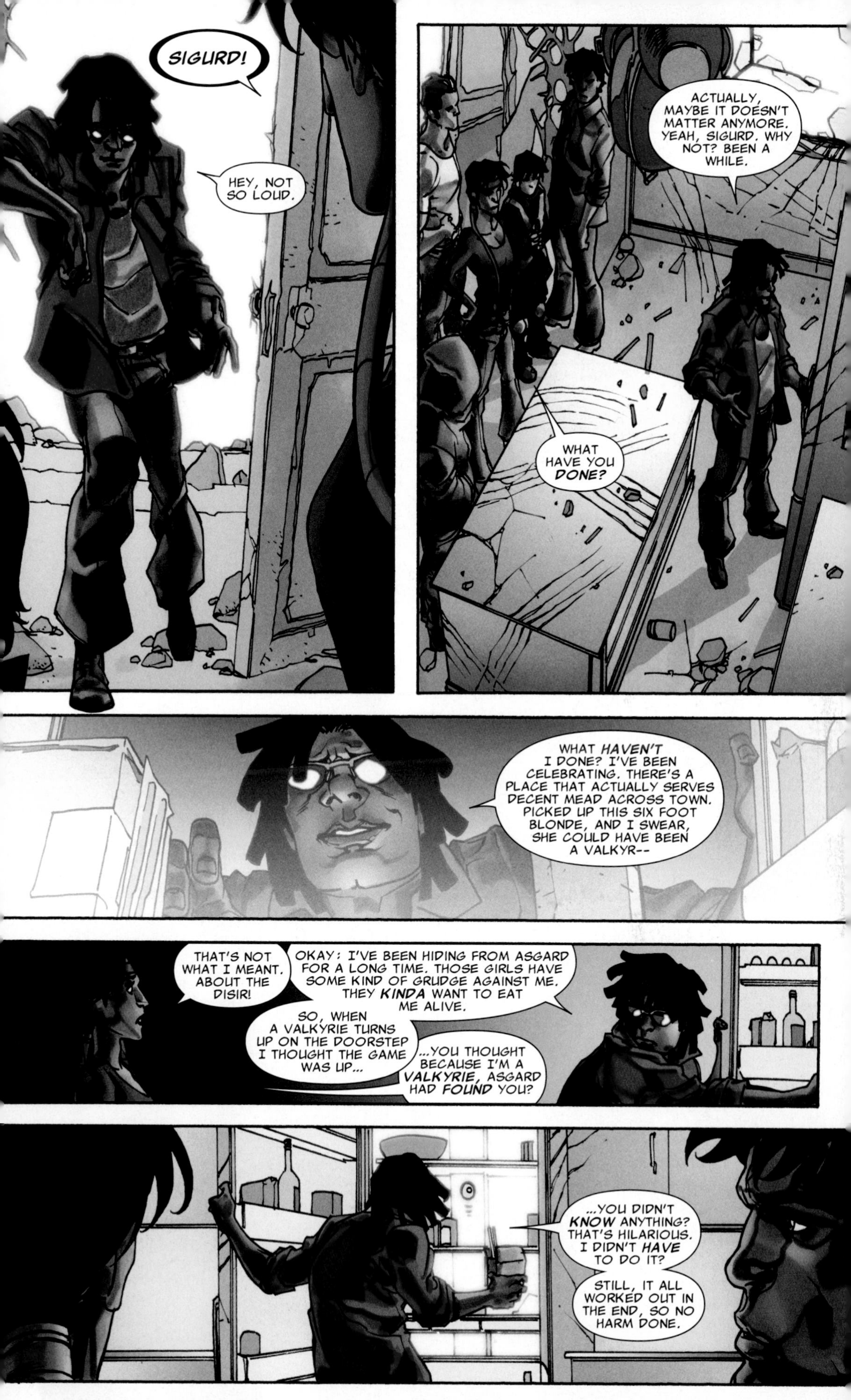
SIGURD!
HEY, NOT SO LOUD.
ACTUALLY, MAYBE IT DOESN'T MATTER ANYMORE. YEAH, SIGURD. WHY NOT? BEEN A WHILE.
WHAT HAVE YOU DONE?
WHAT HAVEN'T I DONE? I'VE BEEN CELEBRATING. THERE'S A PLACE THAT ACTUALLY SERVES DECENT MEAD ACROSS TOWN. PICKED UP THIS SIX FOOT BLONDE, AND I SWEAR, SHE COULD HAVE BEEN A VALKYR--
THAT'S NOT WHAT I MEANT. ABOUT THE DISIR!
OKAY: I'VE BEEN HIDING FROM ASGARD FOR A LONG TIME. THOSE GIRLS HAVE SOME KIND OF GRUDGE AGAINST ME. THEY KINDA WANT TO EAT ME ALIVE.
SO, WHEN A VALKYRIE TURNS UP ON THE DOORSTEP I THOUGHT THE GAME WAS UP...
...YOU THOUGHT BECAUSE I'M A VALKYRIE, ASGARD HAD FOUND YOU?
...YOU DIDN'T KNOW ANYTHING? THAT'S HILARIOUS. I DIDN'T HAVE TO DO IT?
STILL, IT ALL WORKED OUT IN THE END, SO NO HARM DONE.

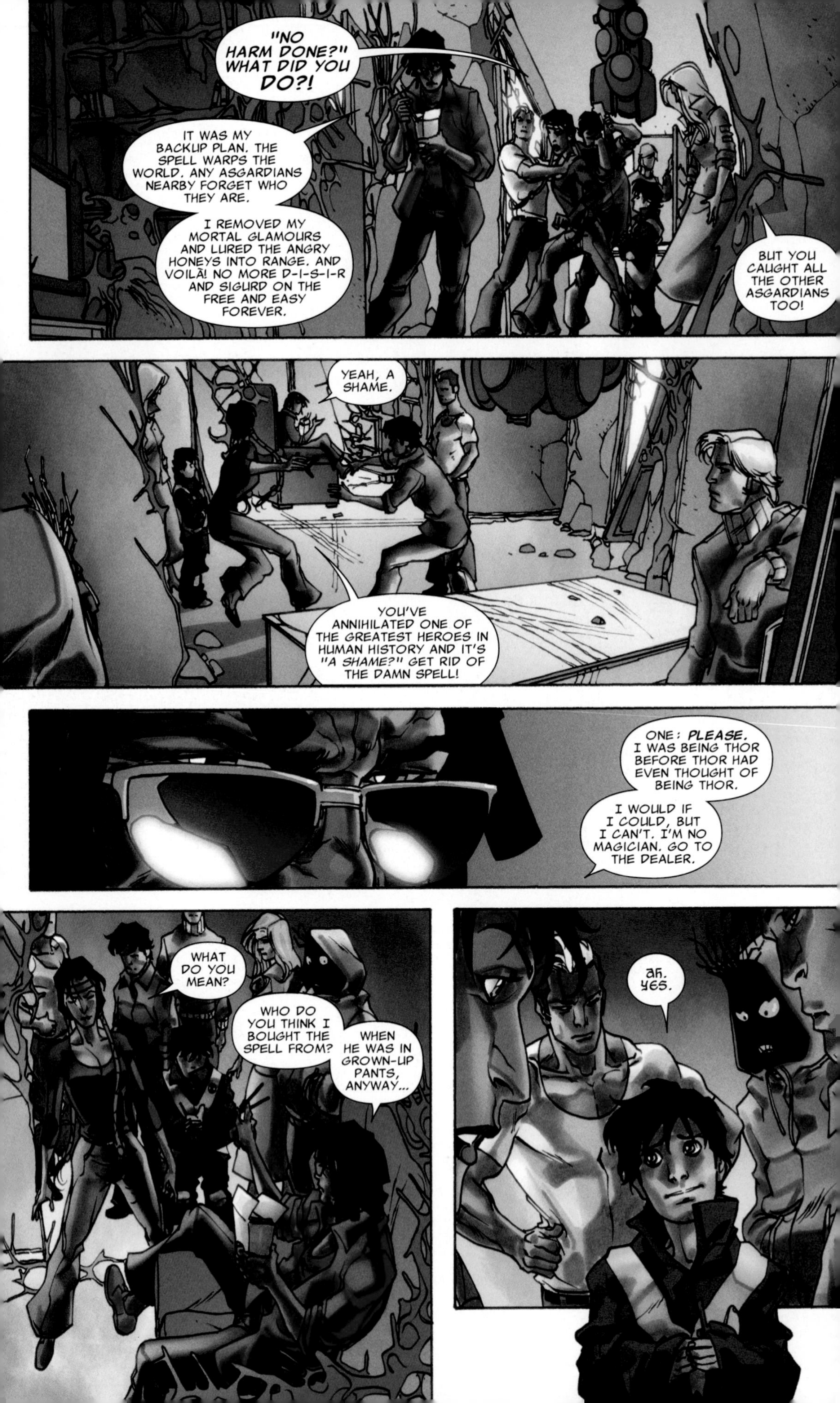

"NO HARM DONE?" WHAT DID YOU DO?!
IT WAS MY BACKUP PLAN. THE SPELL WARPS THE WORLD. ANY ASGARDIANS NEARBY FORGET WHO THEY ARE.
I REMOVED MY MORTAL GLAMOURS AND LURED THE ANGRY HONEYS INTO RANGE. AND VOILÀ! NO MORE D-I-S-I-R AND SIGURD ON THE FREE AND EASY FOREVER.
BUT YOU CAUGHT ALL THE OTHER ASGARDIANS TOO!
YEAH, A SHAME.
YOU'VE ANNIHILATED ONE OF THE GREATEST HEROES IN HUMAN HISTORY AND IT'S "A SHAME?" GET RID OF THE DAMN SPELL!
ONE: PLEASE. I WAS BEING THOR BEFORE THOR HAD EVEN THOUGHT OF BEING THOR.
I WOULD IF I COULD, BUT I CAN'T. I'M NO MAGICIAN. GO TO THE DEALER.
WHAT DO YOU MEAN?
WHO DO YOU THINK I BOUGHT THE SPELL FROM?
WHEN HE WAS IN GROWN-UP PANTS, ANYWAY...
AH. YES.

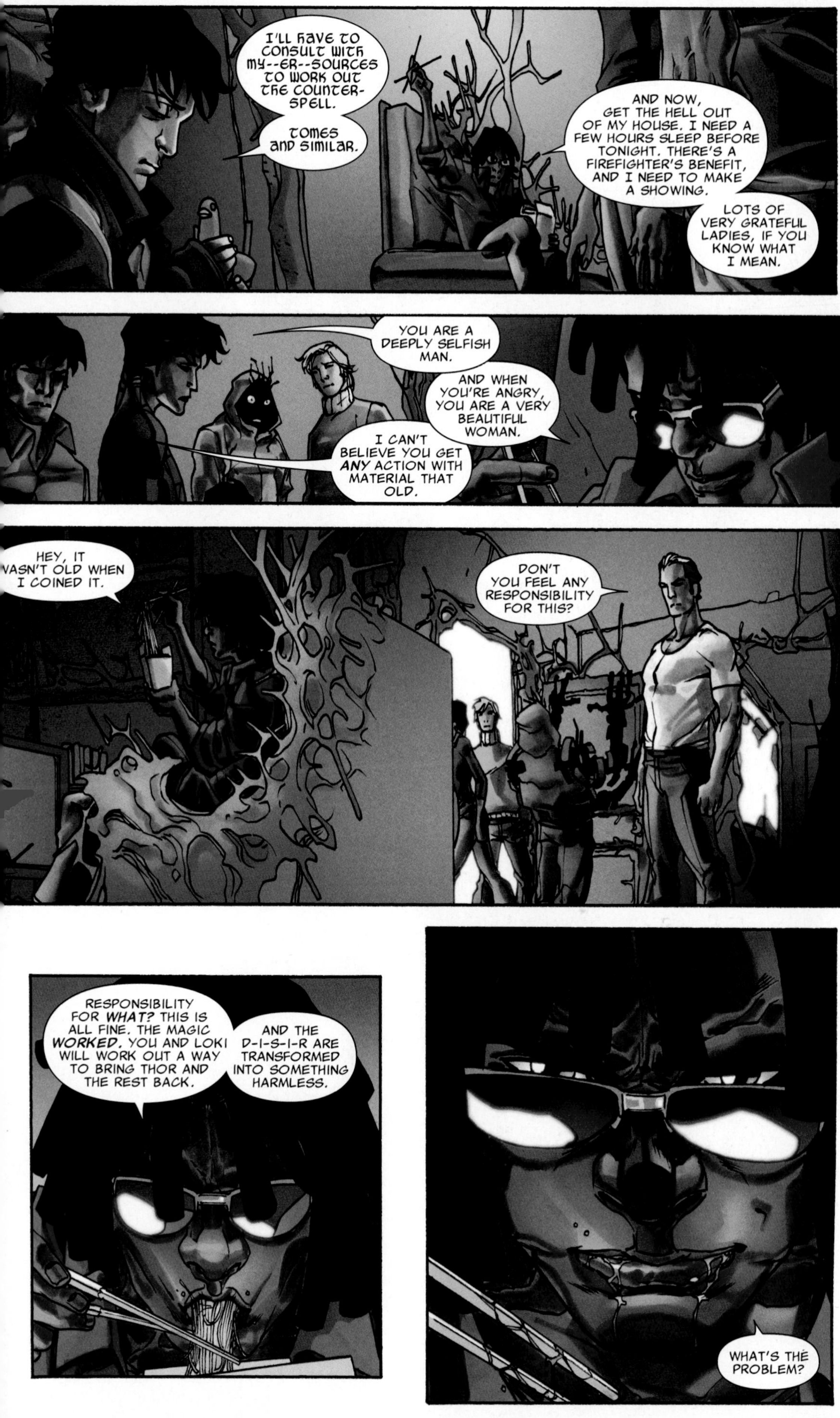
I'LL HAVE TO CONSULT WITH MY--ER--SOURCES TO WORK OUT THE COUNTER-SPELL.
TOMES AND SIMILAR.
AND NOW, GET THE HELL OUT OF MY HOUSE. I NEED A FEW HOURS SLEEP BEFORE TONIGHT. THERE'S A FIREFIGHTER'S BENEFIT, AND I NEED TO MAKE A SHOWING.
LOTS OF VERY GRATEFUL LADIES, IF YOU KNOW WHAT I MEAN.
YOU ARE A DEEPLY SELFISH MAN.
AND WHEN YOU'RE ANGRY, YOU ARE A VERY BEAUTIFUL WOMAN.
I CAN'T BELIEVE YOU GET ANY ACTION WITH MATERIAL THAT OLD.
HEY, IT WASN'T OLD WHEN I COINED IT.
DON'T YOU FEEL ANY RESPONSIBILITY FOR THIS?
RESPONSIBILITY FOR WHAT? THIS IS ALL FINE. THE MAGIC WORKED. YOU AND LOKI WILL WORK OUT A WAY TO BRING THOR AND THE REST BACK.
AND THE D-I-S-I-R ARE TRANSFORMED INTO SOMETHING HARMLESS.
WHAT'S THE PROBLEM?

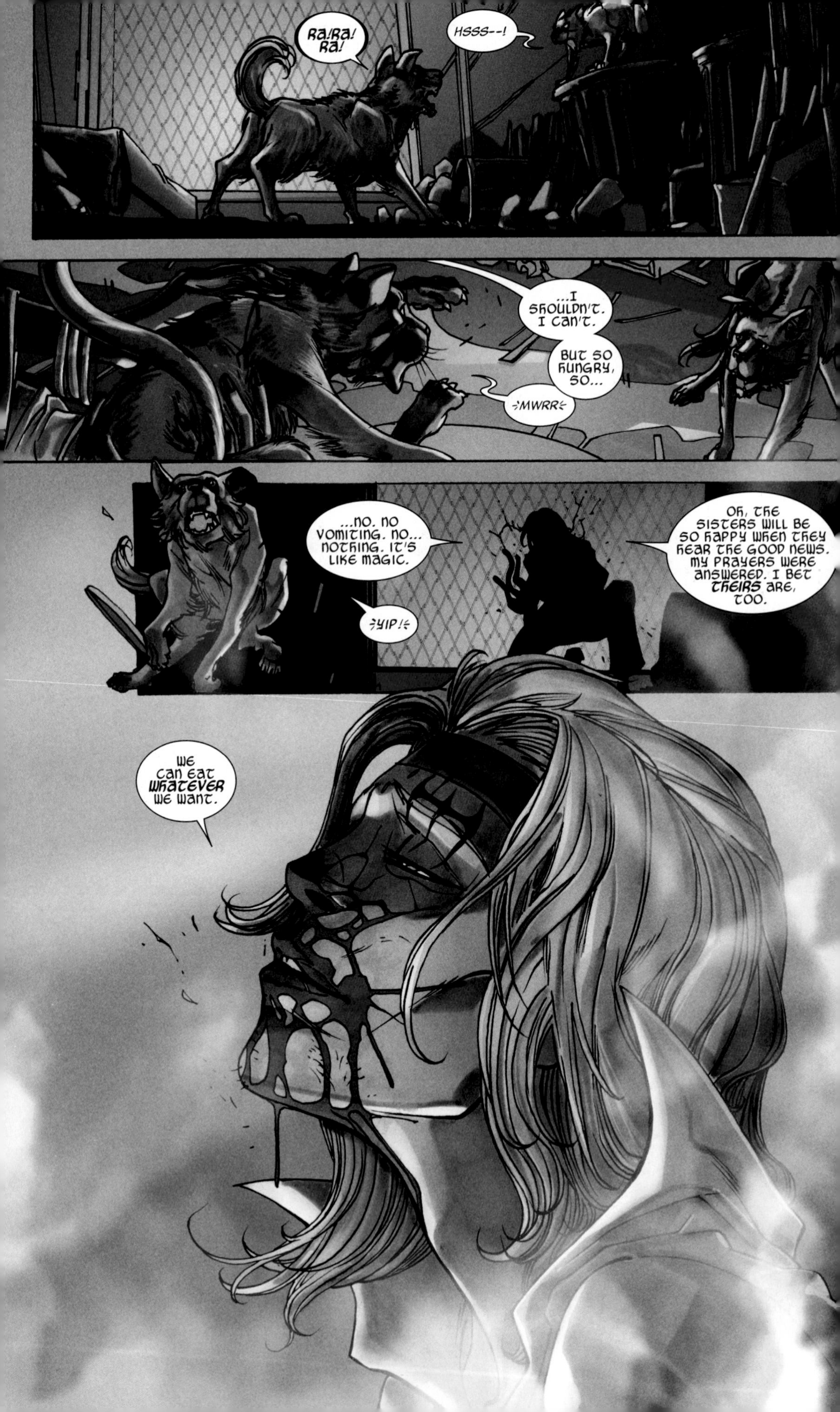
RA!RA! RA!
HSSS--!
...I SHOULDN'T. I CAN'T.
BUT SO HUNGRY, SO...
MWRR
...NO. NO VOMITING. NO... NOTHING. IT'S LIKE MAGIC.
YIP!
OH, THE SISTERS WILL BE SO HAPPY WHEN THEY HEAR THE GOOD NEWS. MY PRAYERS WERE ANSWERED. I BET THEIRS ARE, TOO.
WE CAN EAT WHATEVER WE WANT.

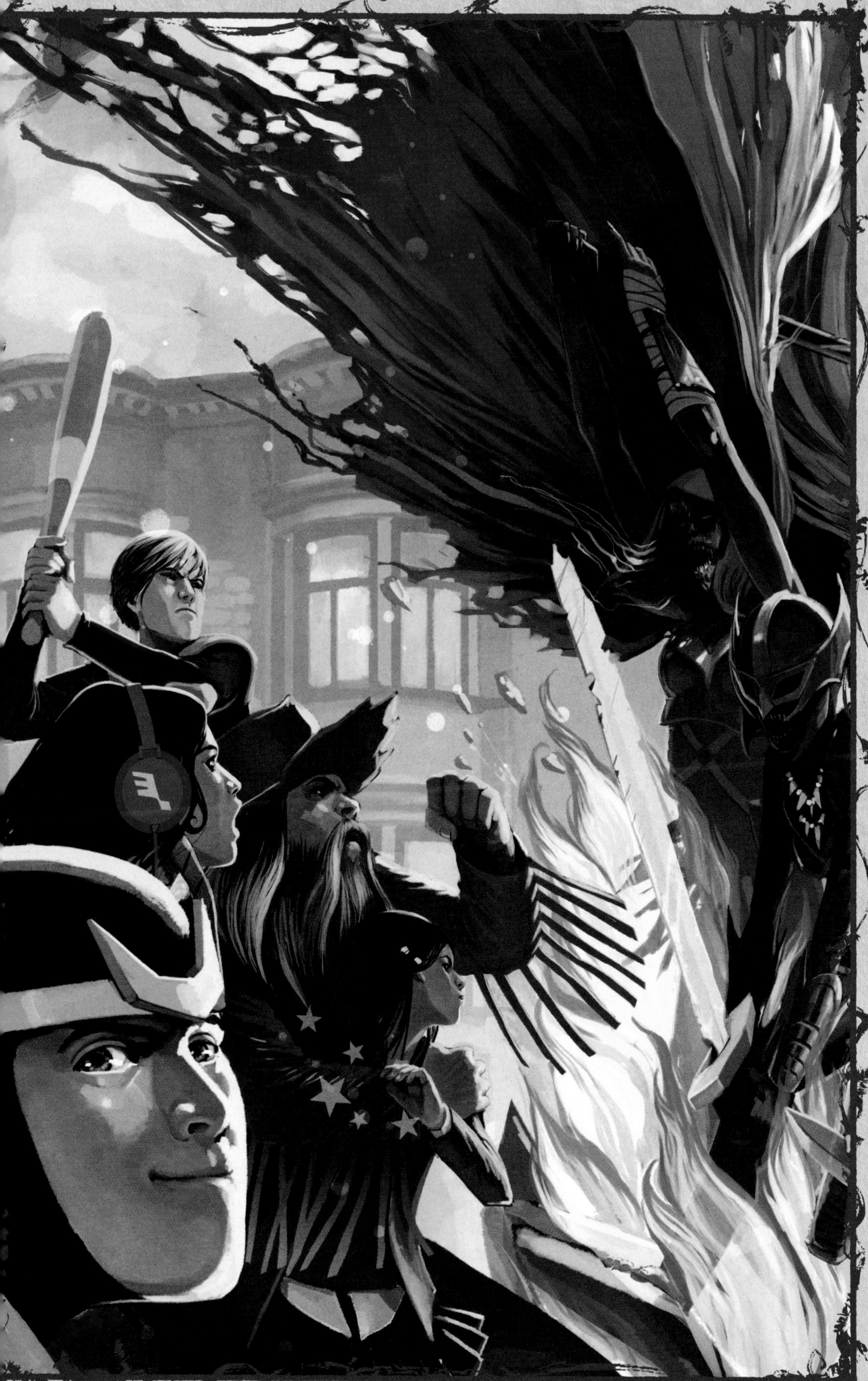

NEW MUTANTS #42: "CANNIBAL TIME BOMB"

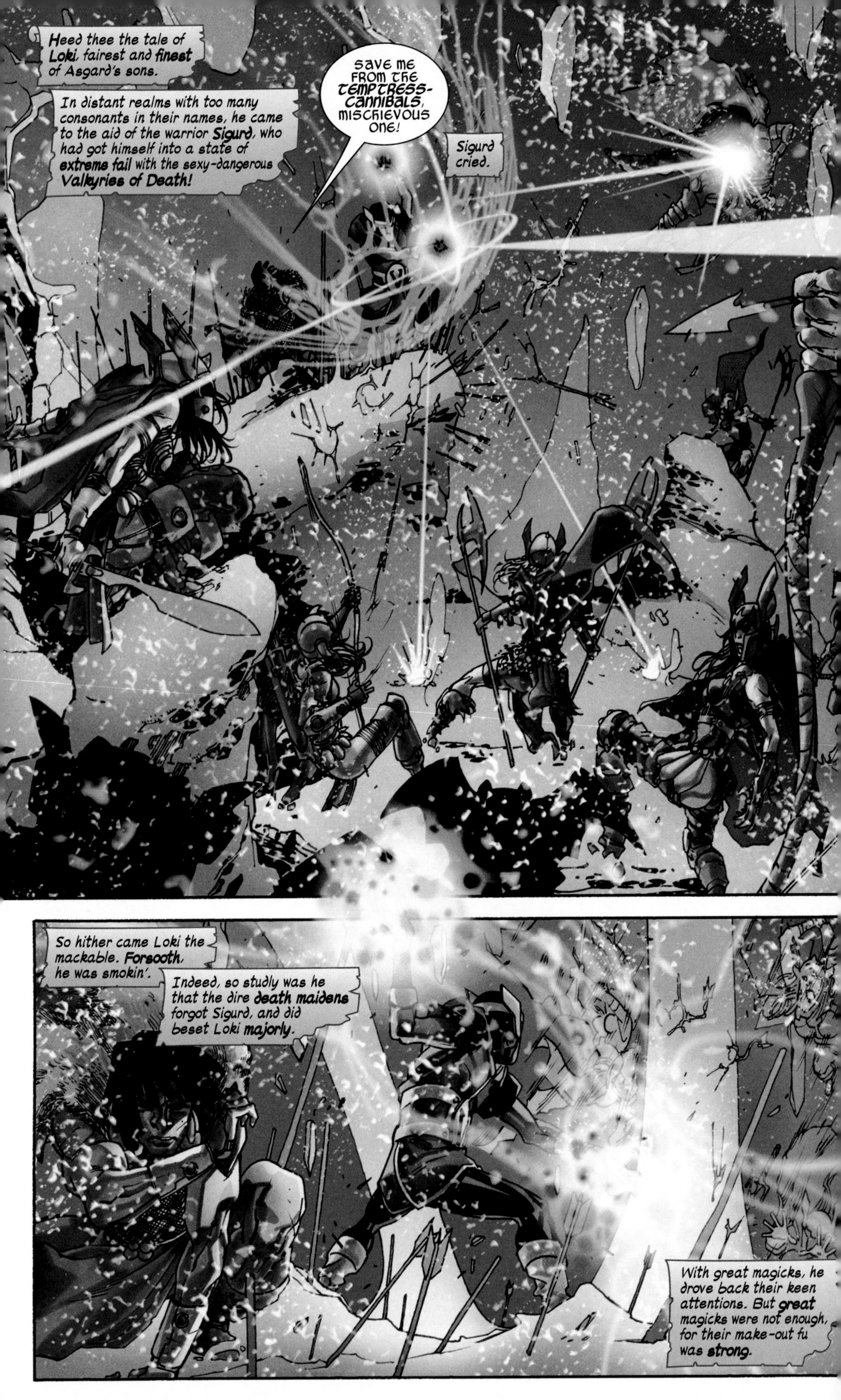
Heed thee the tale of Loki, fairest and finest of Asgard's sons.
In distant realms with too many consonants in their names, he came to the aid of the warrior Sigurd, who had got himself into a state of extreme fail with the sexy-dangerous Valkyries of Death!
SAVE ME FROM THE TEMPTRESS-CANNIBALS, MISCHIEVOUS ONE!
Sigurd cried.
So hither came Loki the mackable. Forsooth, he was smokin'.
Indeed, so studly was he that the dire death maidens forgot Sigurd, and did beset Loki majorly.
With great magicks, he drove back their keen attentions. But great magicks were not enough, for their make-out fu was strong.

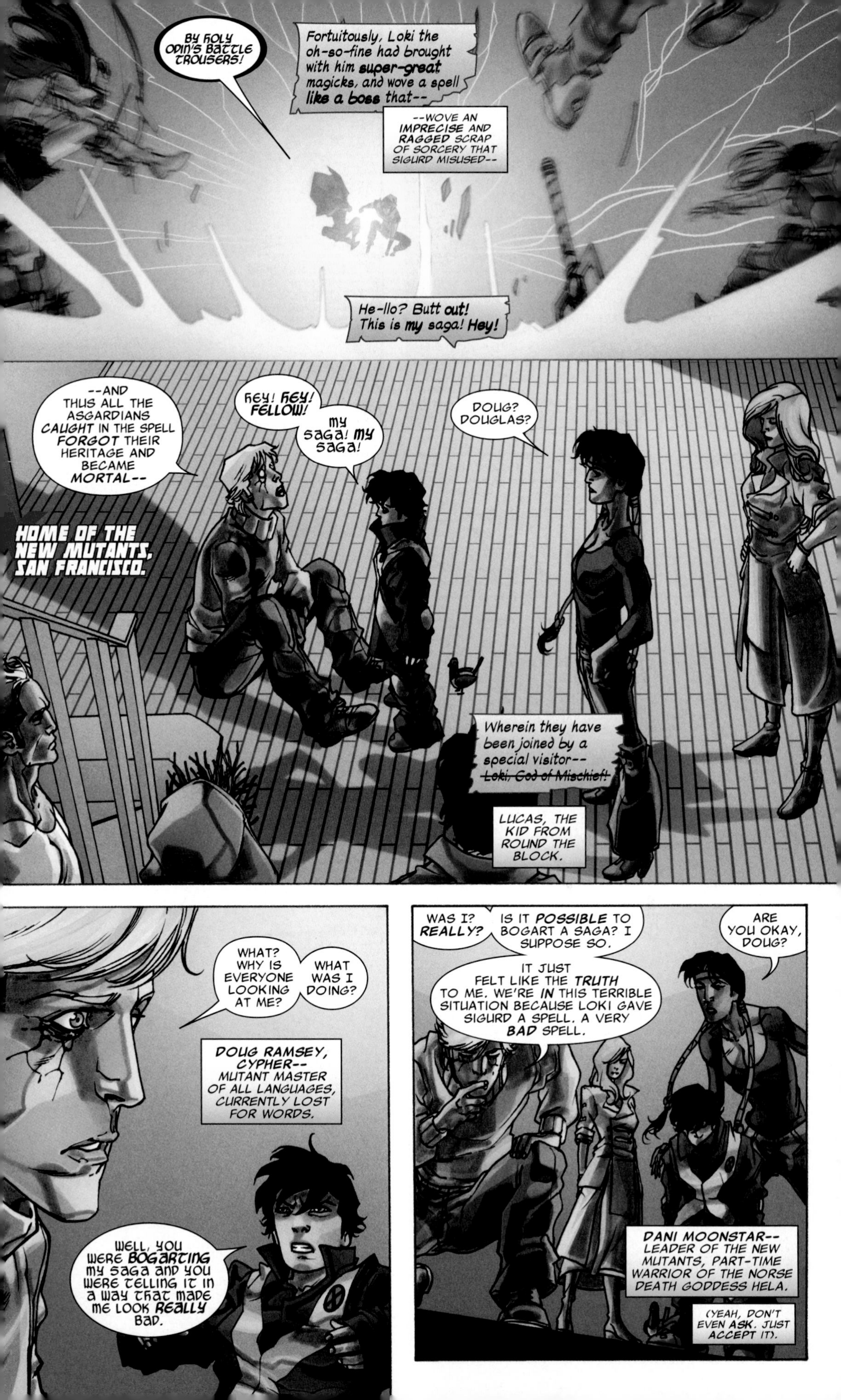
BY HOLY ODIN'S BATTLE TROUSERS!
Fortuitously, Loki the oh-so-fine had brought with him super-great magicks, and wove a spell like a boss that--
--WOVE AN IMPRECISE AND RAGGED SCRAP OF SORCERY THAT SIGURD MISUSED--
He-llo? Butt out! This is my saga! Hey!
--AND THUS ALL THE ASGARDIANS CAUGHT IN THE SPELL FORGOT THEIR HERITAGE AND BECAME MORTAL--
HEY! HEY! FELLOW!
MY SAGA! MY SAGA!
DOUG? DOUGLAS?
HOME OF THE NEW MUTANTS, SAN FRANCISCO.
Wherein they have been joined by a special visitor--
Loki, God of Mischief!
LUCAS, THE KID FROM ROUND THE BLOCK.
WHAT? WHY IS EVERYONE LOOKING AT ME?
WHAT WAS I DOING?
DOUG RAMSEY, CYPHER-- MUTANT MASTER OF ALL LANGUAGES, CURRENTLY LOST FOR WORDS.
WELL, YOU WERE BOGARTING MY SAGA AND YOU WERE TELLING IT IN A WAY THAT MADE ME LOOK REALLY BAD.
WAS I? REALLY?
IS IT POSSIBLE TO BOGART A SAGA? I SUPPOSE SO.
IT JUST FELT LIKE THE TRUTH TO ME. WE'RE IN THIS TERRIBLE SITUATION BECAUSE LOKI GAVE SIGURD A SPELL. A VERY BAD SPELL.
ARE YOU OKAY, DOUG?
DANI MOONSTAR-- LEADER OF THE NEW MUTANTS, PART-TIME WARRIOR OF THE NORSE DEATH GODDESS HELA.
(YEAH, DON'T EVEN ASK. JUST ACCEPT IT).

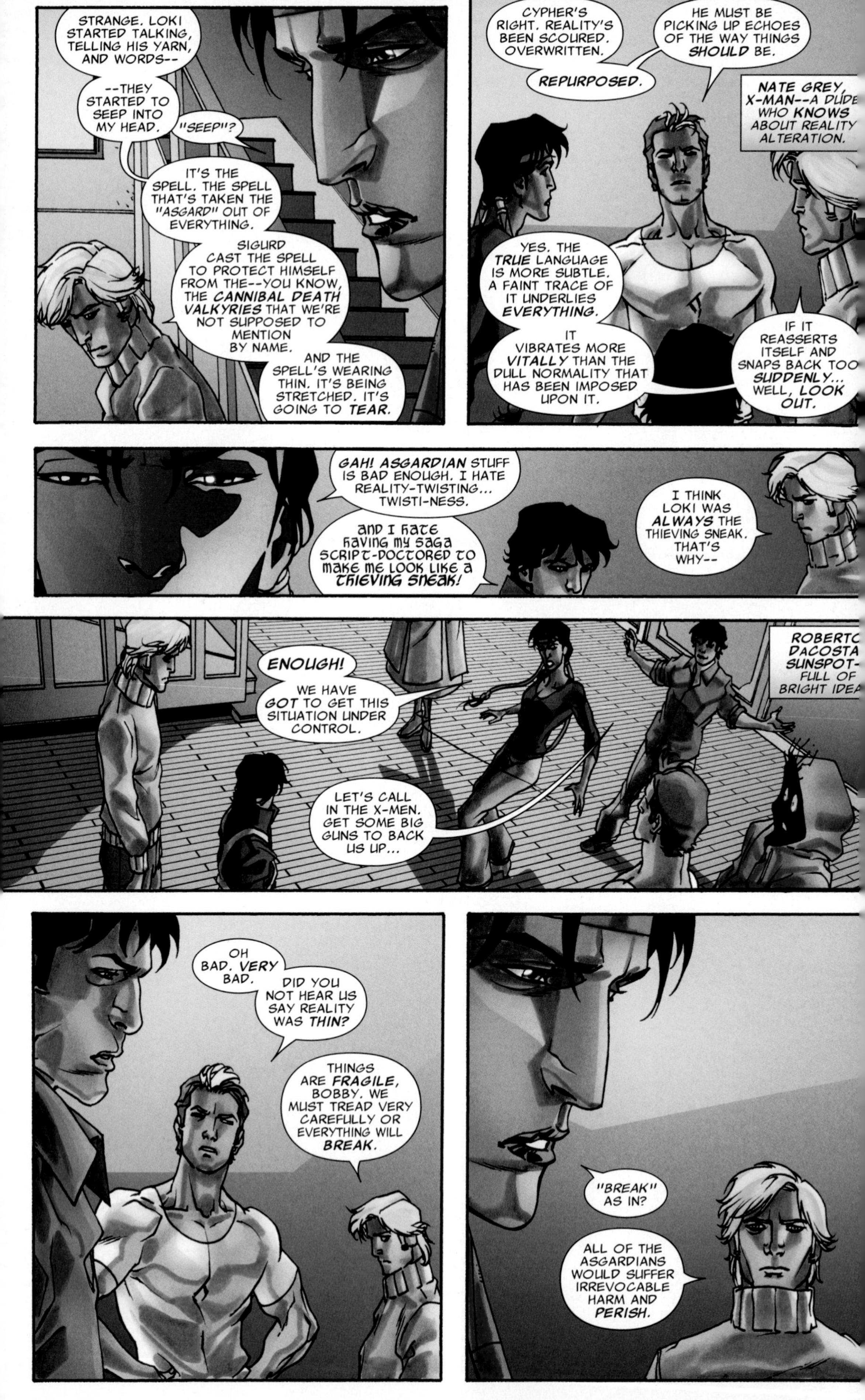
STRANGE. LOKI STARTED TALKING, TELLING HIS YARN, AND WORDS--
--THEY STARTED TO SEEP INTO MY HEAD.
"SEEP"?
IT'S THE SPELL. THE SPELL THAT'S TAKEN THE "ASGARD" OUT OF EVERYTHING.
SIGURD CAST THE SPELL TO PROTECT HIMSELF FROM THE--YOU KNOW, THE CANNIBAL DEATH VALKYRIES THAT WE'RE NOT SUPPOSED TO MENTION BY NAME.
AND THE SPELL'S WEARING THIN. IT'S BEING STRETCHED. IT'S GOING TO TEAR.
CYPHER'S RIGHT. REALITY'S BEEN SCOURED. OVERWRITTEN.
REPURPOSED.
HE MUST BE PICKING UP ECHOES OF THE WAY THINGS SHOULD BE.
NATE GREY, X-MAN--A DUDE WHO KNOWS ABOUT REALITY ALTERATION.
YES. THE TRUE LANGUAGE IS MORE SUBTLE. A FAINT TRACE OF IT UNDERLIES EVERYTHING.
IT VIBRATES MORE VITALLY THAN THE DULL NORMALITY THAT HAS BEEN IMPOSED UPON IT.
IF IT REASSERTS ITSELF AND SNAPS BACK TOO SUDDENLY... WELL, LOOK OUT.
GAH! ASGARDIAN STUFF IS BAD ENOUGH. I HATE REALITY-TWISTING... TWISTI-NESS.
AND I HATE HAVING MY SAGA SCRIPT-DOCTORED TO MAKE ME LOOK LIKE A THIEVING SNEAK!
I THINK LOKI WAS ALWAYS THE THIEVING SNEAK. THAT'S WHY--
ENOUGH! WE HAVE GOT TO GET THIS SITUATION UNDER CONTROL.
ROBERTO DACOSTA SUNSPOT-- FULL OF BRIGHT IDEA
LET'S CALL IN THE X-MEN. GET SOME BIG GUNS TO BACK US UP...
OH BAD. VERY BAD.
DID YOU NOT HEAR US SAY REALITY WAS THIN?
THINGS ARE FRAGILE, BOBBY. WE MUST TREAD VERY CAREFULLY OR EVERYTHING WILL BREAK.
"BREAK" AS IN?
ALL OF THE ASGARDIANS WOULD SUFFER IRREVOCABLE HARM AND PERISH.

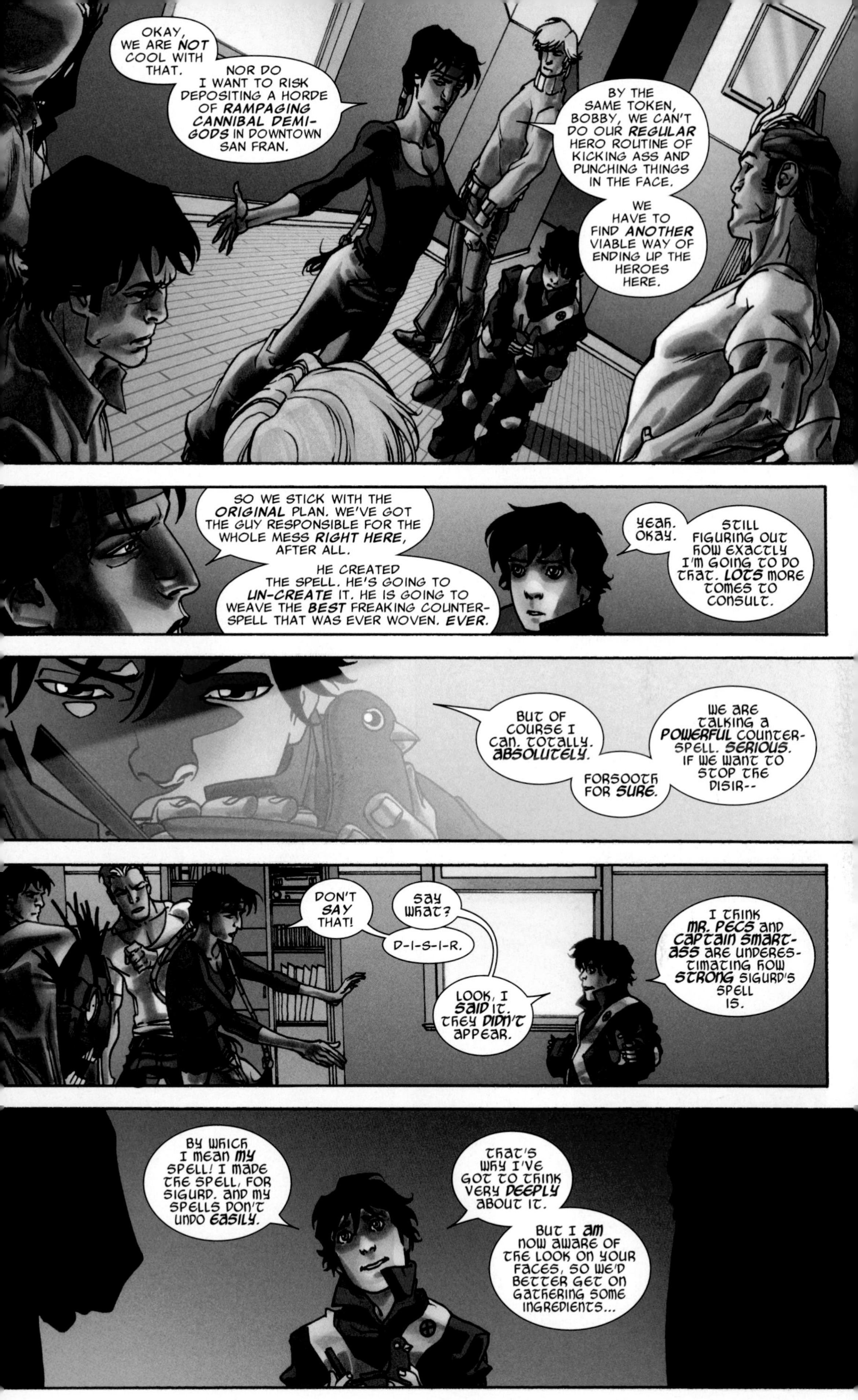
OKAY, WE ARE NOT COOL WITH THAT.
NOR DO I WANT TO RISK DEPOSITING A HORDE OF RAMPAGING CANNIBAL DEMI-GODS IN DOWNTOWN SAN FRAN.
BY THE SAME TOKEN, BOBBY, WE CAN'T DO OUR REGULAR HERO ROUTINE OF KICKING ASS AND PUNCHING THINGS IN THE FACE.
WE HAVE TO FIND ANOTHER VIABLE WAY OF ENDING UP THE HEROES HERE.
SO WE STICK WITH THE ORIGINAL PLAN. WE'VE GOT THE GUY RESPONSIBLE FOR THE WHOLE MESS RIGHT HERE, AFTER ALL.
HE CREATED THE SPELL. HE'S GOING TO UN-CREATE IT. HE IS GOING TO WEAVE THE BEST FREAKING COUNTER-SPELL THAT WAS EVER WOVEN. EVER.
YEAH. OKAY.
STILL FIGURING OUT HOW EXACTLY I'M GOING TO DO THAT. LOTS MORE TOMES TO CONSULT.
BUT OF COURSE I CAN. TOTALLY. ABSOLUTELY.
FORSOOTH FOR SURE.
WE ARE TALKING A POWERFUL COUNTER-SPELL. SERIOUS. IF WE WANT TO STOP THE DISIR--
DON'T SAY THAT!
SAY WHAT?
D-I-S-I-R.
LOOK, I SAID IT. THEY DIDN'T APPEAR.
I THINK MR. PECS AND CAPTAIN SMART-ASS ARE UNDERES-TIMATING HOW STRONG SIGURD'S SPELL IS.
BY WHICH I MEAN MY SPELL! I MADE THE SPELL, FOR SIGURD. AND MY SPELLS DON'T UNDO EASILY.
THAT'S WHY I'VE GOT TO THINK VERY DEEPLY ABOUT IT.
BUT I AM NOW AWARE OF THE LOOK ON YOUR FACES, SO WE'D BETTER GET ON GATHERING SOME INGREDIENTS...

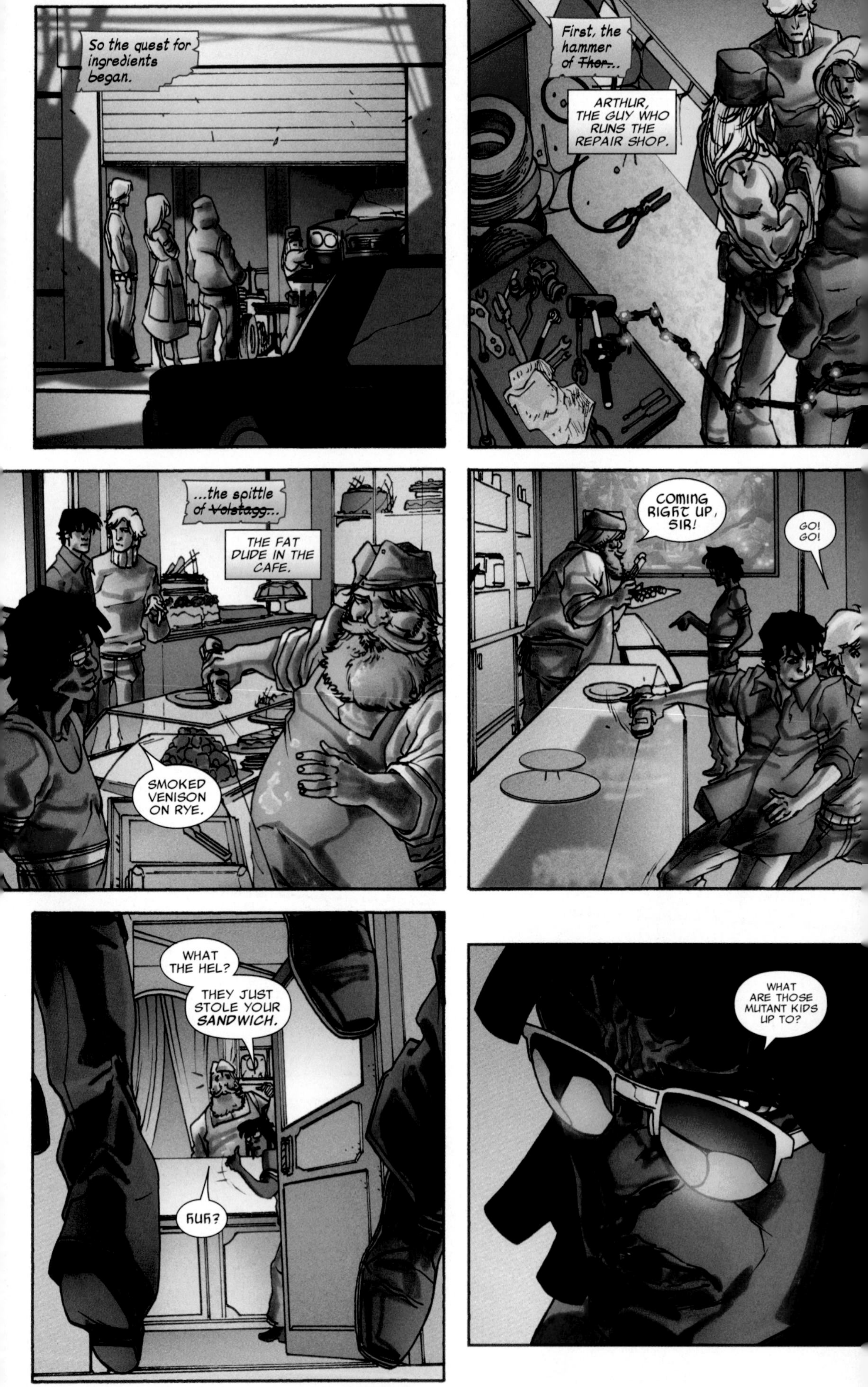
So the quest for ingredients began.
First, the hammer of ~~Thor~~...
ARTHUR, THE GUY WHO RUNS THE REPAIR SHOP.
...the spittle of ~~Volstagg~~...
THE FAT DUDE IN THE CAFE.
SMOKED VENISON ON RYE.
COMING RIGHT UP, SIR!
GO! GO!
WHAT THE HEL?
THEY JUST STOLE YOUR SANDWICH.
HUH?
WHAT ARE THOSE MUTANT KIDS UP TO?

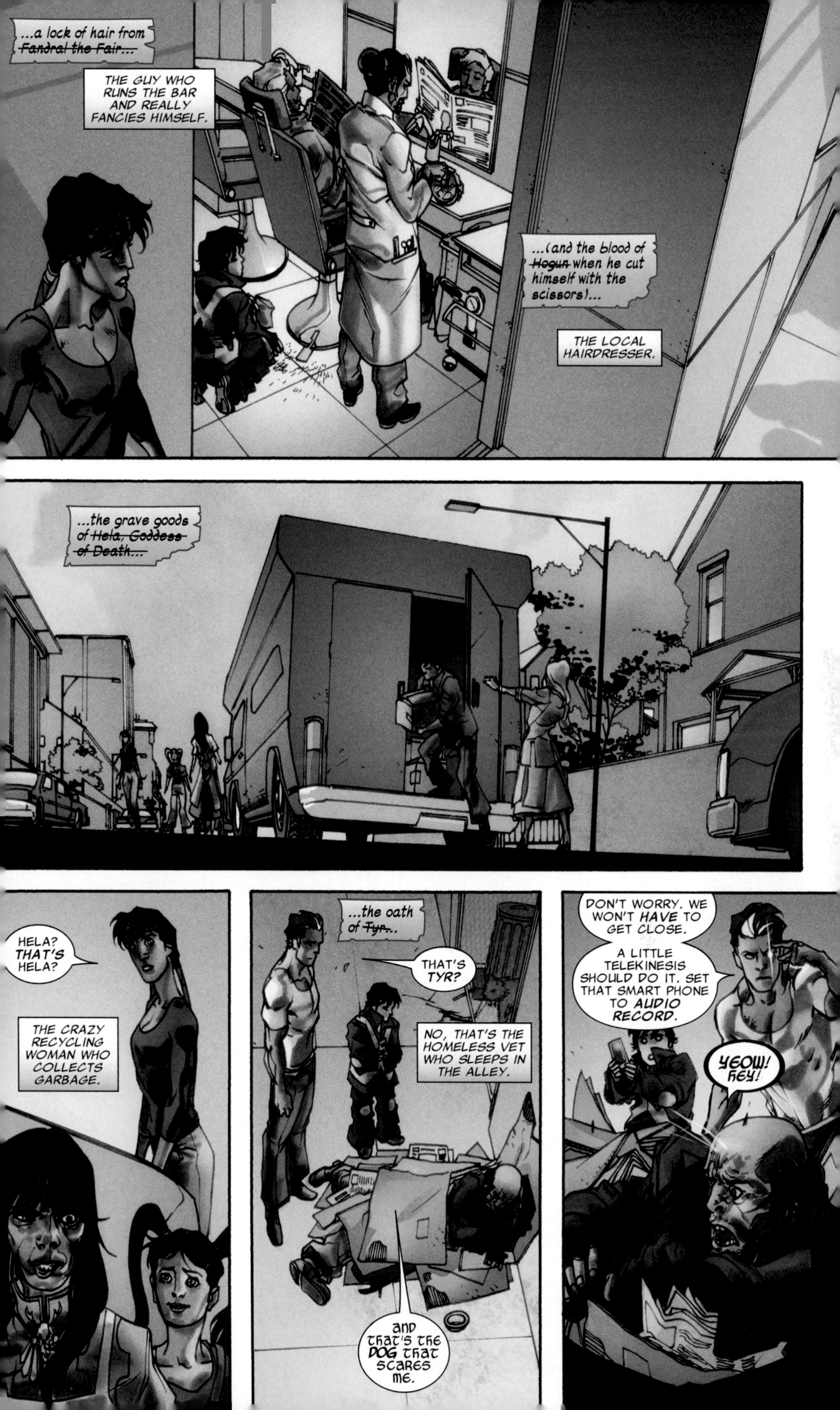
...a lock of hair from ~~Fandral the Fair~~...
THE GUY WHO RUNS THE BAR AND REALLY FANCIES HIMSELF.
...(and the blood of ~~Hogun~~ when he cut himself with the scissors)...
THE LOCAL HAIRDRESSER.
...the grave goods of ~~Hela, Goddess of Death~~...
HELA? THAT'S HELA?
THE CRAZY RECYCLING WOMAN WHO COLLECTS GARBAGE.
...the oath of ~~Tyr~~...
THAT'S TYR?
NO, THAT'S THE HOMELESS VET WHO SLEEPS IN THE ALLEY.
AND THAT'S THE DOG THAT SCARES ME.
DON'T WORRY. WE WON'T HAVE TO GET CLOSE.
A LITTLE TELEKINESIS SHOULD DO IT. SET THAT SMART PHONE TO AUDIO RECORD.
YEOW! HEY!

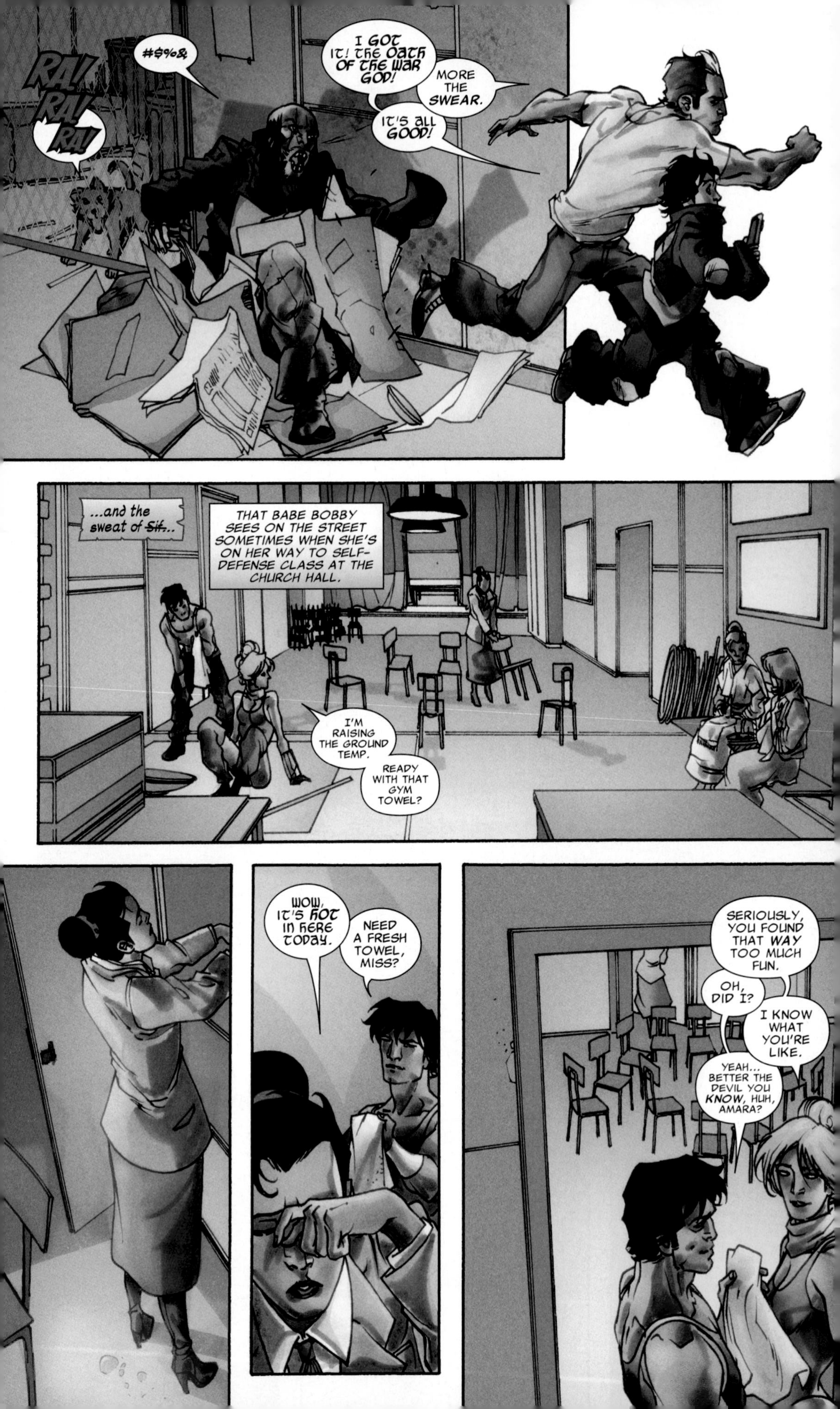
RA! RA! RA!
#$%&
I GOT IT! THE OATH OF THE WAR GOD!
MORE THE SWEAR.
IT'S ALL GOOD!
...and the sweat of Sif...
THAT BABE BOBBY SEES ON THE STREET SOMETIMES WHEN SHE'S ON HER WAY TO SELF-DEFENSE CLASS AT THE CHURCH HALL.
I'M RAISING THE GROUND TEMP.
READY WITH THAT GYM TOWEL?
WOW, IT'S HOT IN HERE TODAY.
NEED A FRESH TOWEL, MISS?
SERIOUSLY, YOU FOUND THAT WAY TOO MUCH FUN.
OH, DID I?
I KNOW WHAT YOU'RE LIKE.
YEAH... BETTER THE DEVIL YOU KNOW, HUH, AMARA?

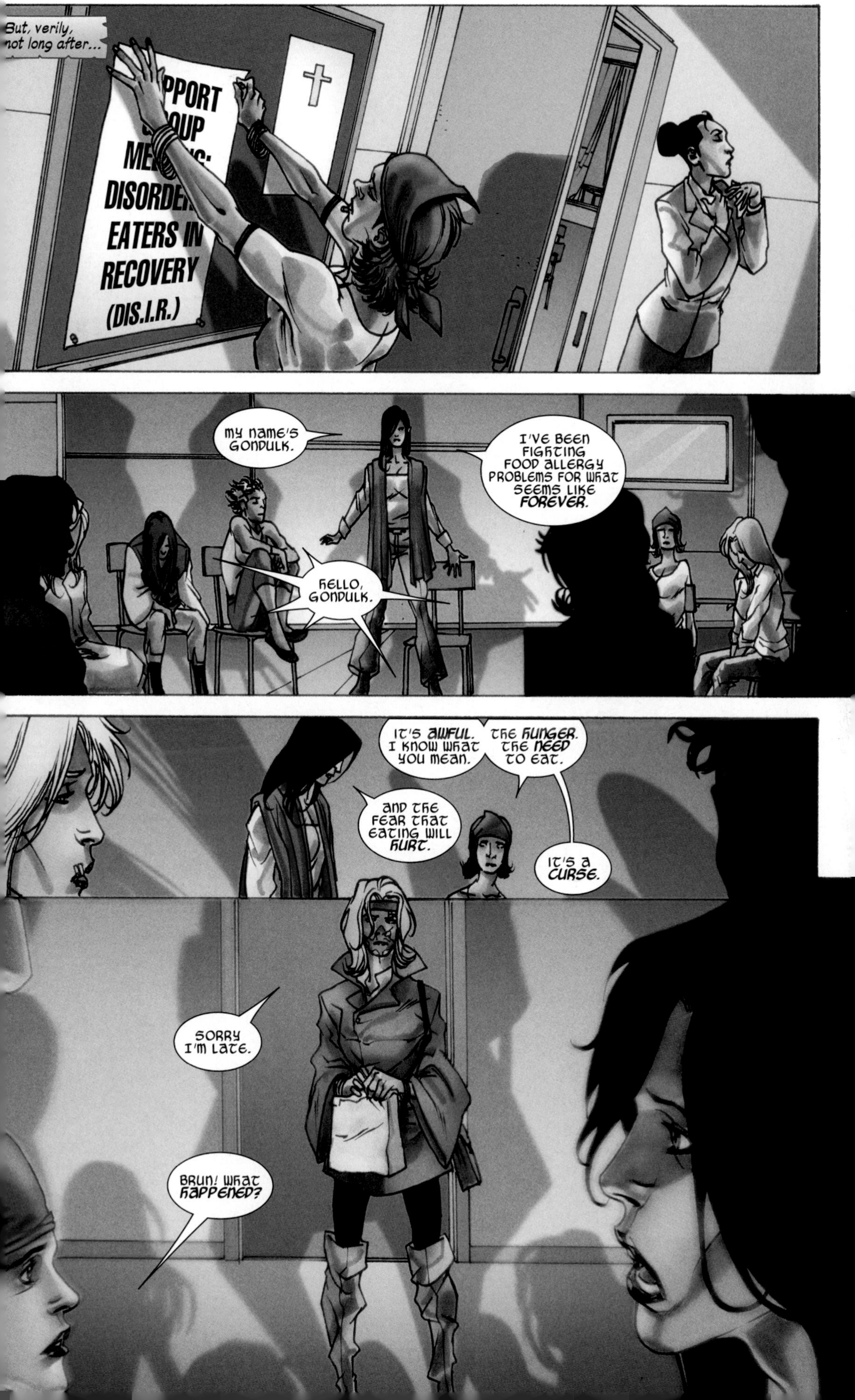

But, verily, not long after...
SUPPORT GROUP MEETING: DISORDERED EATERS IN RECOVERY (DIS.I.R.)
MY NAME'S GONDULK.
I'VE BEEN FIGHTING FOOD ALLERGY PROBLEMS FOR WHAT SEEMS LIKE FOREVER.
HELLO, GONDULK.
IT'S AWFUL. I KNOW WHAT YOU MEAN.
THE HUNGER. THE NEED TO EAT.
AND THE FEAR THAT EATING WILL HURT.
IT'S A CURSE.
SORRY I'M LATE.
BRUN! WHAT HAPPENED?

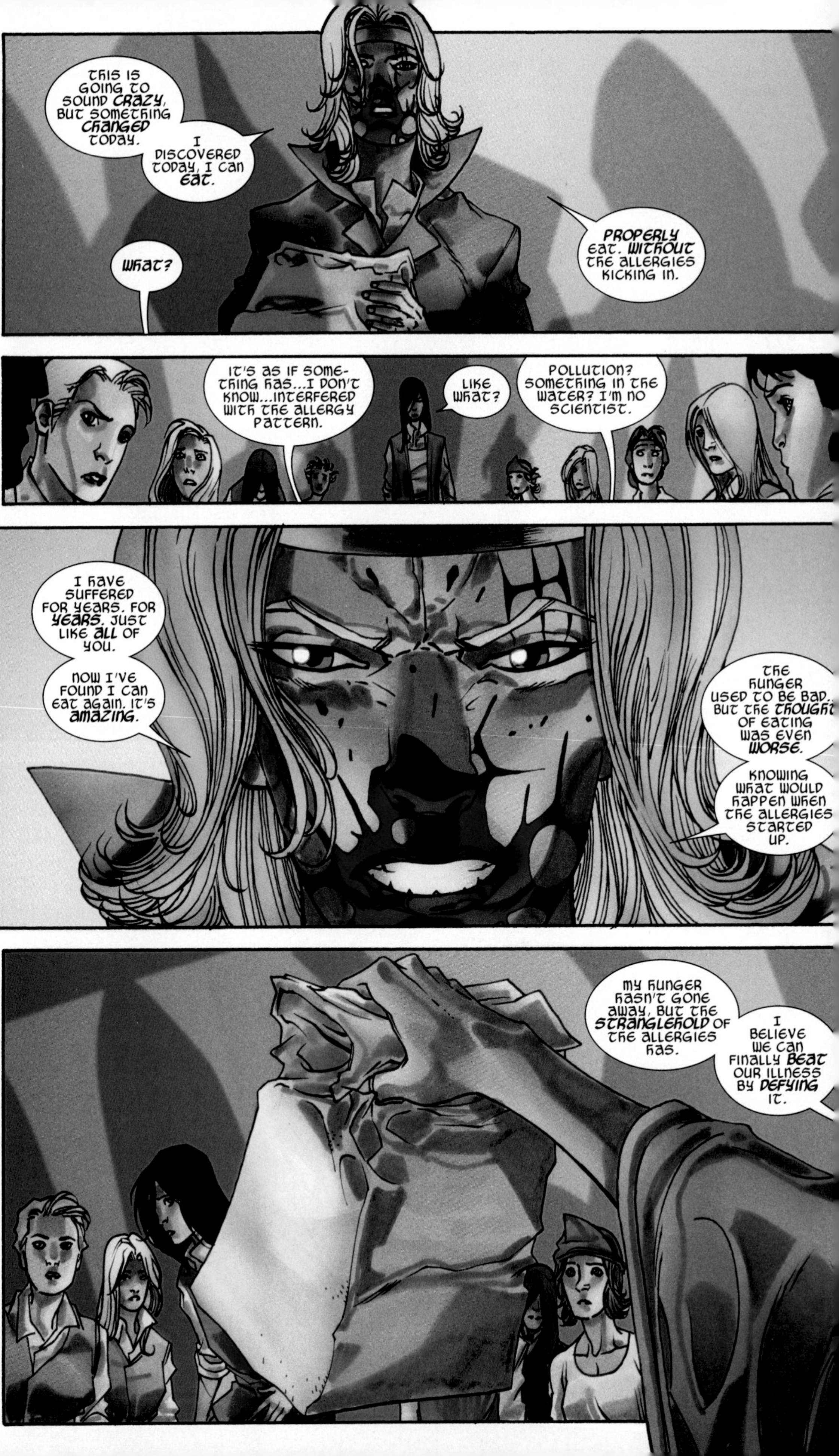
THIS IS GOING TO SOUND CRAZY, BUT SOMETHING CHANGED TODAY.
I DISCOVERED TODAY, I CAN EAT.
WHAT?
PROPERLY EAT. WITHOUT THE ALLERGIES KICKING IN.
IT'S AS IF SOME-THING HAS...I DON'T KNOW...INTERFERED WITH THE ALLERGY PATTERN.
LIKE WHAT?
POLLUTION? SOMETHING IN THE WATER? I'M NO SCIENTIST.
I HAVE SUFFERED FOR YEARS. FOR YEARS. JUST LIKE ALL OF YOU.
NOW I'VE FOUND I CAN EAT AGAIN. IT'S AMAZING.
THE HUNGER USED TO BE BAD... BUT THE THOUGHT OF EATING WAS EVEN WORSE.
KNOWING WHAT WOULD HAPPEN WHEN THE ALLERGIES STARTED UP.
MY HUNGER HASN'T GONE AWAY, BUT THE STRANGLEHOLD OF THE ALLERGIES HAS.
I BELIEVE WE CAN FINALLY BEAT OUR ILLNESS BY DEFYING IT.

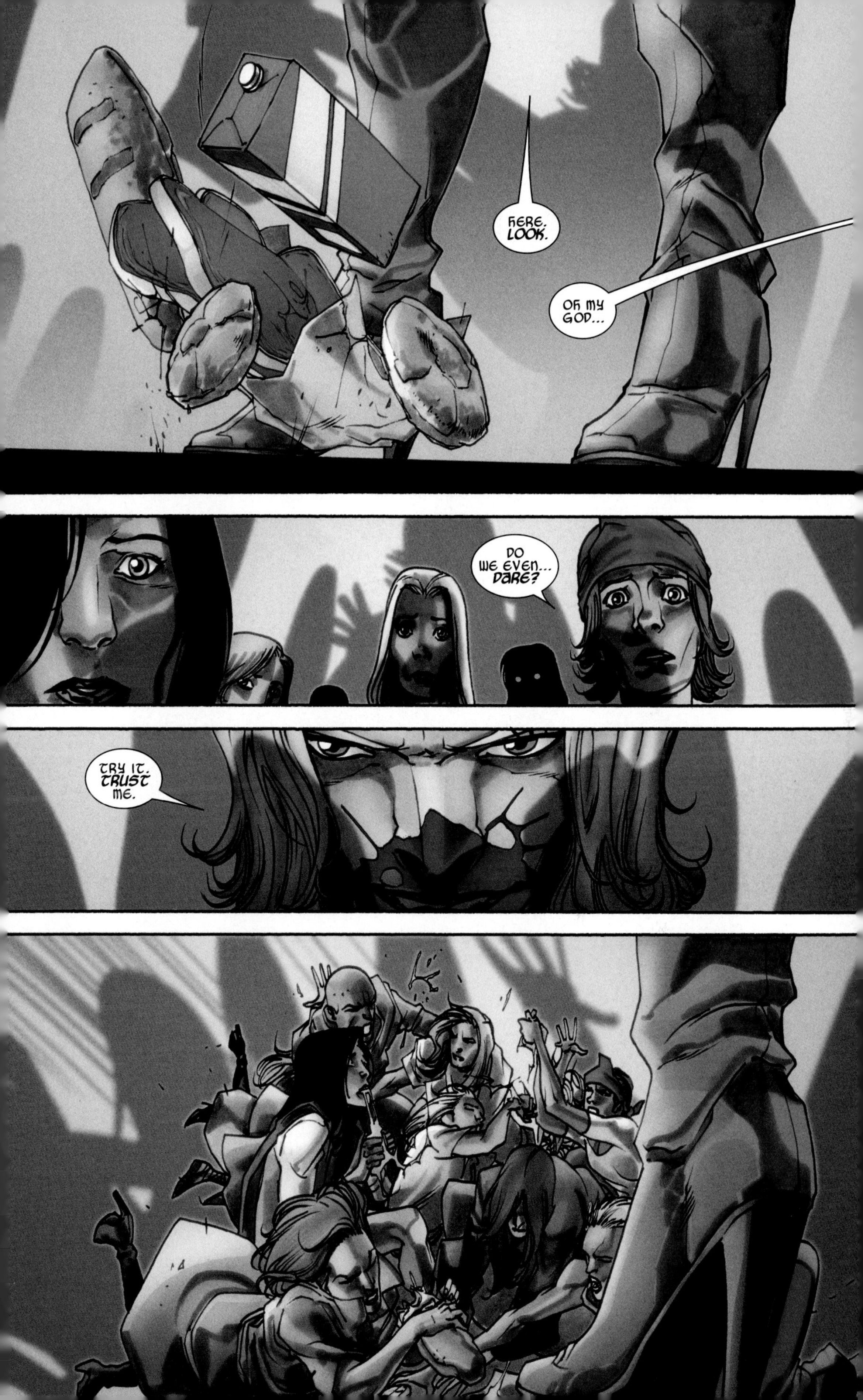
HERE. LOOK.
OH MY GOD...
DO WE EVEN... DARE?
TRY IT. TRUST ME.

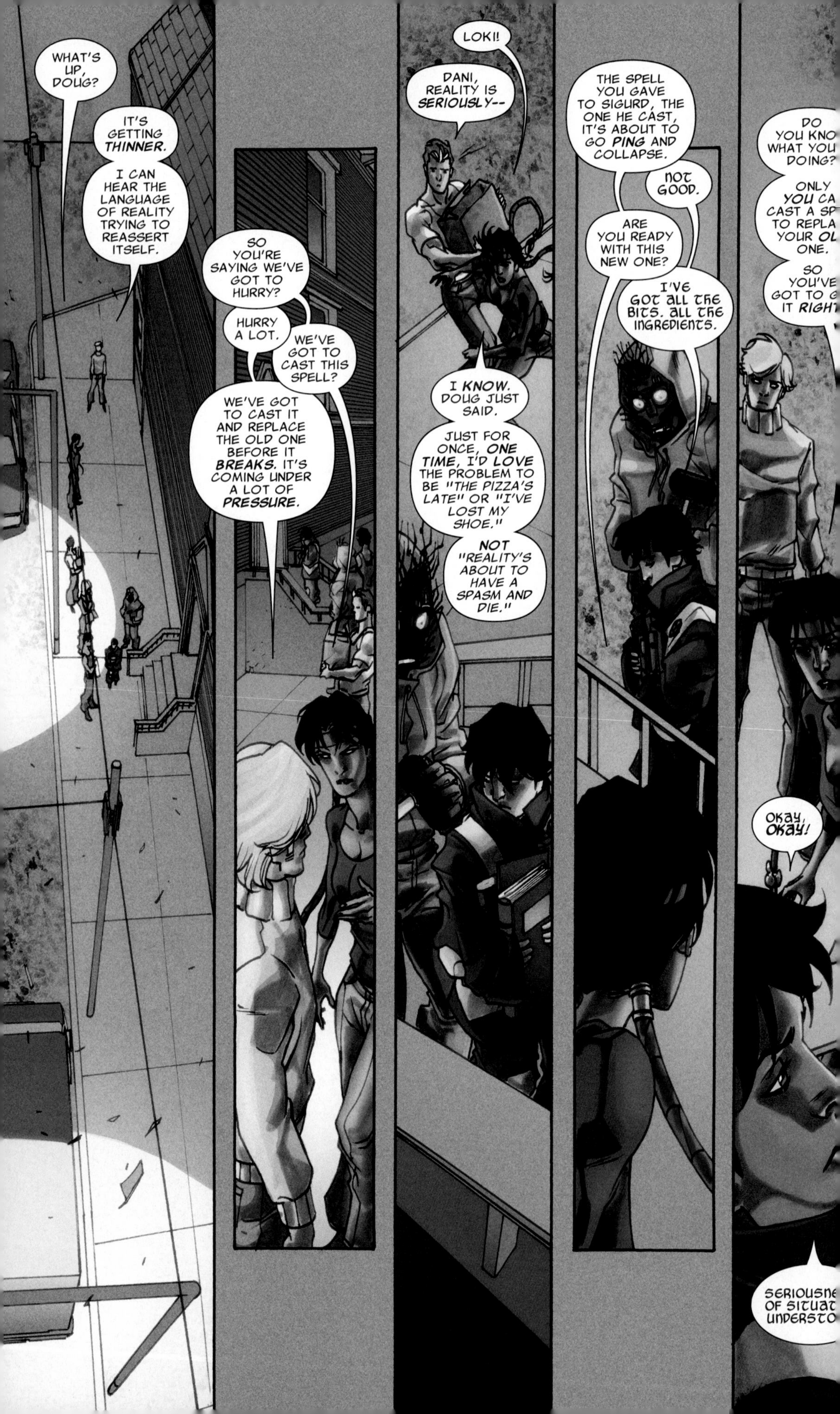

WHAT'S UP, DOUG?
IT'S GETTING THINNER.
I CAN HEAR THE LANGUAGE OF REALITY TRYING TO REASSERT ITSELF.
SO YOU'RE SAYING WE'VE GOT TO HURRY?
HURRY A LOT.
WE'VE GOT TO CAST THIS SPELL?
WE'VE GOT TO CAST IT AND REPLACE THE OLD ONE BEFORE IT BREAKS. IT'S COMING UNDER A LOT OF PRESSURE.
LOKI!
DANI, REALITY IS SERIOUSLY--
I KNOW. DOUG JUST SAID.
JUST FOR ONCE, ONE TIME, I'D LOVE THE PROBLEM TO BE "THE PIZZA'S LATE" OR "I'VE LOST MY SHOE."
NOT "REALITY'S ABOUT TO HAVE A SPASM AND DIE."
THE SPELL YOU GAVE TO SIGURD, THE ONE HE CAST, IT'S ABOUT TO GO PING AND COLLAPSE.
NOT GOOD.
ARE YOU READY WITH THIS NEW ONE?
I'VE GOT ALL THE BITS. ALL THE INGREDIENTS.
OKAY, OKAY!

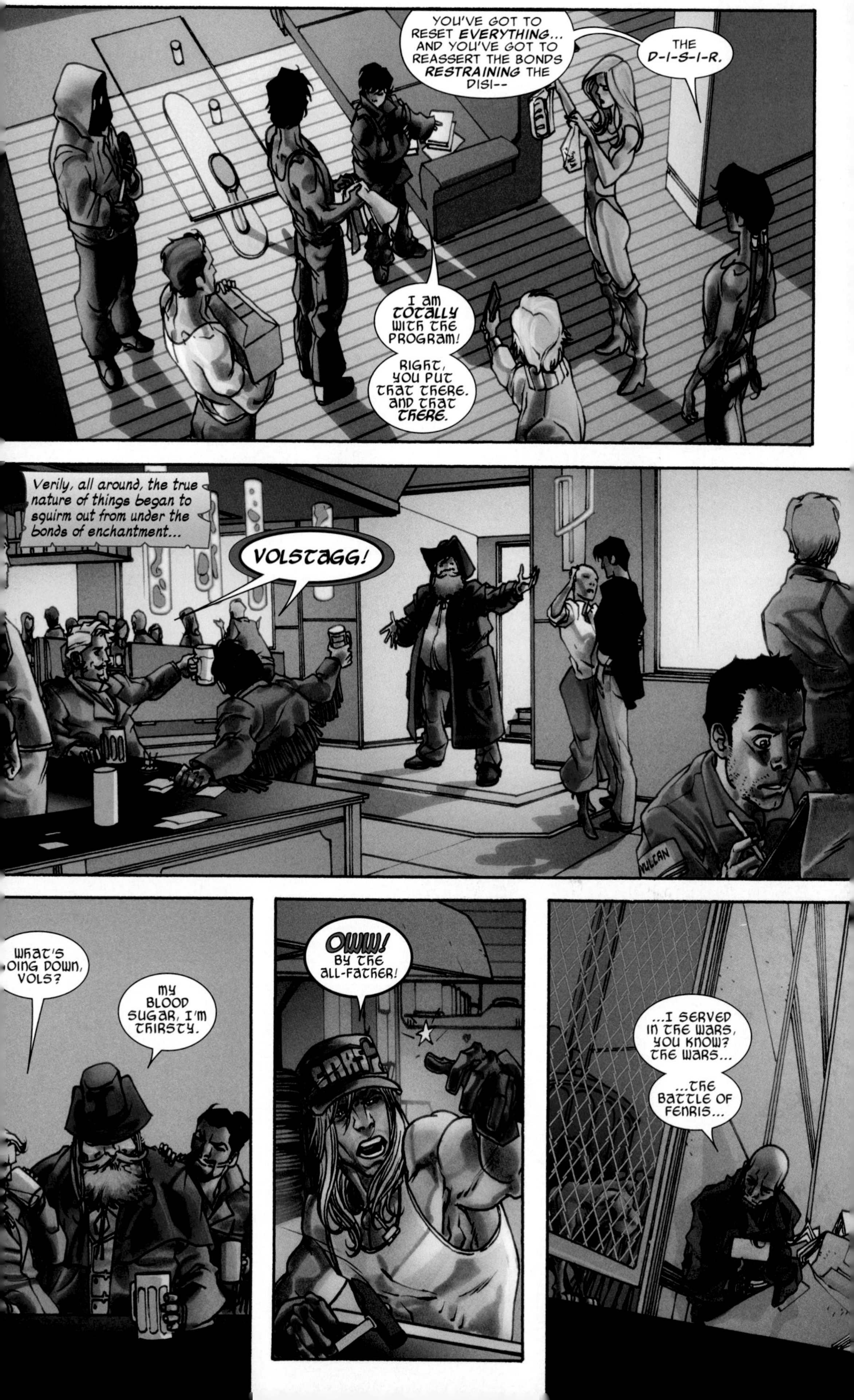

YOU'VE GOT TO RESET EVERYTHING... AND YOU'VE GOT TO REASSERT THE BONDS RESTRAINING THE DISI--
THE D-I-S-I-R.
I AM TOTALLY WITH THE PROGRAM!
RIGHT, YOU PUT THAT THERE. AND THAT THERE.
Verily, all around, the true nature of things began to squirm out from under the bonds of enchantment...
VOLSTAGG!
VULCAN
WHAT'S OING DOWN, VOLS?
MY BLOOD SUGAR, I'M THIRSTY.
OWW! BY THE ALL-FATHER!
...I SERVED IN THE WARS, YOU KNOW? THE WARS...
...THE BATTLE OF FENRIS...

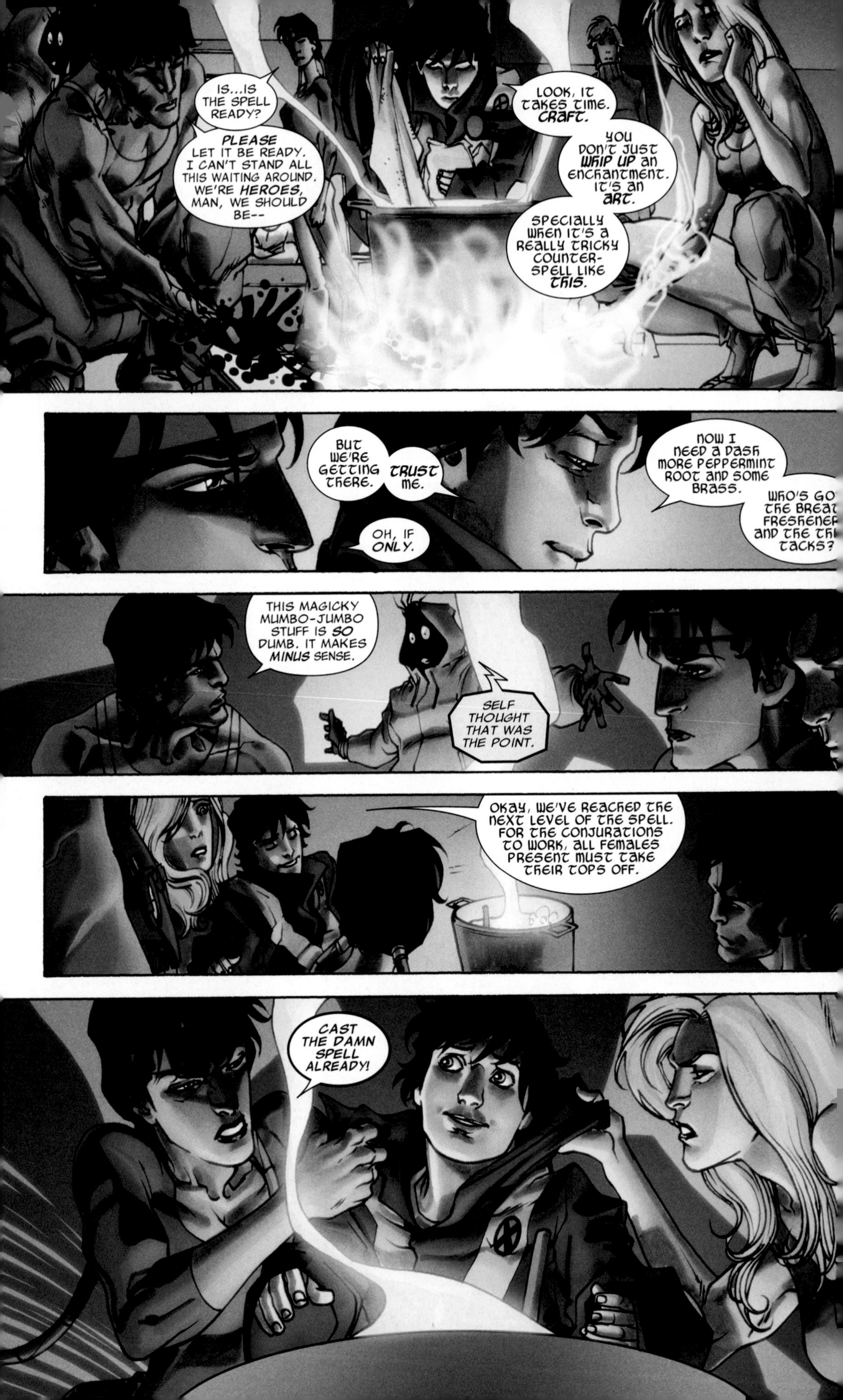
IS...IS THE SPELL READY?
PLEASE LET IT BE READY. I CAN'T STAND ALL THIS WAITING AROUND. WE'RE HEROES, MAN, WE SHOULD BE--
LOOK, IT TAKES TIME. CRAFT.
YOU DON'T JUST WHIP UP AN ENCHANTMENT. IT'S AN ART.
SPECIALLY WHEN IT'S A REALLY TRICKY COUNTER-SPELL LIKE THIS.
BUT WE'RE GETTING THERE.
TRUST ME.
OH, IF ONLY.
NOW I NEED A DASH MORE PEPPERMINT ROOT AND SOME BRASS.
WHO'S GO THE BREAT FRESHENER AND THE TH TACKS?
THIS MAGICKY MUMBO-JUMBO STUFF IS SO DUMB. IT MAKES MINUS SENSE.
SELF THOUGHT THAT WAS THE POINT.
OKAY, WE'VE REACHED THE NEXT LEVEL OF THE SPELL. FOR THE CONJURATIONS TO WORK, ALL FEMALES PRESENT MUST TAKE THEIR TOPS OFF.
CAST THE DAMN SPELL ALREADY!

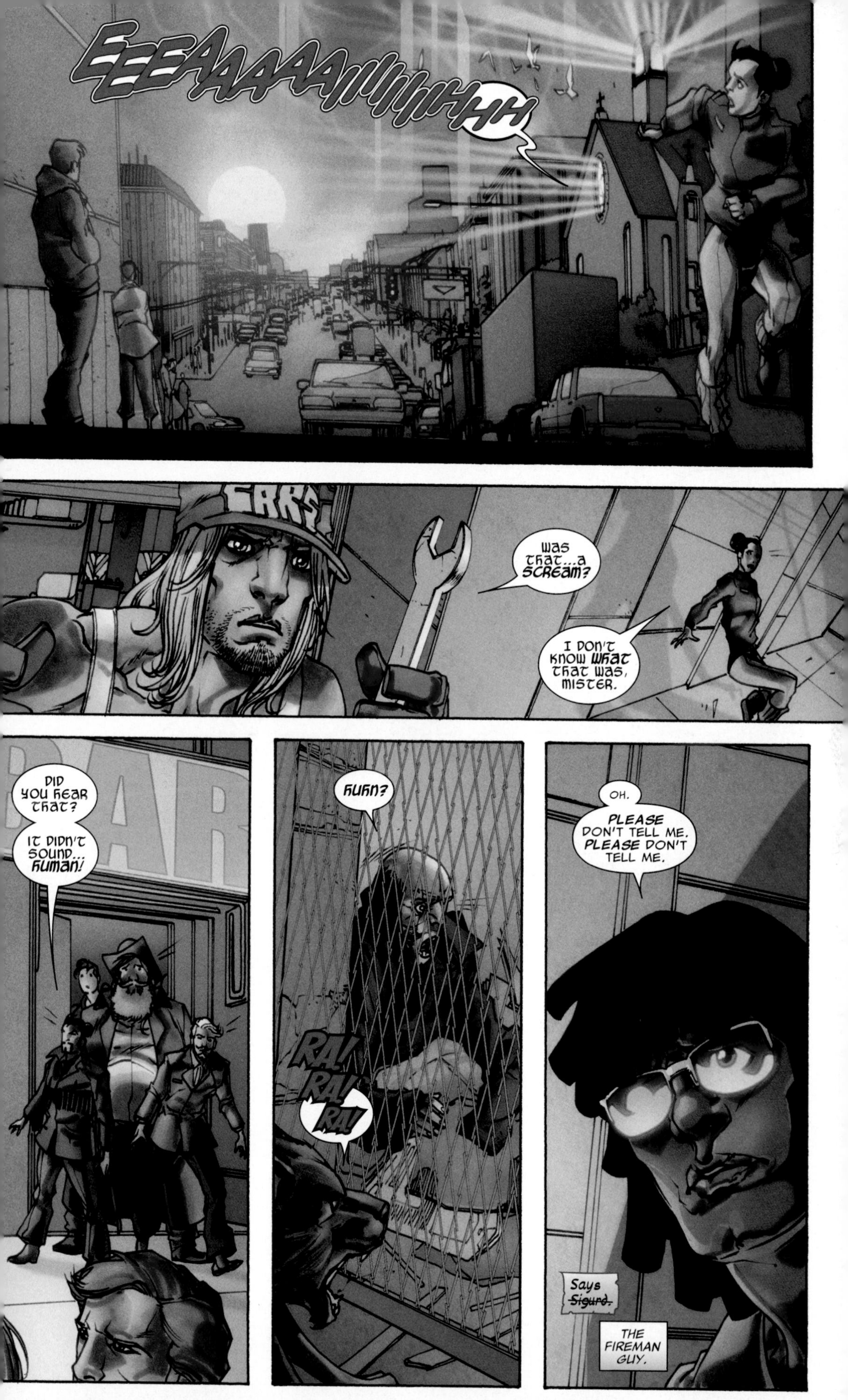
EEEAAAAAIIIIIIHHH
WAS THAT...A SCREAM?
I DON'T KNOW WHAT THAT WAS, MISTER.
DID YOU HEAR THAT?
IT DIDN'T SOUND... HUMAN!
HUHN?
RA! RA! RA!
OH.
PLEASE DON'T TELL ME. PLEASE DON'T TELL ME.
Says Sigurd.
THE FIREMAN GUY.

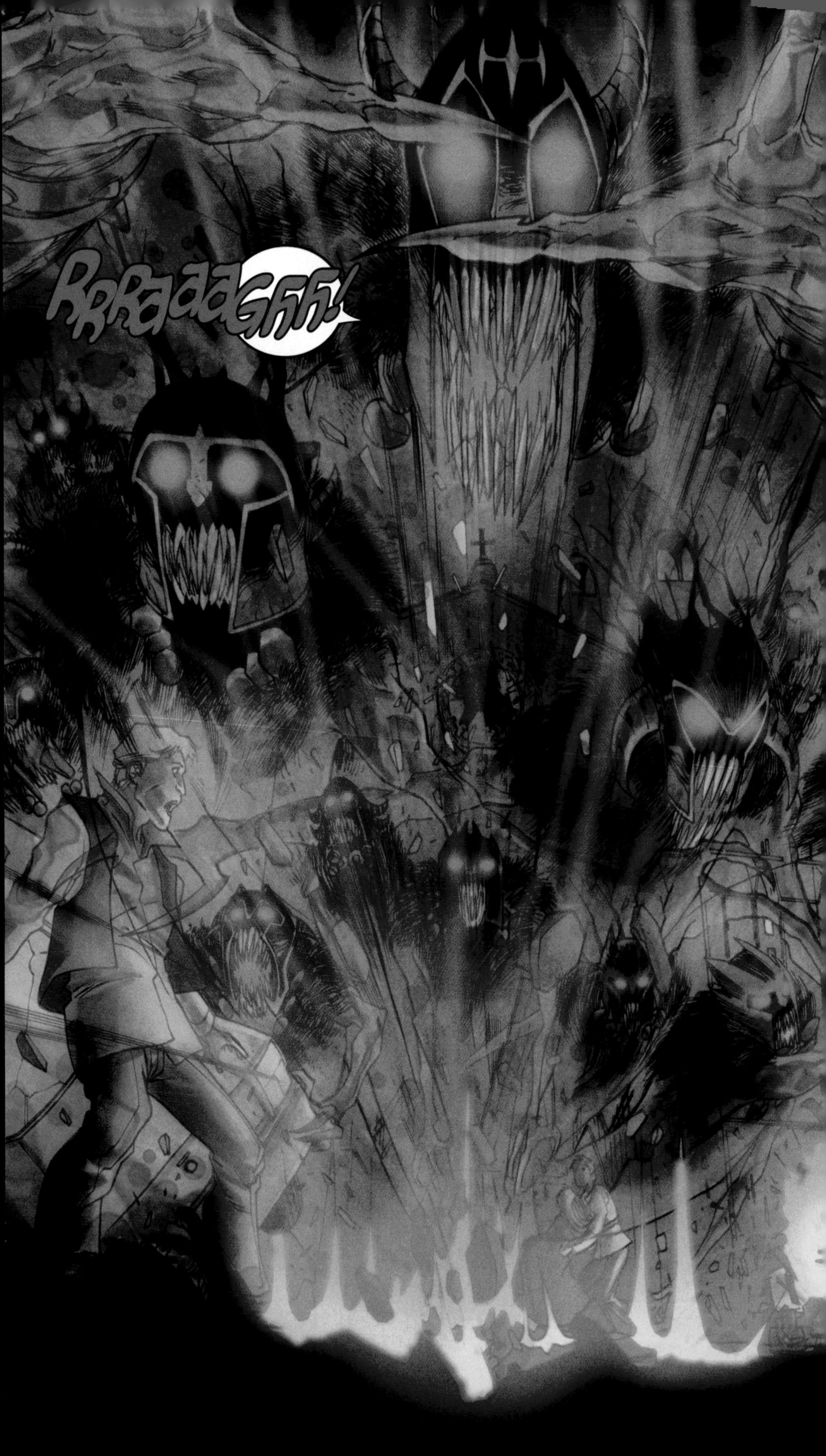
RRRAAAAGHH!

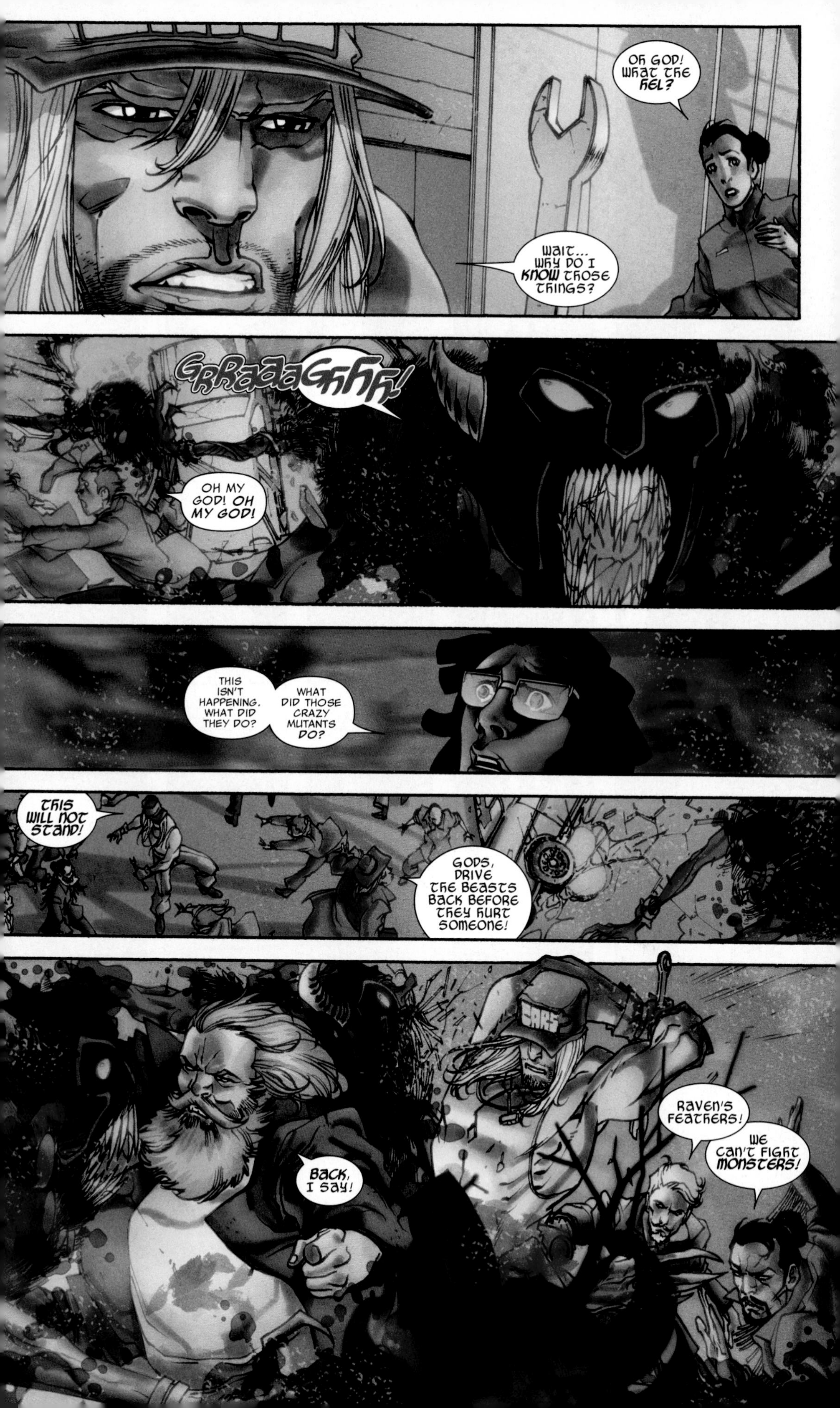

OH GOD! WHAT THE HEL?
WAIT... WHY DO I KNOW THOSE THINGS?
GRRAAAAGHHH!
OH MY GOD! OH MY GOD!
THIS ISN'T HAPPENING. WHAT DID THEY DO?
WHAT DID THOSE CRAZY MUTANTS DO?
THIS WILL NOT STAND!
GODS, DRIVE THE BEASTS BACK BEFORE THEY HURT SOMEONE!
BACK, I SAY!
RAVEN'S FEATHERS!
WE CAN'T FIGHT MONSTERS!

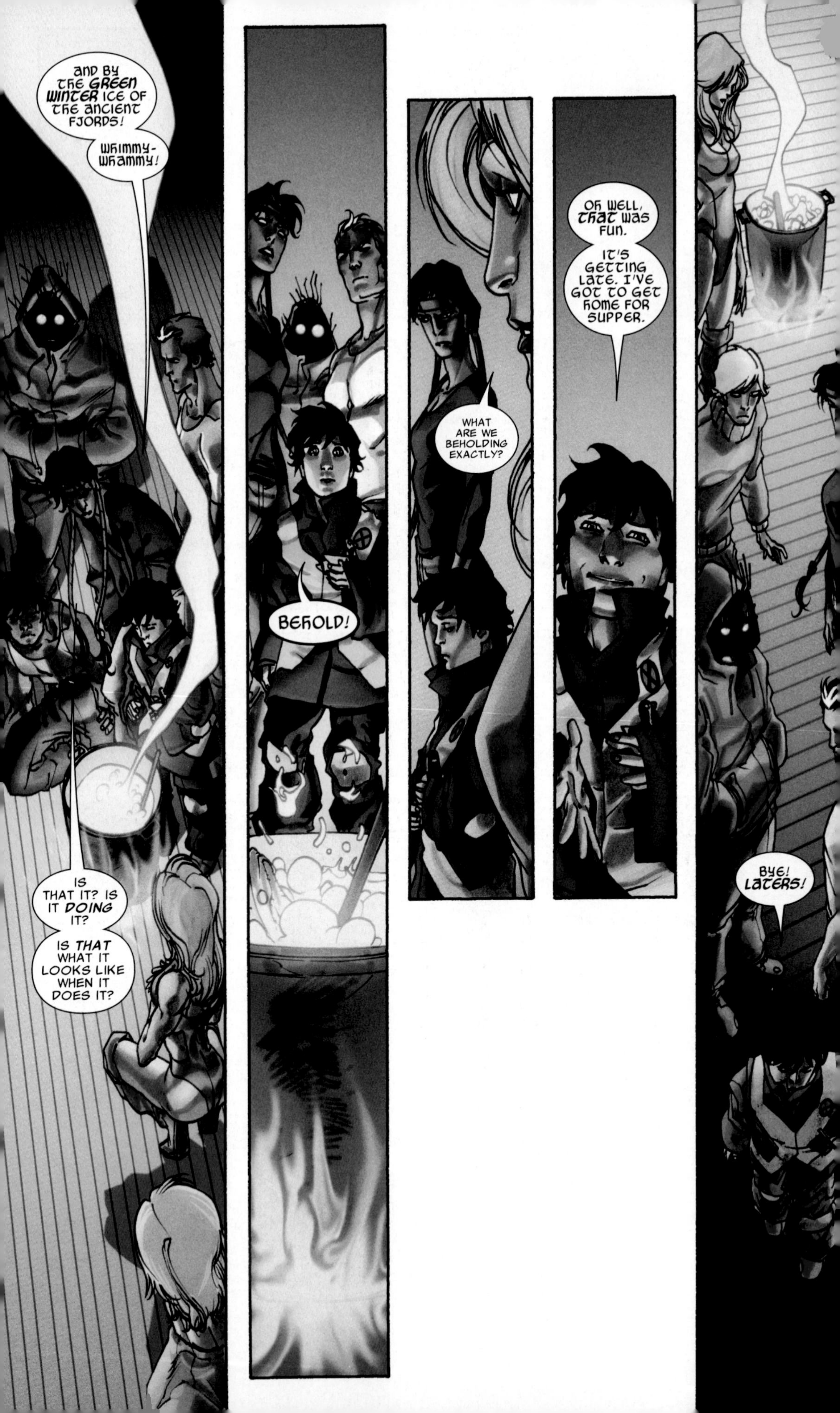
AND BY THE GREEN WINTER ICE OF THE ANCIENT FJORDS!
WHIMMY-WHAMMY!
IS THAT IT? IS IT DOING IT?
IS THAT WHAT IT LOOKS LIKE WHEN IT DOES IT?
BEHOLD!
WHAT ARE WE BEHOLDING EXACTLY?
OH WELL, THAT WAS FUN.
IT'S GETTING LATE. I'VE GOT TO GET HOME FOR SUPPER.
BYE! LATERS!

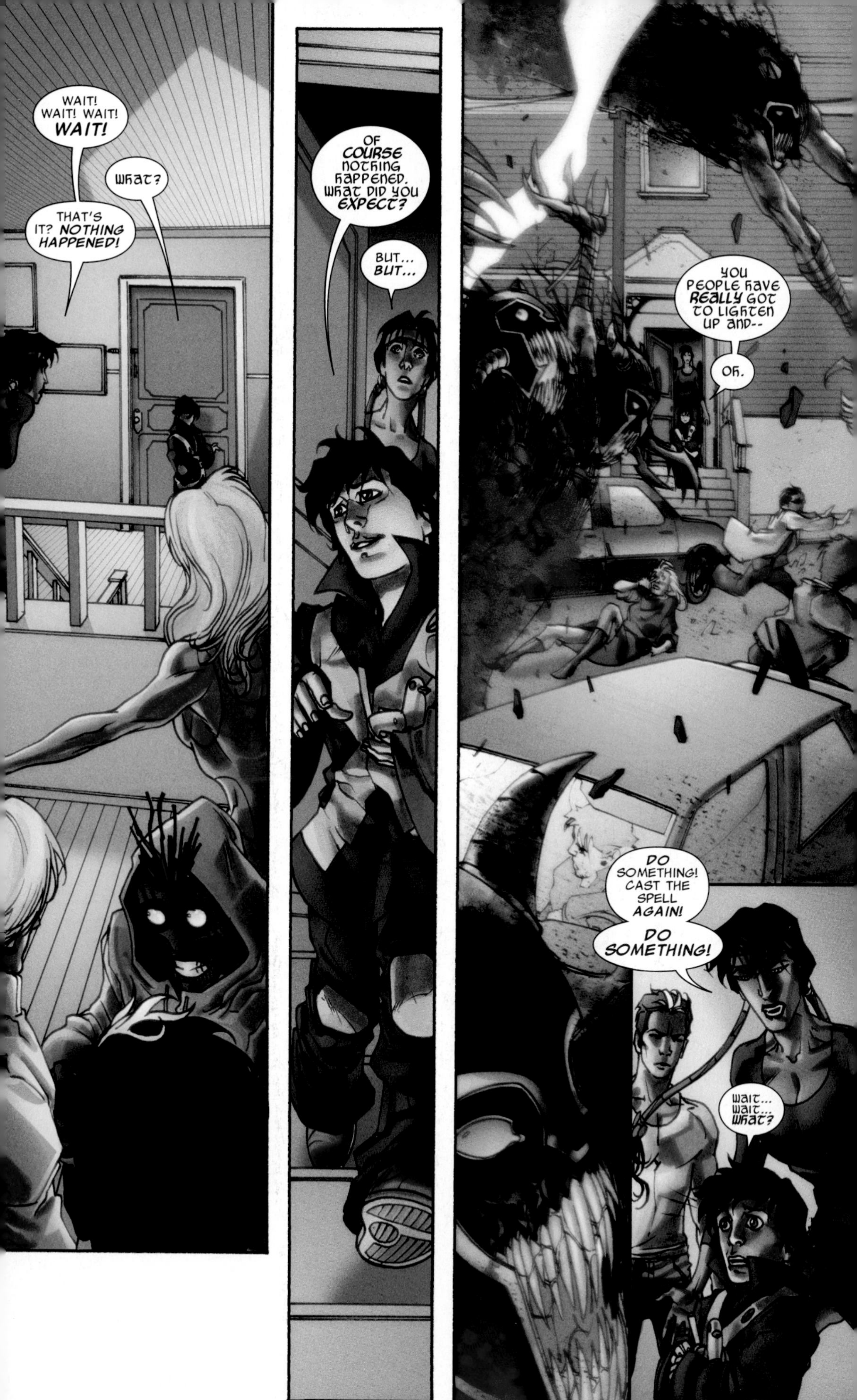
WAIT! WAIT! WAIT! WAIT!
WHAT?
THAT'S IT? NOTHING HAPPENED!
OF COURSE NOTHING HAPPENED. WHAT DID YOU EXPECT?
BUT... BUT...
YOU PEOPLE HAVE REALLY GOT TO LIGHTEN UP AND--
OH.
DO SOMETHING! CAST THE SPELL AGAIN!
DO SOMETHING!
WAIT... WAIT... WHAT?

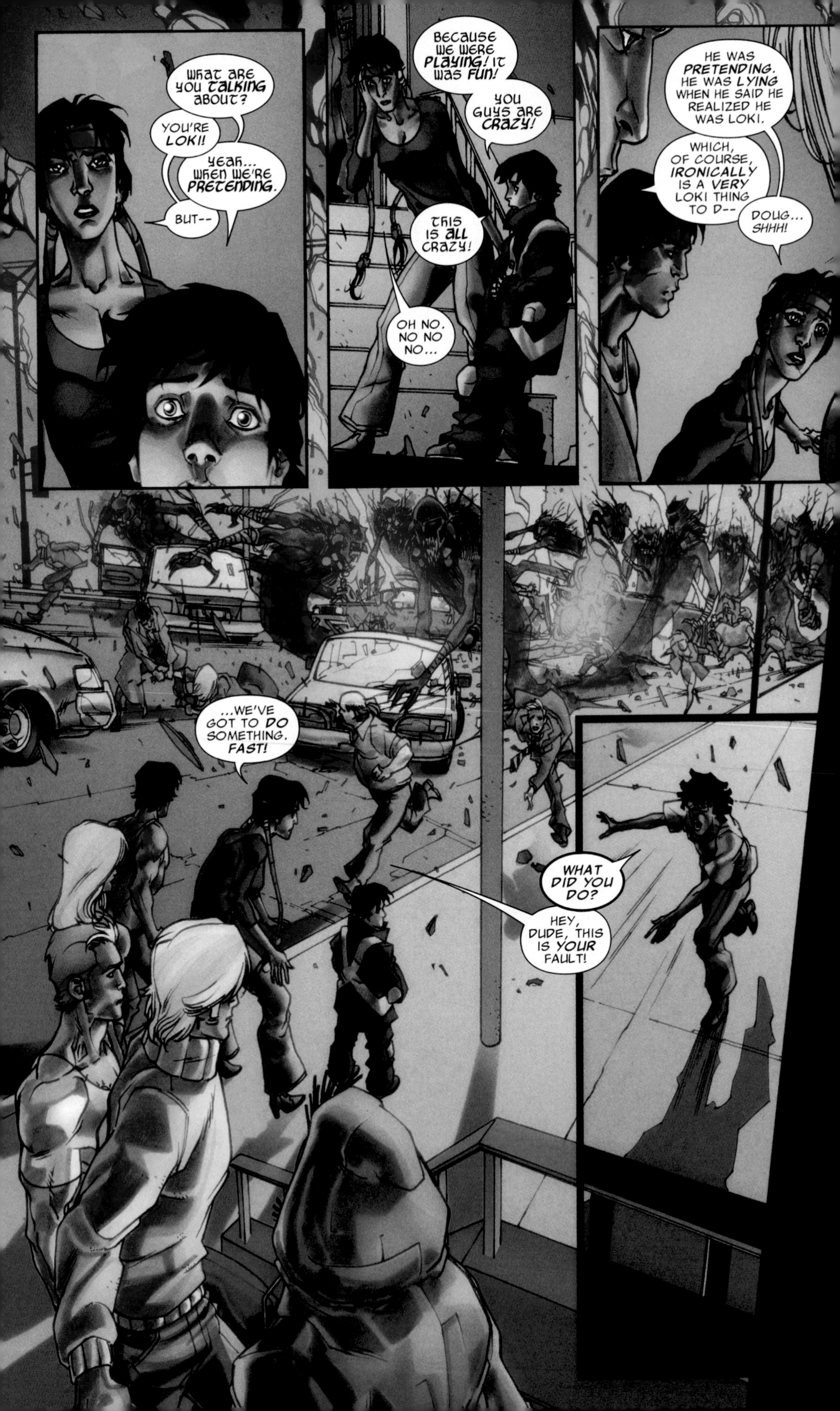
WHAT ARE YOU TALKING ABOUT?
YOU'RE LOKI!
YEAH... WHEN WE'RE PRETENDING.
BUT--
BECAUSE WE WERE PLAYING! IT WAS FUN!
YOU GUYS ARE CRAZY!
THIS IS ALL CRAZY!
OH NO. NO NO NO...
HE WAS PRETENDING. HE WAS LYING WHEN HE SAID HE REALIZED HE WAS LOKI.
WHICH, OF COURSE, IRONICALLY IS A VERY LOKI THING TO D--
DOUG... SHHH!
...WE'VE GOT TO DO SOMETHING. FAST!
WHAT DID YOU DO?
HEY, DUDE, THIS IS YOUR FAULT!

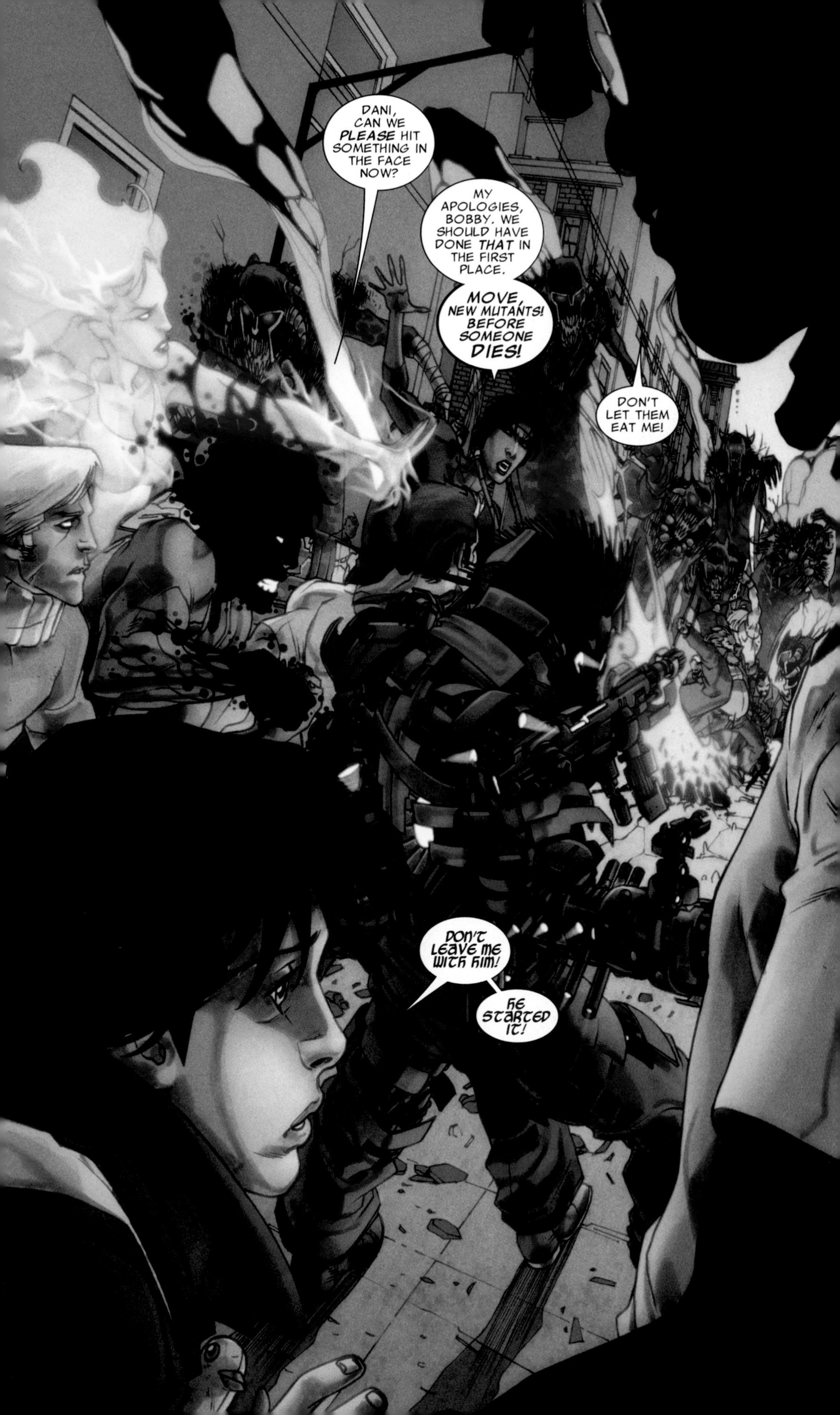
DANI, CAN WE PLEASE HIT SOMETHING IN THE FACE NOW?
MY APOLOGIES, BOBBY. WE SHOULD HAVE DONE THAT IN THE FIRST PLACE.
MOVE, NEW MUTANTS! BEFORE SOMEONE DIES!
DON'T LET THEM EAT ME!
DON'T LEAVE ME WITH HIM!
HE STARTED IT!

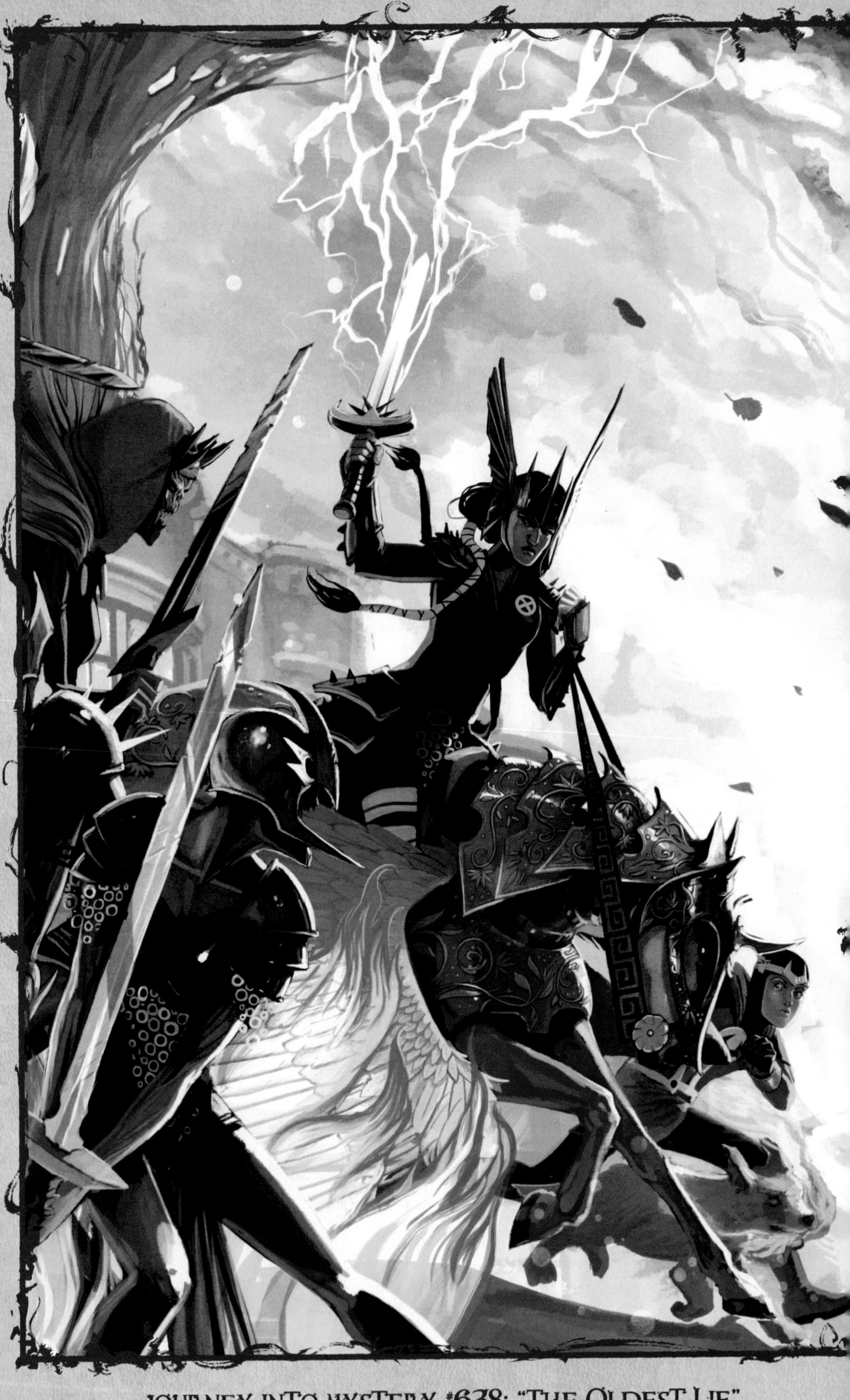

JOURNEY INTO MYSTERY #638: "THE OLDEST LIE"

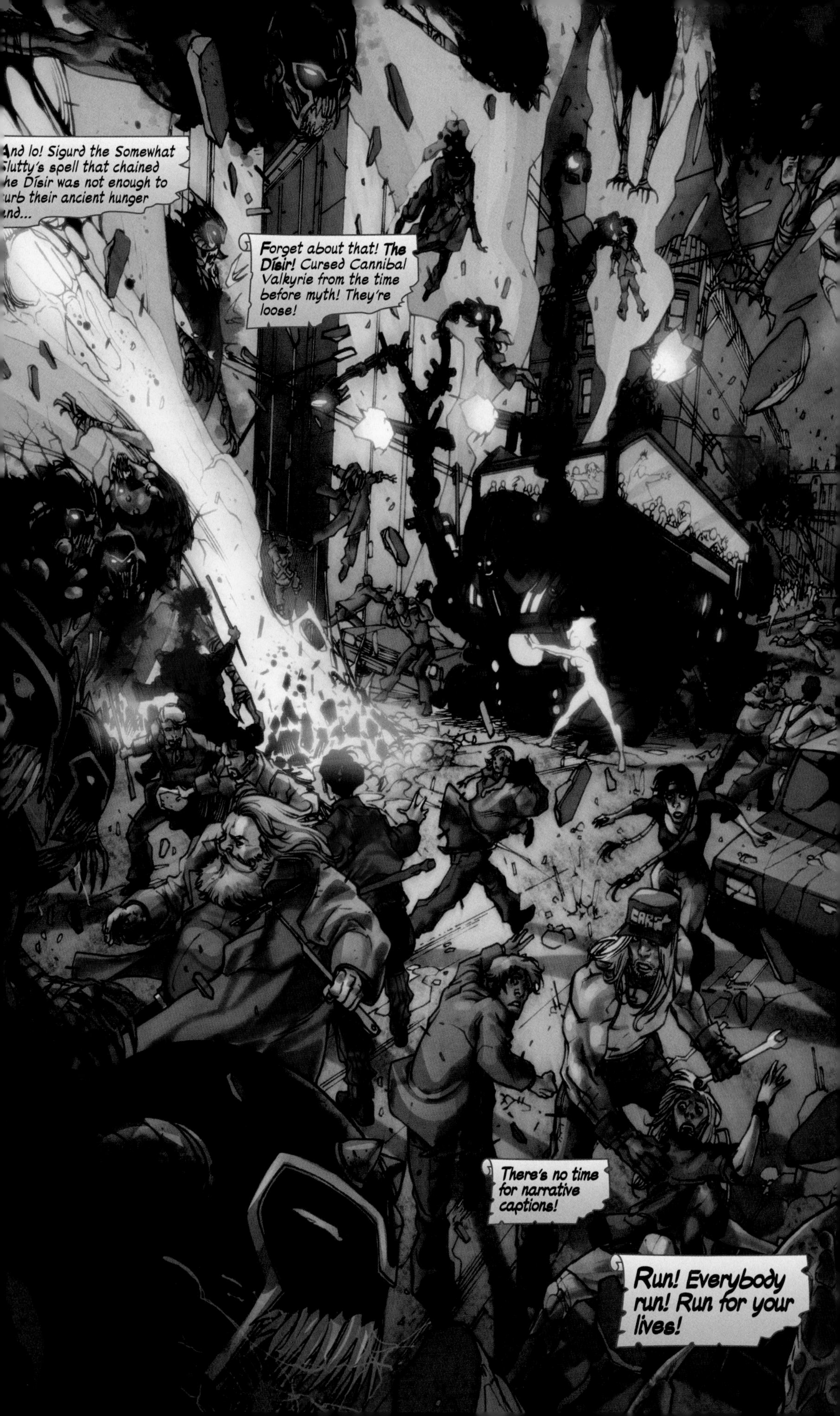
And lo! Sigurd the Somewhat lutty's spell that chained he Dísir was not enough to urb their ancient hunger nd...
Forget about that! The Dísir! Cursed Cannibal Valkyrie from the time before myth! They're loose!
There's no time for narrative captions!
Run! Everybody run! Run for your lives!

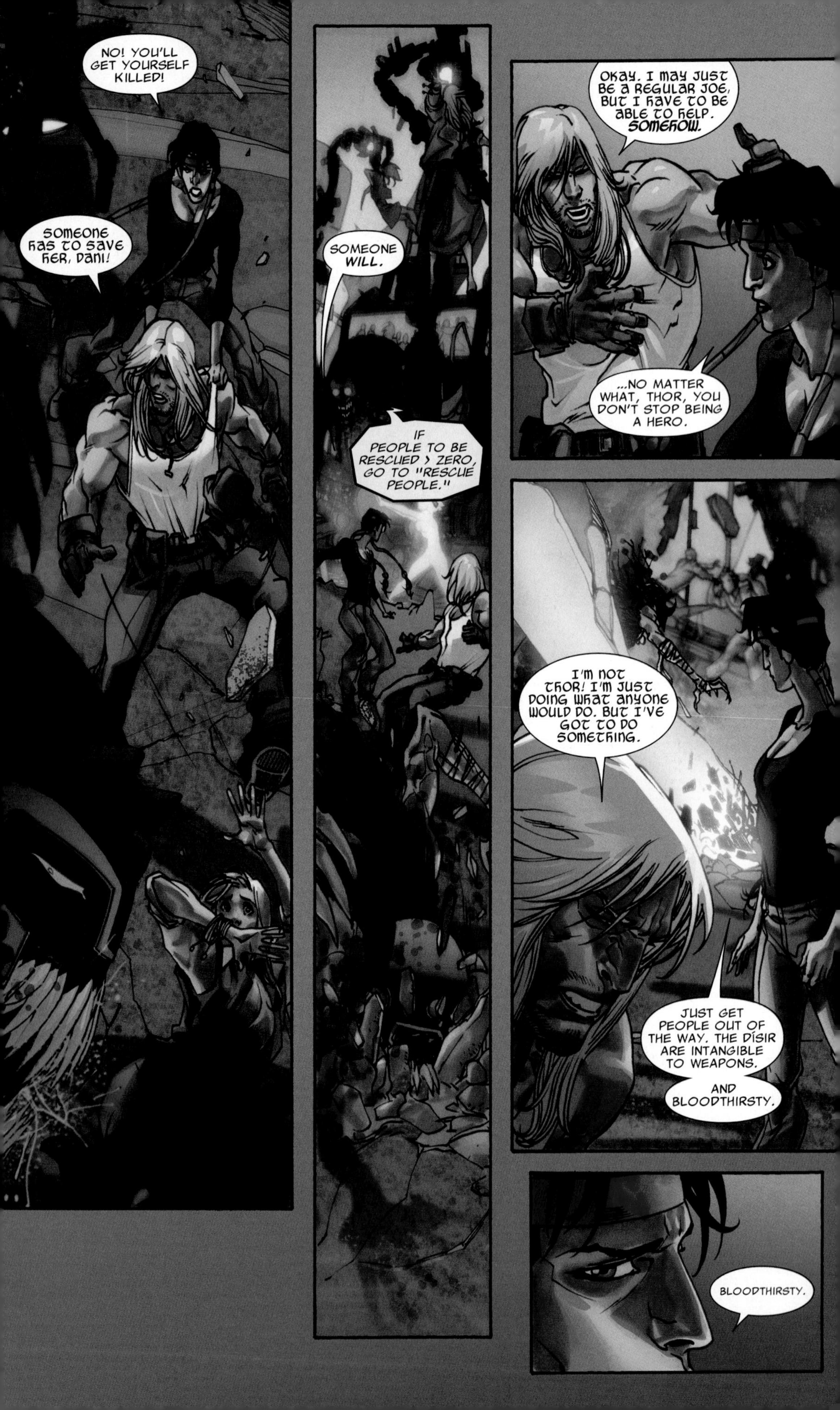

NO! YOU'LL GET YOURSELF KILLED!
SOMEONE HAS TO SAVE HER, DANI!
SOMEONE WILL.
IF PEOPLE TO BE RESCUED > ZERO, GO TO "RESCUE PEOPLE."
OKAY. I MAY JUST BE A REGULAR JOE, BUT I HAVE TO BE ABLE TO HELP. SOMEHOW.
...NO MATTER WHAT, THOR, YOU DON'T STOP BEING A HERO.
I'M NOT THOR! I'M JUST DOING WHAT ANYONE WOULD DO. BUT I'VE GOT TO DO SOMETHING.
JUST GET PEOPLE OUT OF THE WAY. THE DÍSIR ARE INTANGIBLE TO WEAPONS.
AND BLOODTHIRSTY.
BLOODTHIRSTY.

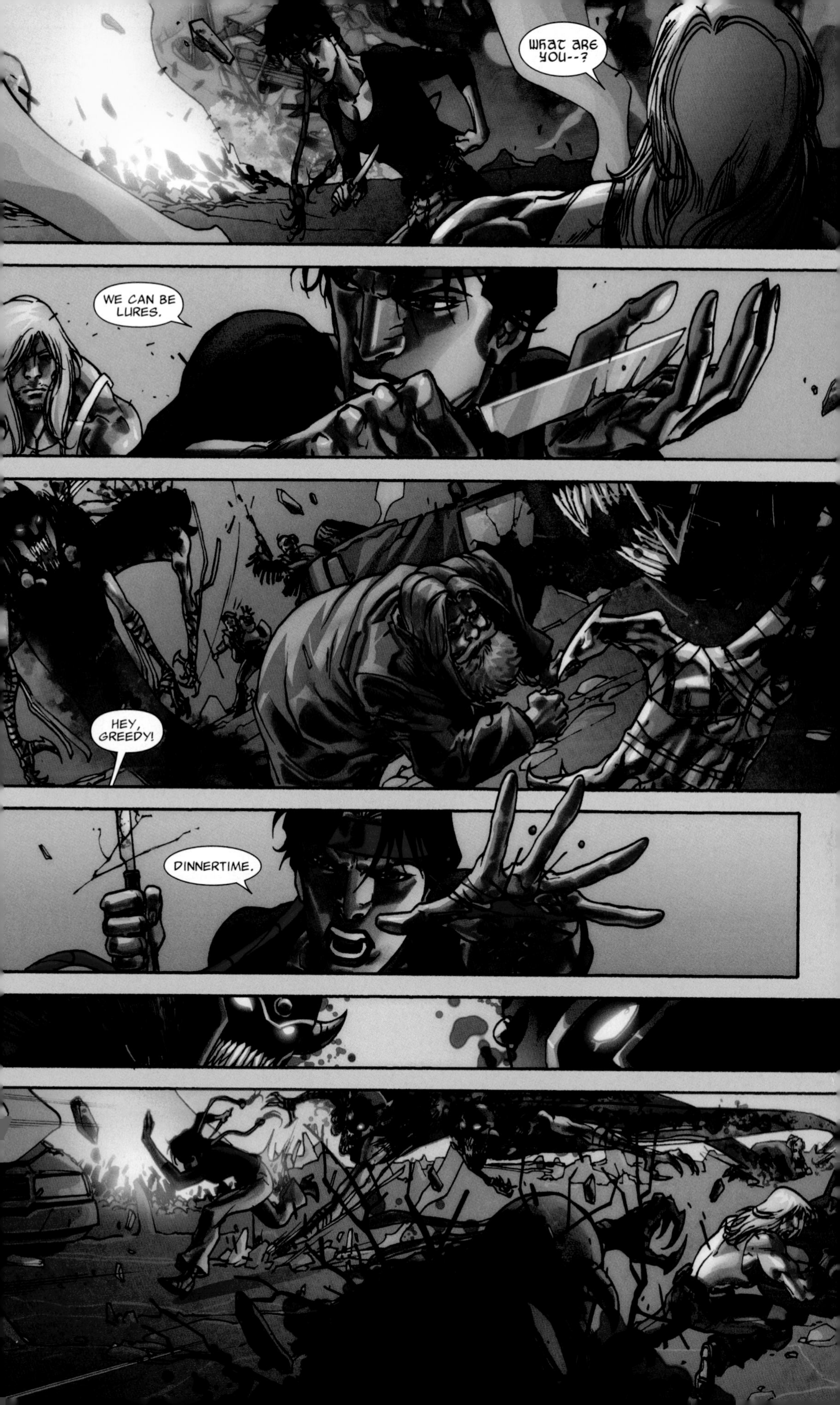
WHAT ARE YOU--?
WE CAN BE LURES.
HEY, GREEDY!
DINNERTIME.

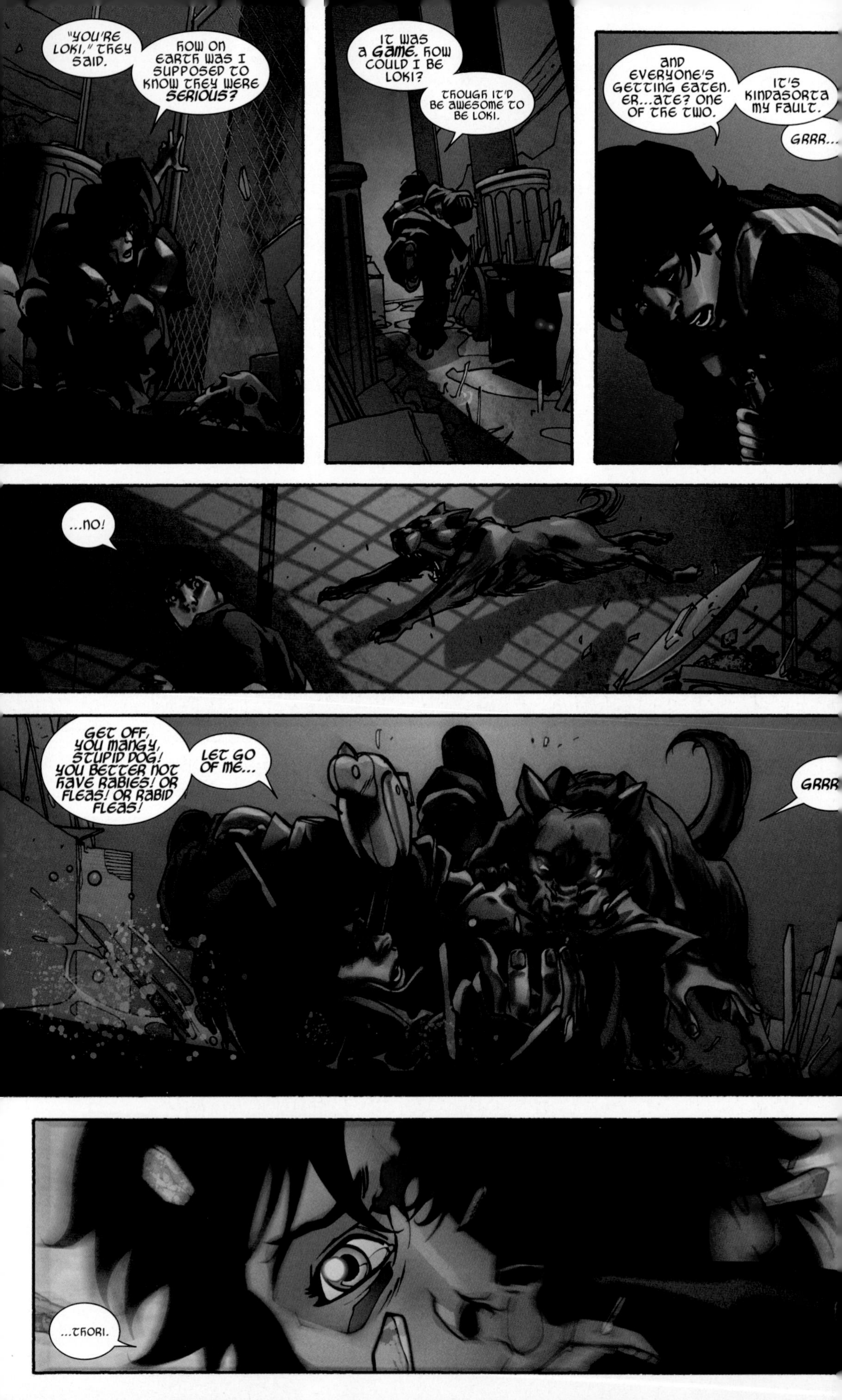
"YOU'RE LOKI," THEY SAID.
HOW ON EARTH WAS I SUPPOSED TO KNOW THEY WERE SERIOUS?
IT WAS A GAME. HOW COULD I BE LOKI?
THOUGH IT'D BE AWESOME TO BE LOKI.
AND EVERYONE'S GETTING EATEN. ER...ATE? ONE OF THE TWO.
IT'S KINDASORTA MY FAULT.
GRRR...
...NO!
GET OFF, YOU MANGY, STUPID DOG! YOU BETTER NOT HAVE RABIES! OR FLEAS! OR RABID FLEAS!
LET GO OF ME...
GRRR
...THORI.

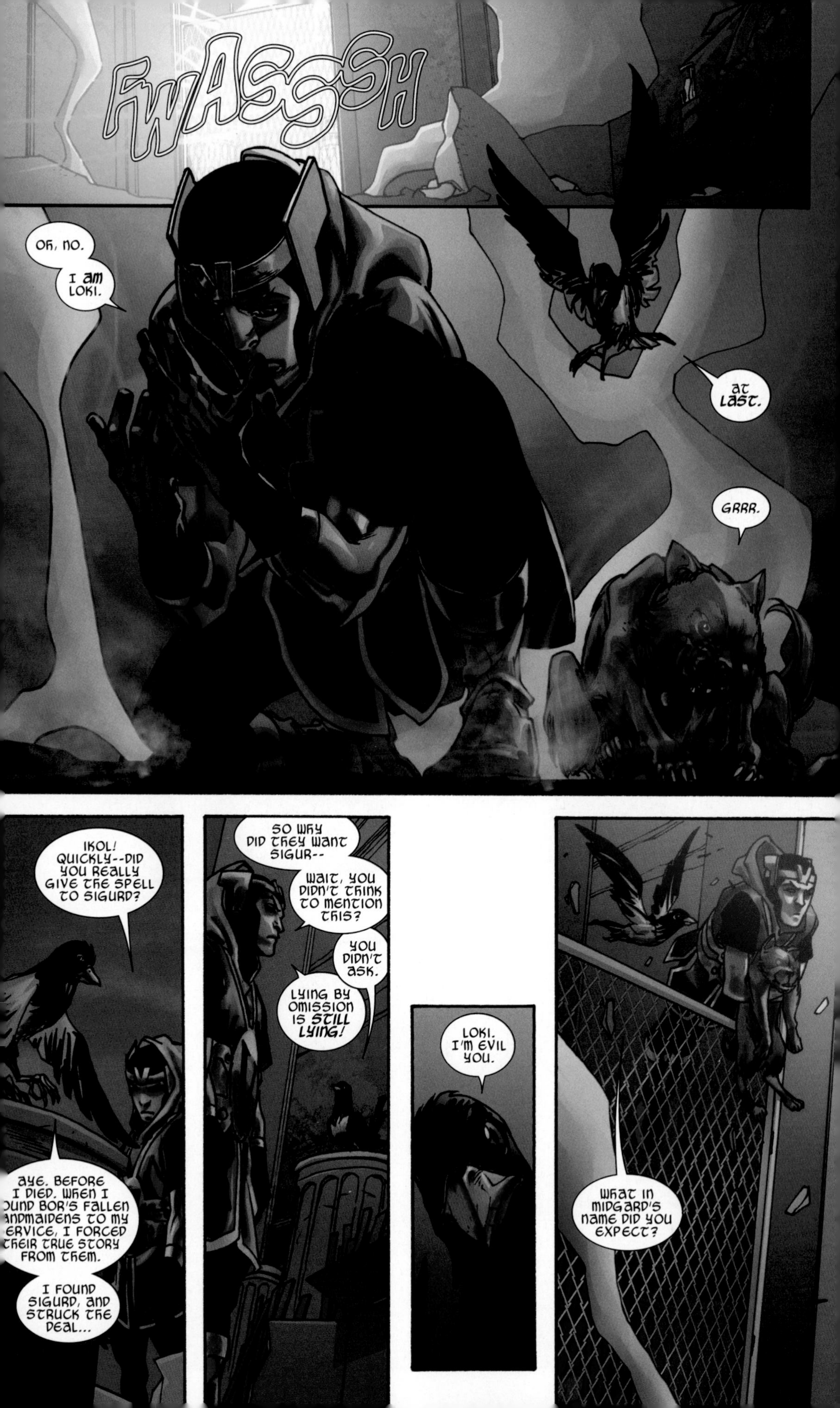
FWASSSH
OH, NO.
I AM LOKI.
AT LAST.
GRRR.
IKOL! QUICKLY--DID YOU REALLY GIVE THE SPELL TO SIGURD?
AYE. BEFORE I DIED. WHEN I FOUND BOR'S FALLEN HANDMAIDENS TO MY SERVICE, I FORCED THEIR TRUE STORY FROM THEM.
I FOUND SIGURD, AND STRUCK THE DEAL...
SO WHY DID THEY WANT SIGUR--
WAIT, YOU DIDN'T THINK TO MENTION THIS?
YOU DIDN'T ASK.
LYING BY OMISSION IS STILL LYING!
LOKI. I'M EVIL YOU.
WHAT IN MIDGARD'S NAME DID YOU EXPECT?

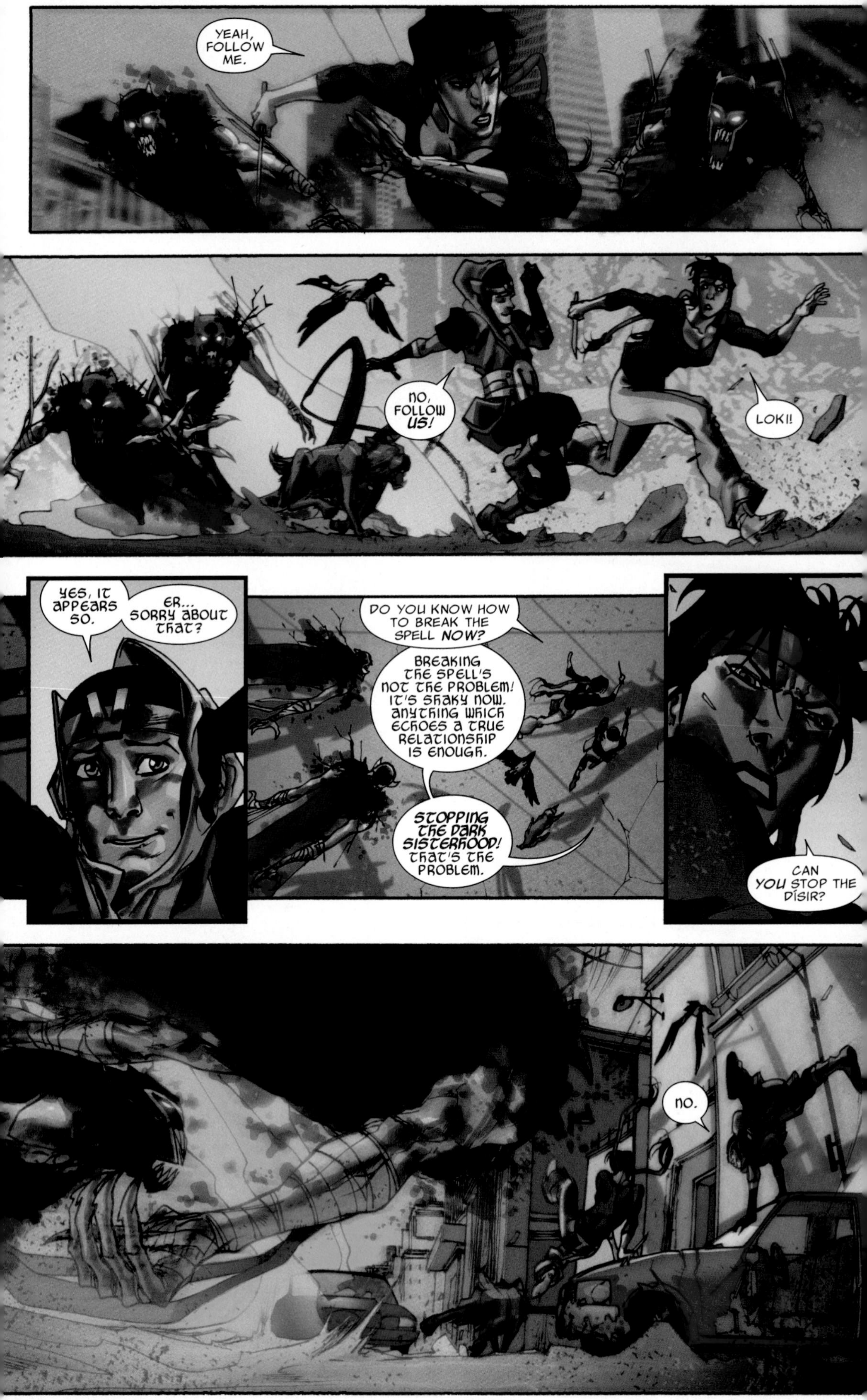
YEAH, FOLLOW ME.
NO, FOLLOW US!
LOKI!
YES, IT APPEARS SO.
ER... SORRY ABOUT THAT?
DO YOU KNOW HOW TO BREAK THE SPELL NOW?
BREAKING THE SPELL'S NOT THE PROBLEM! IT'S SHAKY NOW. ANYTHING WHICH ECHOES A TRUE RELATIONSHIP IS ENOUGH.
STOPPING THE DARK SISTERHOOD! THAT'S THE PROBLEM.
CAN YOU STOP THE DÍSIR?
NO.

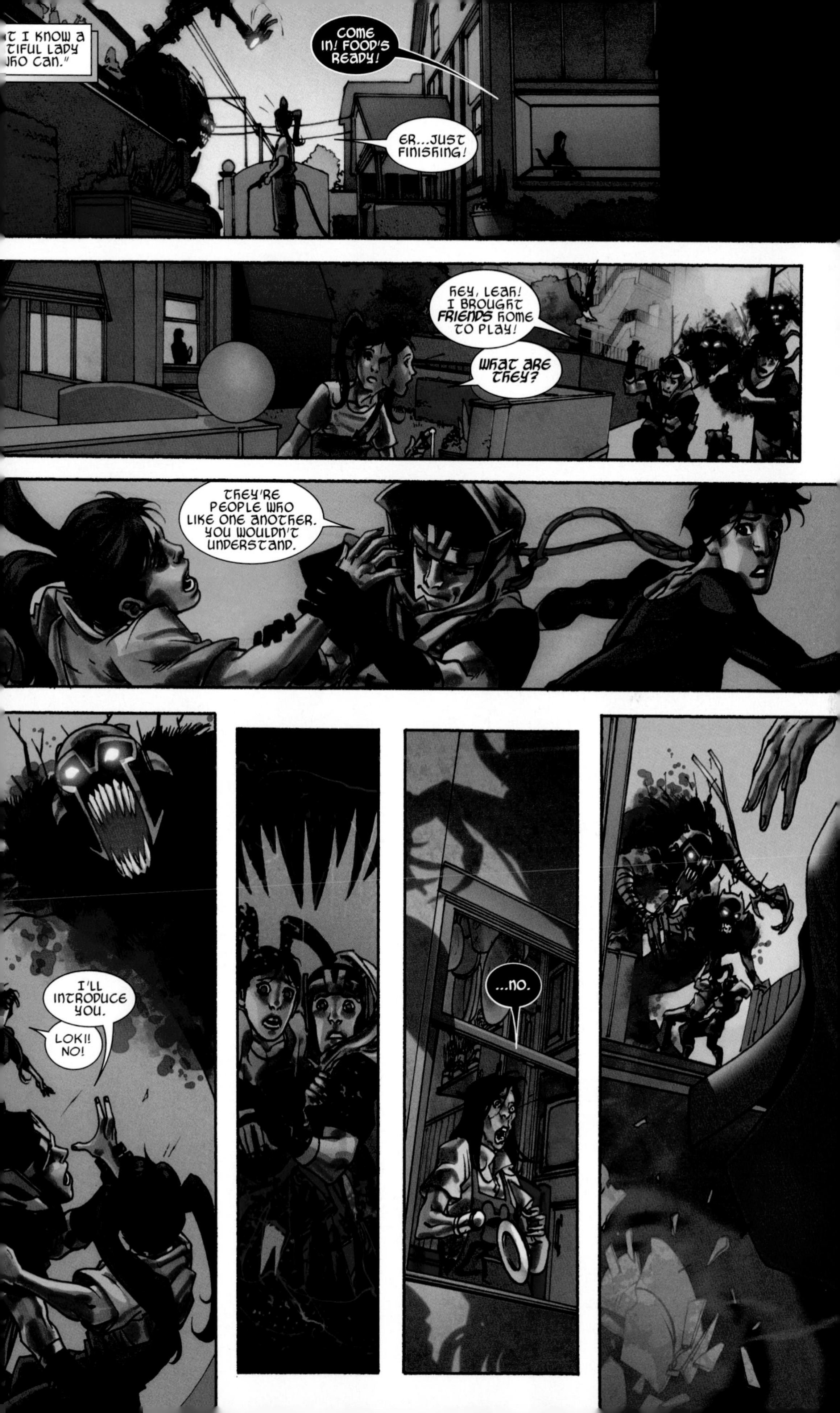

T I KNOW A
TIFUL LADY
HO CAN."
COME IN! FOOD'S READY!
ER...JUST FINISHING!
HEY, LEAH! I BROUGHT FRIENDS HOME TO PLAY!
WHAT ARE THEY?
THEY'RE PEOPLE WHO LIKE ONE ANOTHER. YOU WOULDN'T UNDERSTAND.
I'LL INTRODUCE YOU.
LOKI! NO!
...NO.

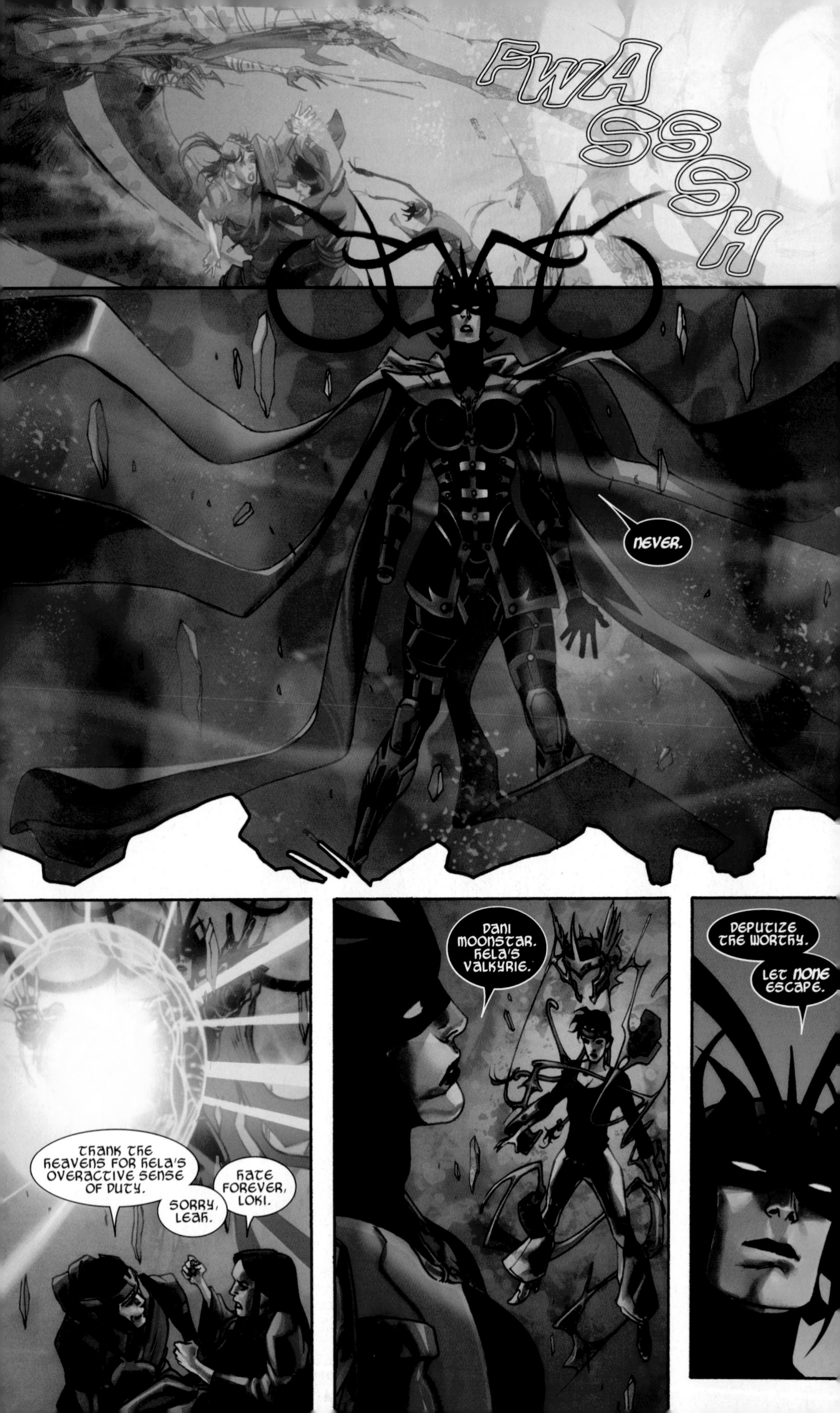
FWASSSH
NEVER.
THANK THE HEAVENS FOR HELA'S OVERACTIVE SENSE OF DUTY.
SORRY, LEAH.
HATE FOREVER, LOKI.
DANI MOONSTAR. HELA'S VALKYRIE.
DEPUTIZE THE WORTHY.
LET NONE ESCAPE.

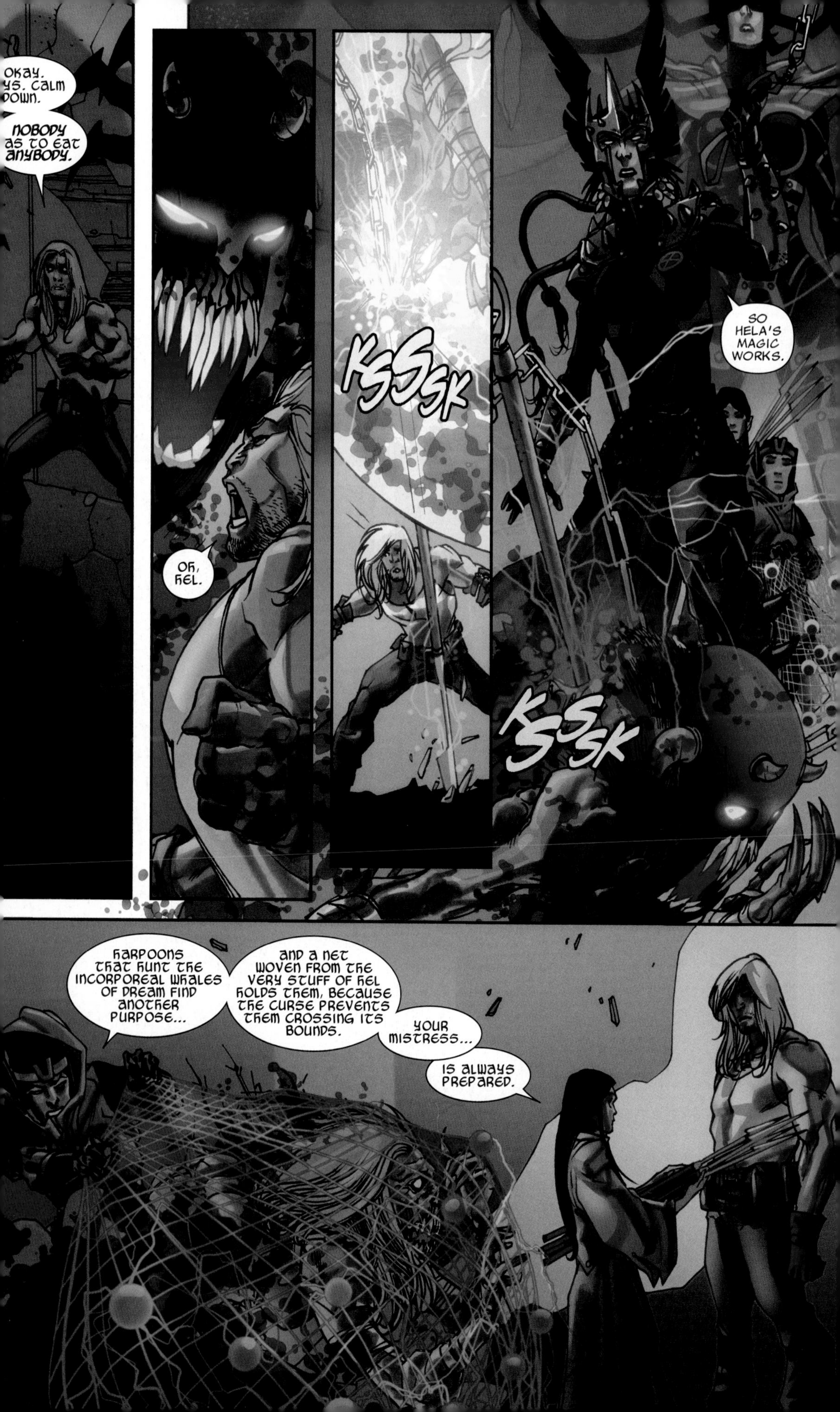

OKAY.
YS. CALM
DOWN.
NOBODY
AS TO EAT
ANYBODY.
OH, HEL.
KSSSK
SO HELA'S MAGIC WORKS.
KSSSK
HARPOONS THAT HUNT THE INCORPOREAL WHALES OF DREAM FIND ANOTHER PURPOSE...
AND A NET WOVEN FROM THE VERY STUFF OF HEL HOLDS THEM, BECAUSE THE CURSE PREVENTS THEM CROSSING ITS BOUNDS.
YOUR MISTRESS...
IS ALWAYS PREPARED.

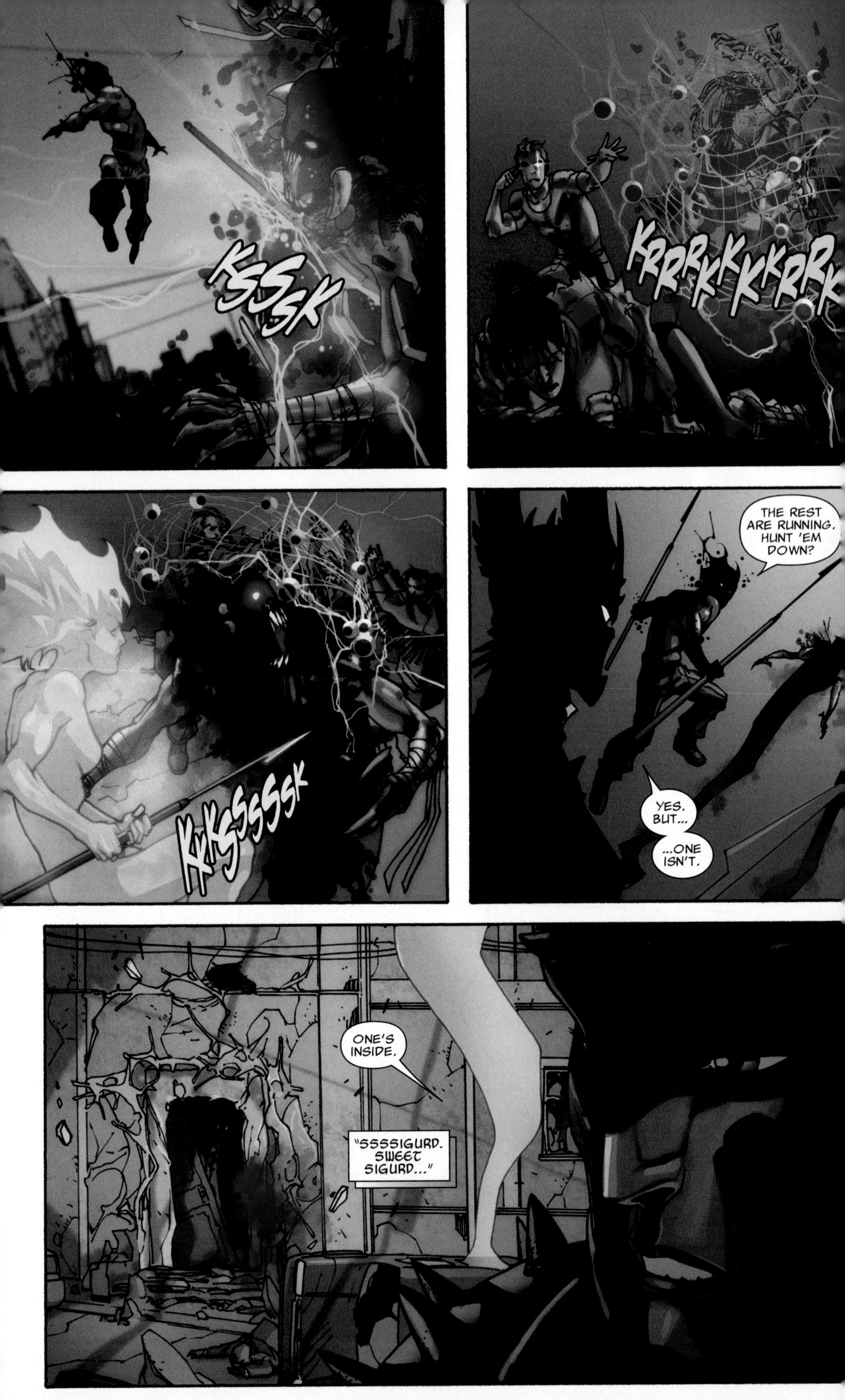
KSSSK
KRRRKKKKRRK
KKKSSSSSK
THE REST ARE RUNNING. HUNT 'EM DOWN?
YES. BUT...
...ONE ISN'T.
ONE'S INSIDE.
"SSSSIGURD. SWEET SIGURD..."

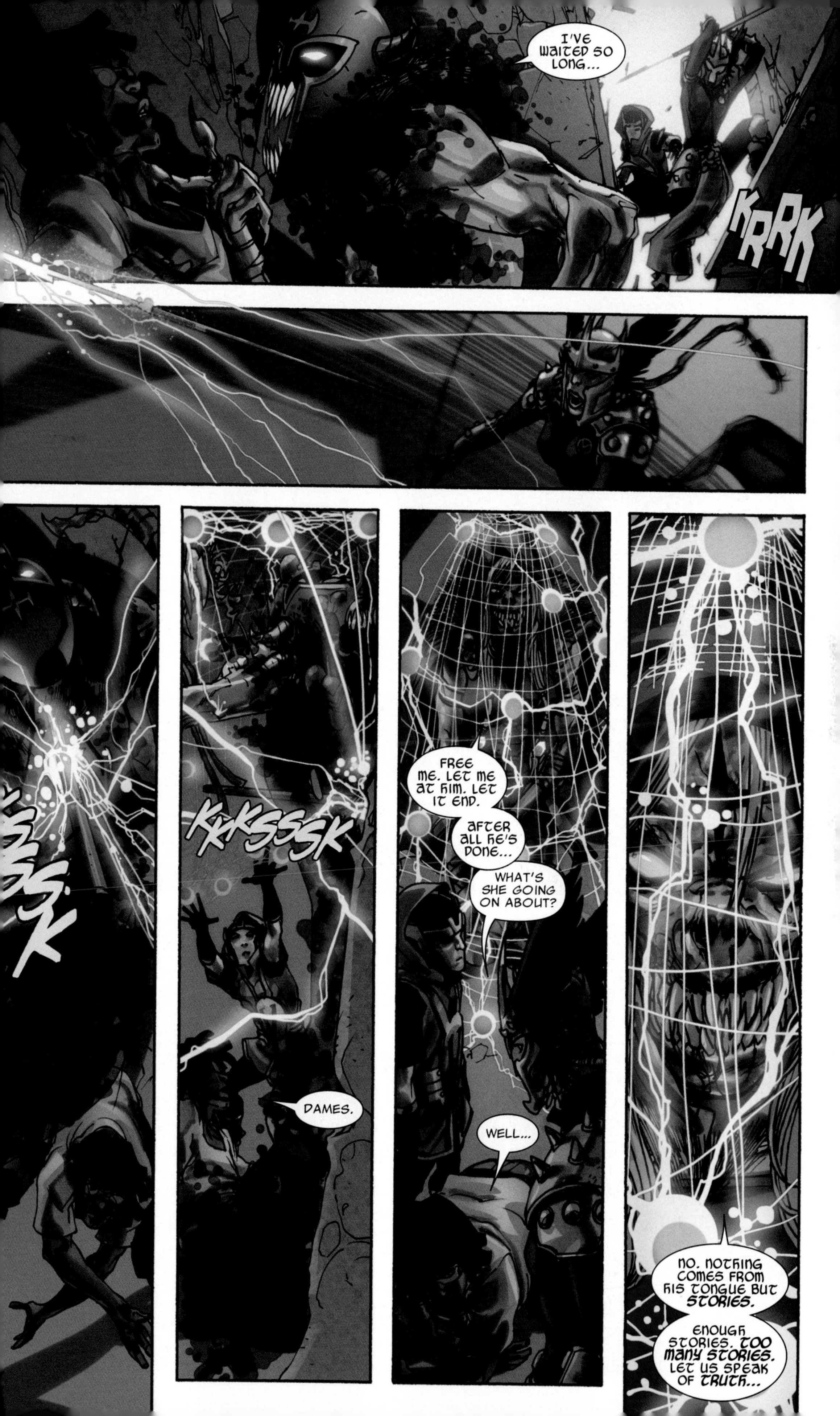
I'VE WAITED SO LONG...
KRRK
KKKSSSK
DAMES.
FREE ME. LET ME AT HIM. LET IT END.
AFTER ALL HE'S DONE...
WHAT'S SHE GOING ON ABOUT?
WELL...
NO. NOTHING COMES FROM HIS TONGUE BUT STORIES.
ENOUGH STORIES. TOO MANY STORIES. LET US SPEAK OF TRUTH...

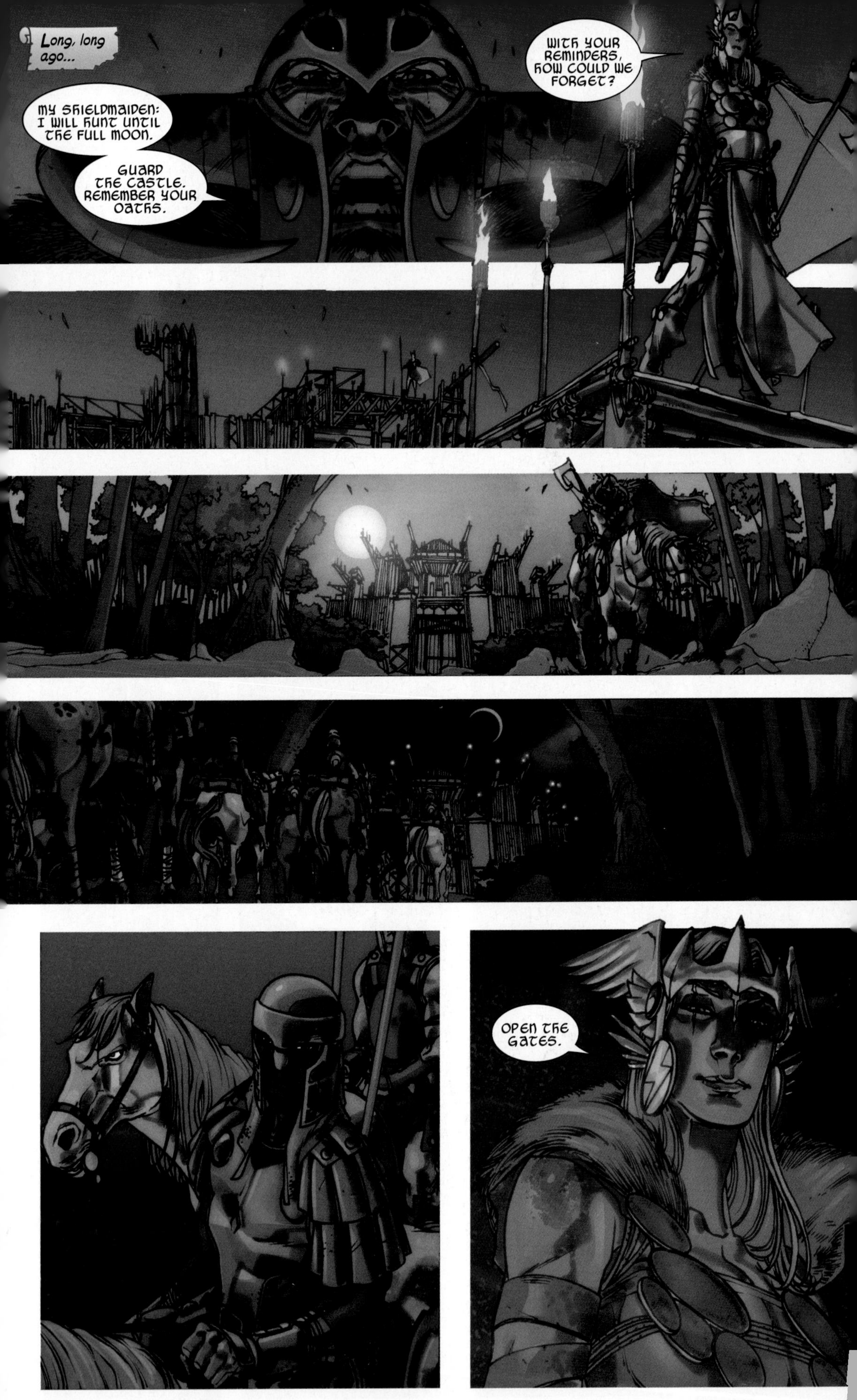
Long, long ago...
MY SHIELDMAIDEN: I WILL HUNT UNTIL THE FULL MOON.
GUARD THE CASTLE. REMEMBER YOUR OATHS.
WITH YOUR REMINDERS, HOW COULD WE FORGET?
OPEN THE GATES.

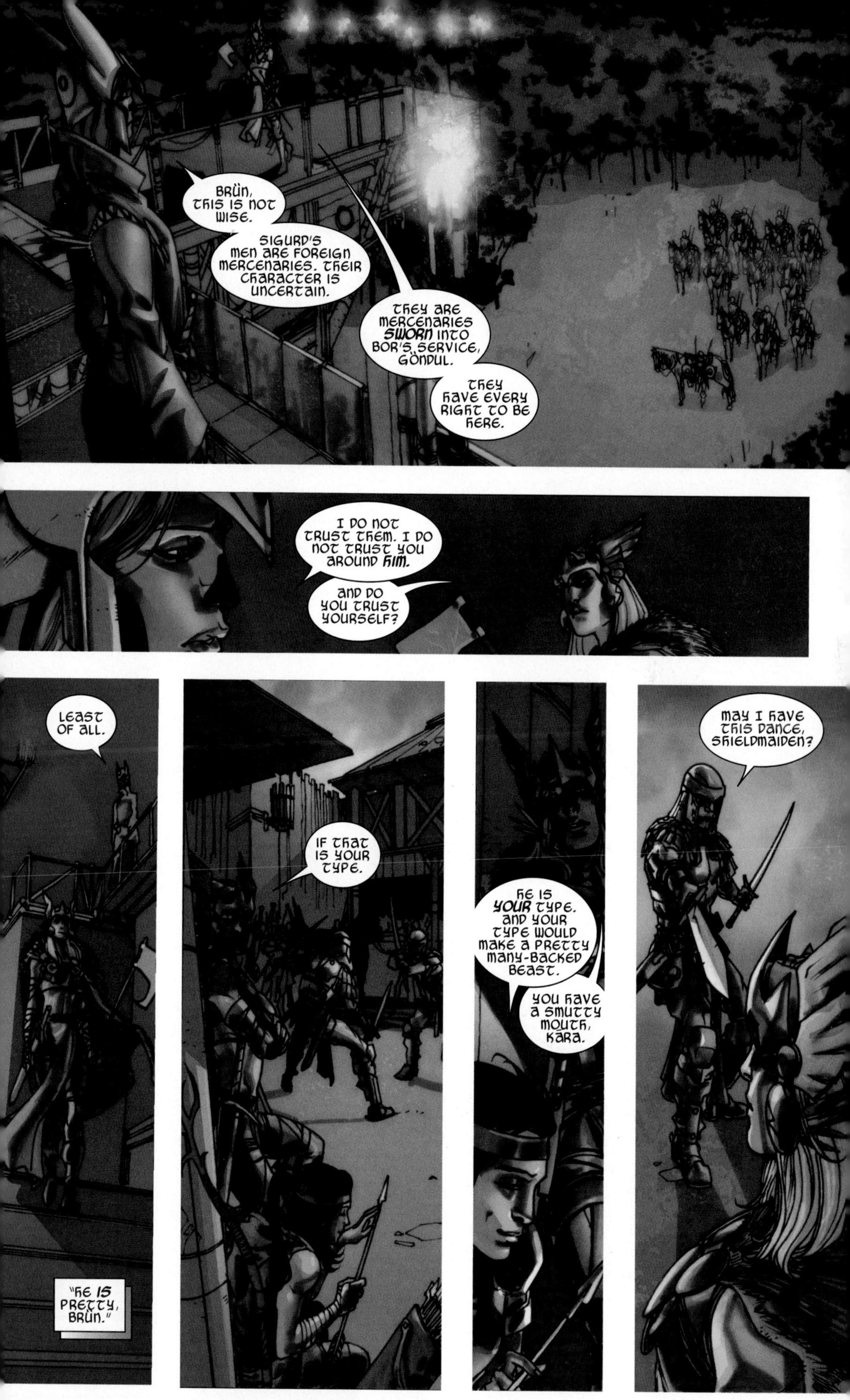
BRÜN, THIS IS NOT WISE.
SIGURD'S MEN ARE FOREIGN MERCENARIES. THEIR CHARACTER IS UNCERTAIN.
THEY ARE MERCENARIES SWORN INTO BOR'S SERVICE, GÖNDUL.
THEY HAVE EVERY RIGHT TO BE HERE.
I DO NOT TRUST THEM. I DO NOT TRUST YOU AROUND HIM.
AND DO YOU TRUST YOURSELF?
LEAST OF ALL.
"HE IS PRETTY, BRÜN."
IF THAT IS YOUR TYPE.
HE IS YOUR TYPE. AND YOUR TYPE WOULD MAKE A PRETTY MANY-BACKED BEAST.
YOU HAVE A SMUTTY MOUTH, KARA.
MAY I HAVE THIS DANCE, SHIELDMAIDEN?

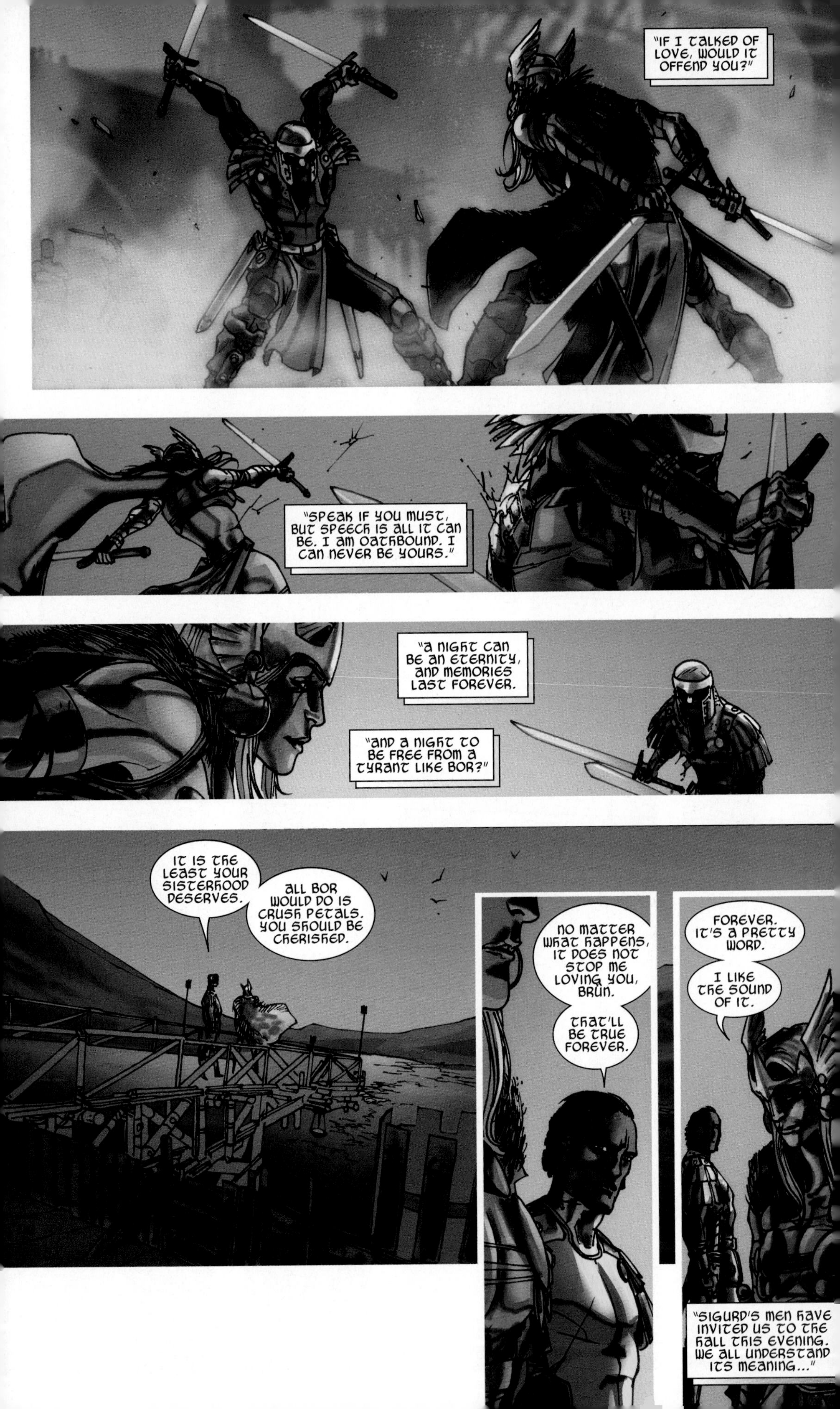
"IF I TALKED OF LOVE, WOULD IT OFFEND YOU?"
"SPEAK IF YOU MUST, BUT SPEECH IS ALL IT CAN BE. I AM OATHBOUND. I CAN NEVER BE YOURS."
"A NIGHT CAN BE AN ETERNITY, AND MEMORIES LAST FOREVER.
"AND A NIGHT TO BE FREE FROM A TYRANT LIKE BOR?"
IT IS THE LEAST YOUR SISTERHOOD DESERVES.
ALL BOR WOULD DO IS CRUSH PETALS. YOU SHOULD BE CHERISHED.
NO MATTER WHAT HAPPENS, IT DOES NOT STOP ME LOVING YOU, BRUN.
THAT'LL BE TRUE FOREVER.
FOREVER. IT'S A PRETTY WORD.
I LIKE THE SOUND OF IT.
"SIGURD'S MEN HAVE INVITED US TO THE HALL THIS EVENING. WE ALL UNDERSTAND ITS MEANING..."

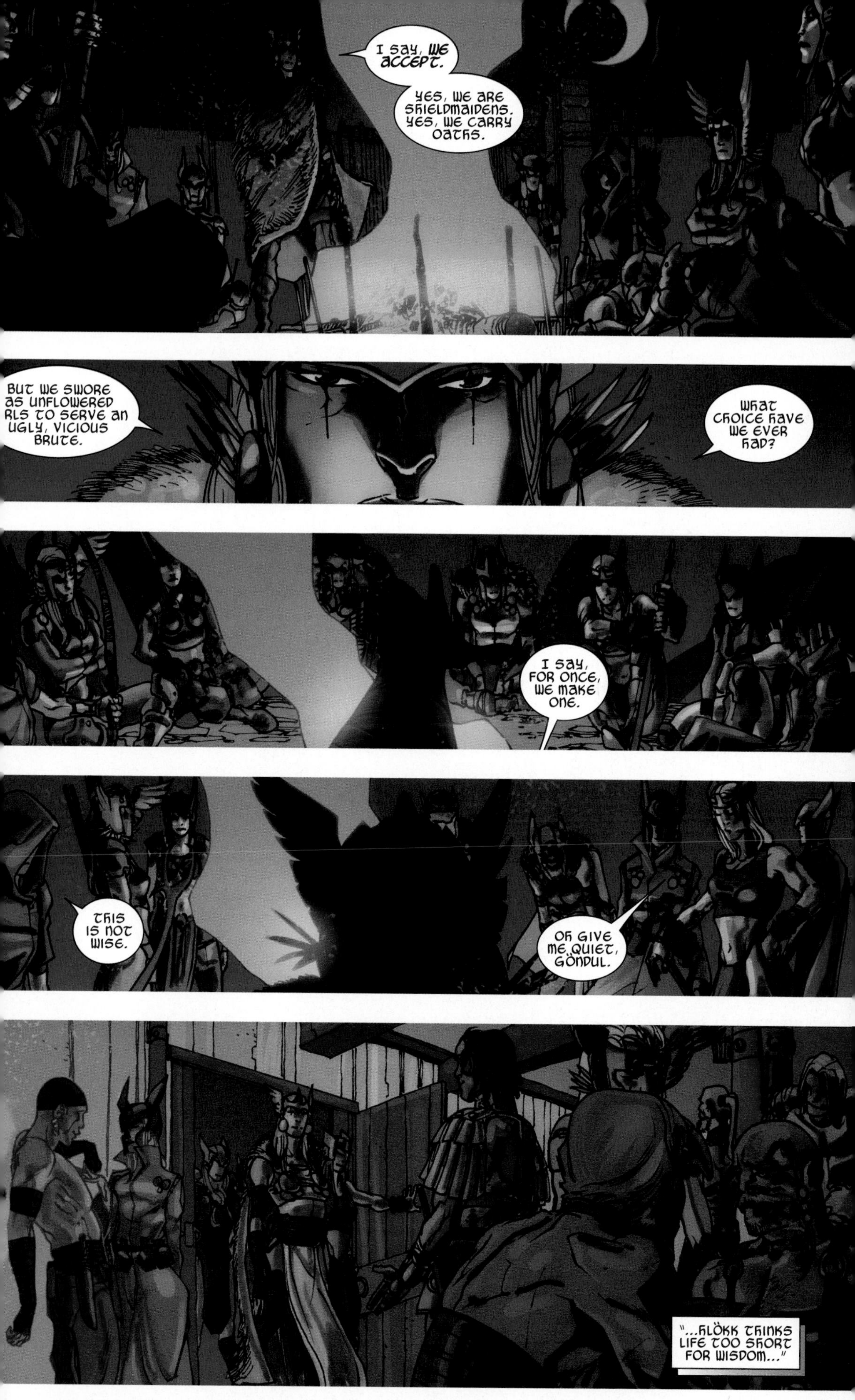
I SAY, WE ACCEPT.
YES, WE ARE SHIELDMAIDENS. YES, WE CARRY OATHS.
BUT WE SWORE AS UNFLOWERED RLS TO SERVE AN UGLY, VICIOUS BRUTE.
WHAT CHOICE HAVE WE EVER HAD?
I SAY, FOR ONCE, WE MAKE ONE.
THIS IS NOT WISE.
OH GIVE ME QUIET, GÖNDUL.
"...HLÖKK THINKS LIFE TOO SHORT FOR WISDOM..."

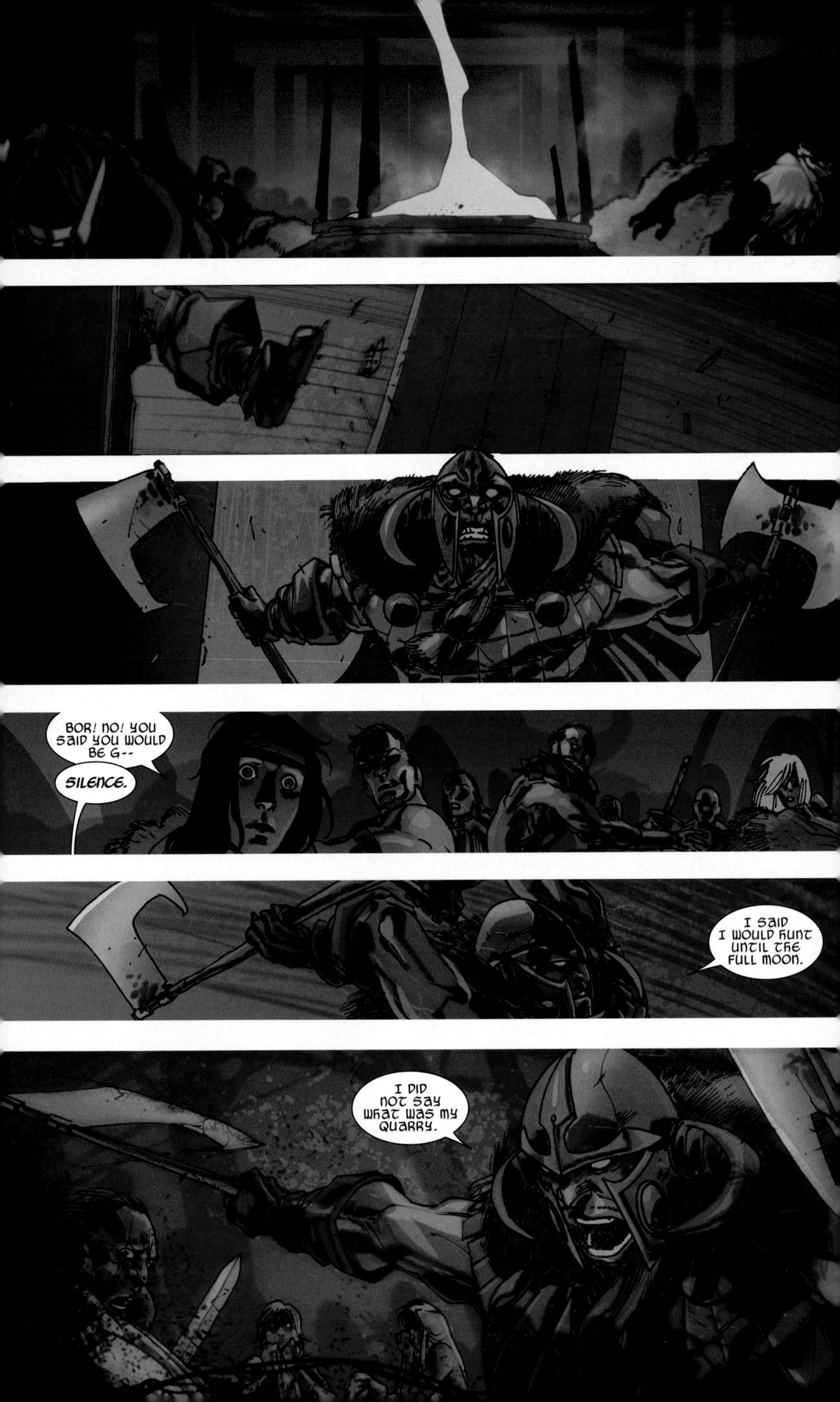
BOR! NO! YOU SAID YOU WOULD BE G--
SILENCE.
I SAID I WOULD HUNT UNTIL THE FULL MOON.
I DID NOT SAY WHAT WAS MY QUARRY.

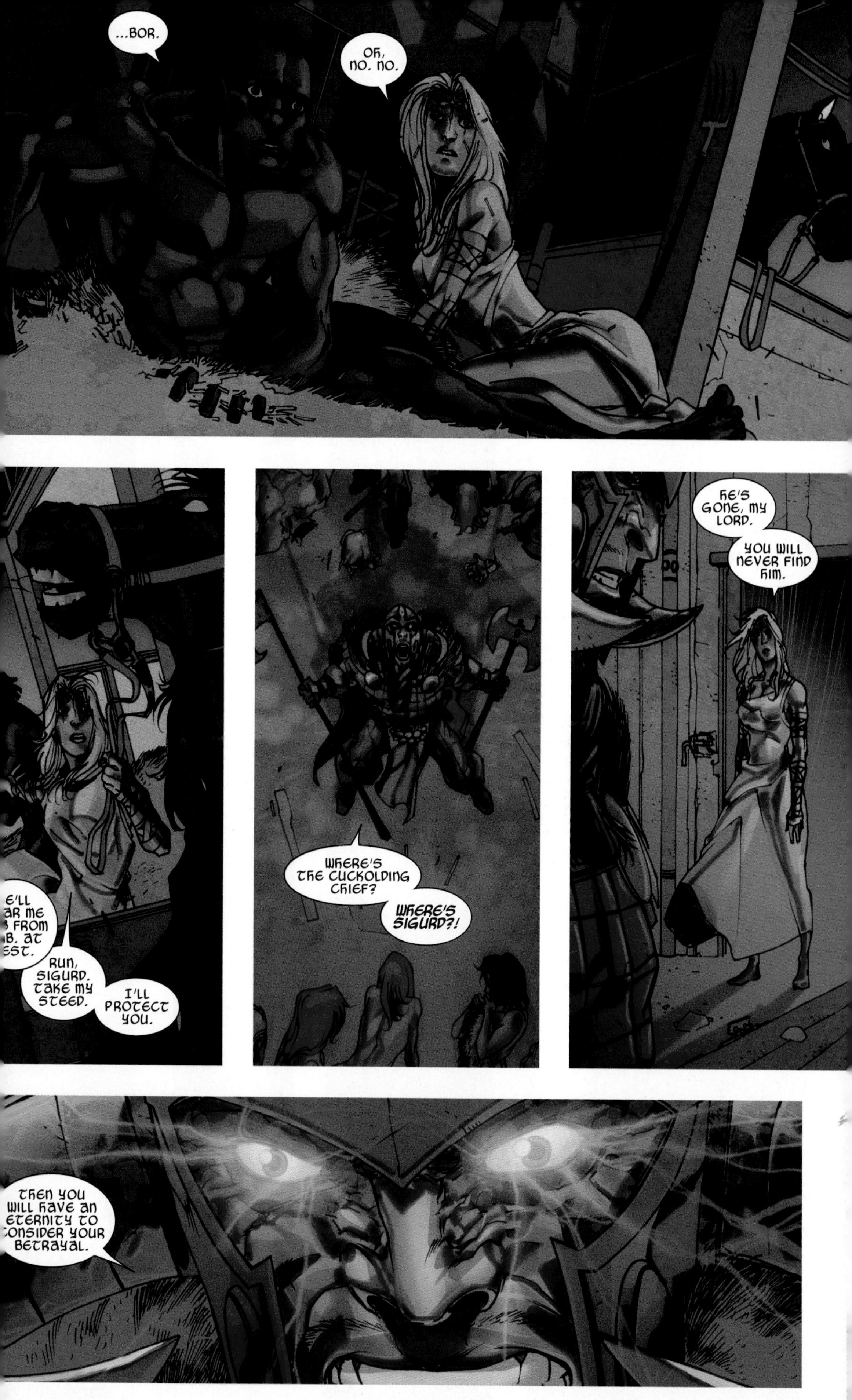
...BOR.
OH, NO. NO.
E'LL AR ME FROM B. AT EST.
RUN, SIGURD. TAKE MY STEED.
I'LL PROTECT YOU.
WHERE'S THE CUCKOLDING CHIEF?
WHERE'S SIGURD?!
HE'S GONE, MY LORD.
YOU WILL NEVER FIND HIM.
THEN YOU WILL HAVE AN ETERNITY TO CONSIDER YOUR BETRAYAL.

YOU LET YOUR HUNGER FOR FLESH OVERCOME YOU?

THEN YOU WILL LIVE WITH THAT FOREVER.

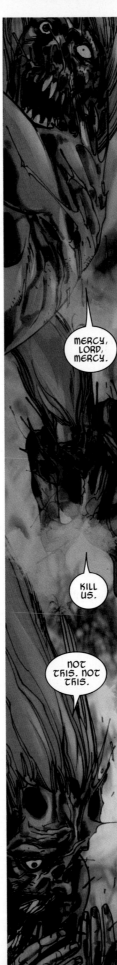

MERCY, LORD, MERCY.

KILL US.

NOT THIS. NOT THIS.

NO. HEL IS TOO GOOD FOR YOU.

BUT HERE'S HOW YOU CAN ESCAPE THE CURSE...

ENSURE SIGURD'S BLADE IS FOREVER SAFELY SHEATHED. END HIS LIFE OR BE HIS WIFE. EITHER WOULD SATISFY ME.

AND I THINK FOR HIM, A WIFE WOULD BE THE GREATER BURDEN.

"AND SO BEGAN ETERNITY."

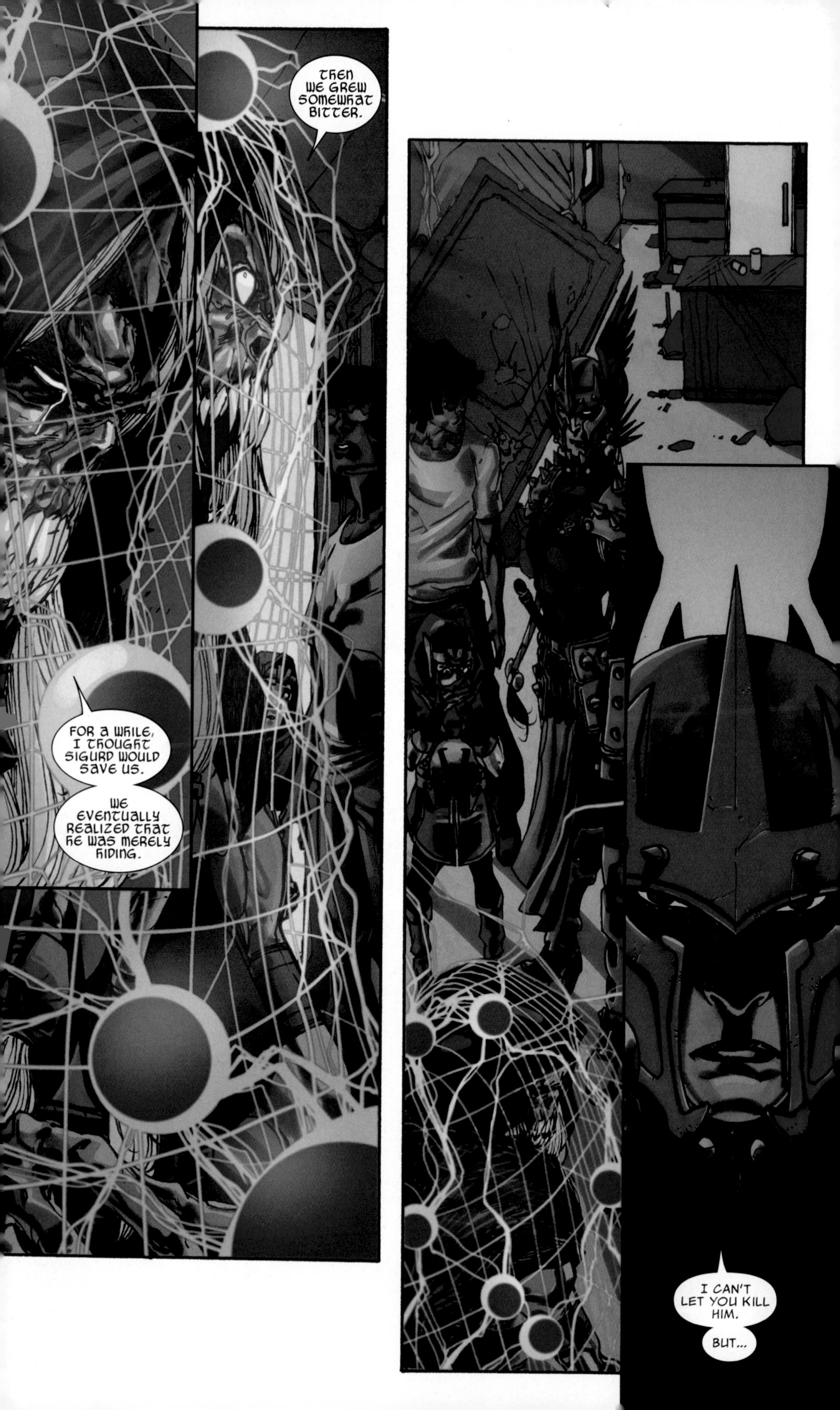
THEN WE GREW SOMEWHAT BITTER.
FOR A WHILE, I THOUGHT SIGURD WOULD SAVE US.
WE EVENTUALLY REALIZED THAT HE WAS MERELY HIDING.
I CAN'T LET YOU KILL HIM.
BUT...

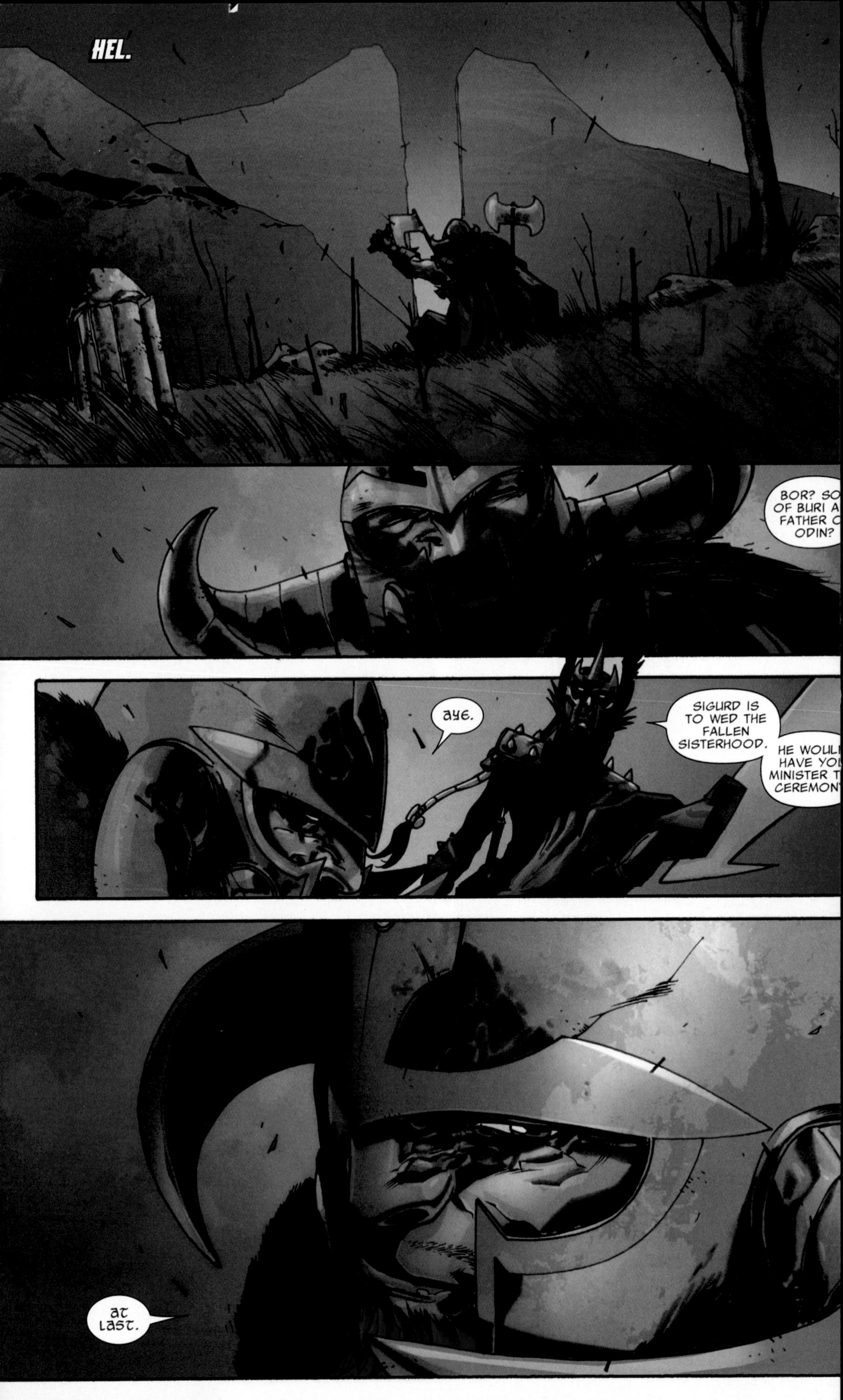
HEL.
BOR? SO OF BURI A FATHER O ODIN?
AYE.
SIGURD IS TO WED THE FALLEN SISTERHOOD.
HE WOUL HAVE YO MINISTER T CEREMON
AT LAST.

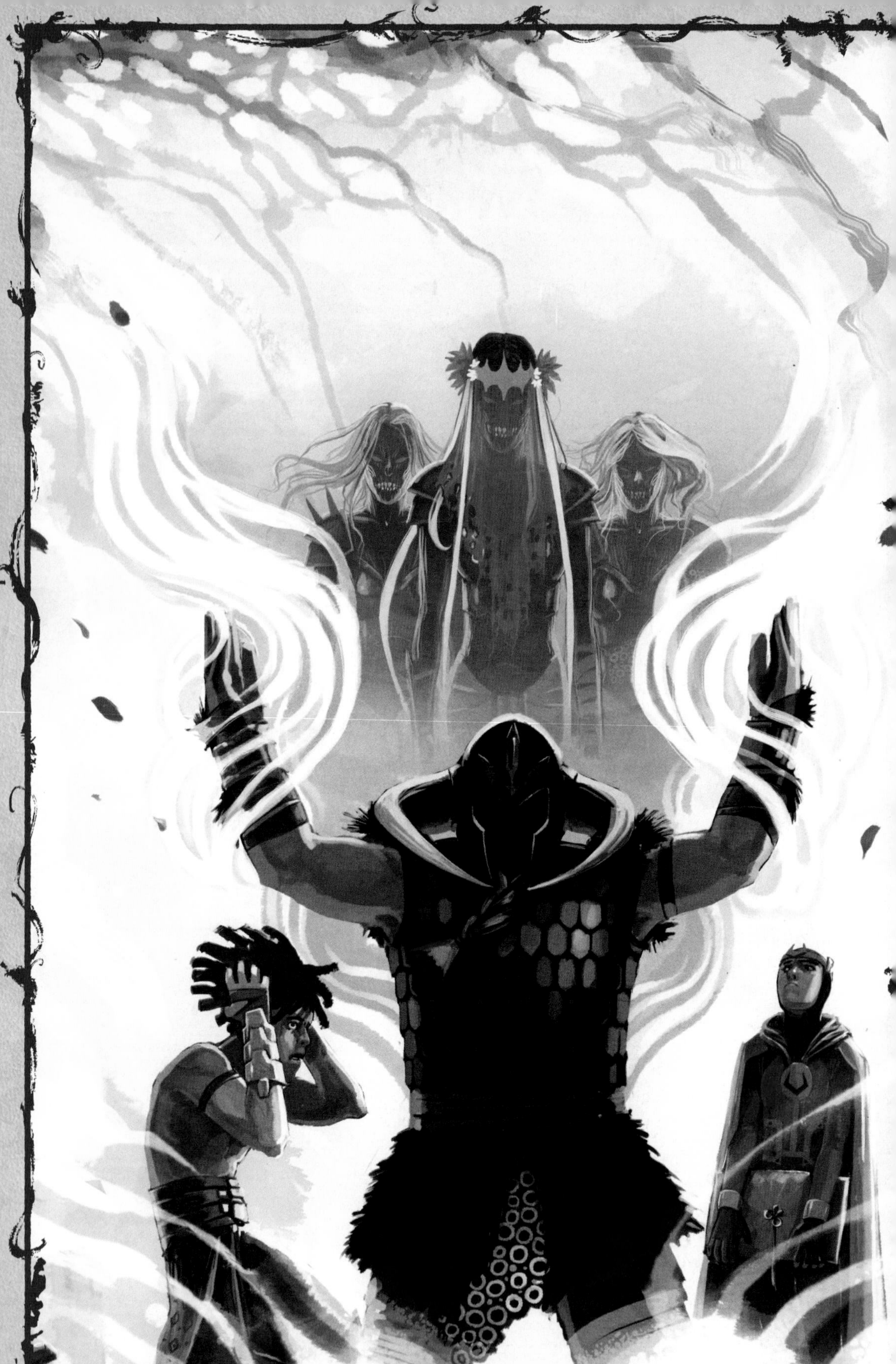

NEW MUTANTS #43: "UNHAPPILY EVER AFTER"

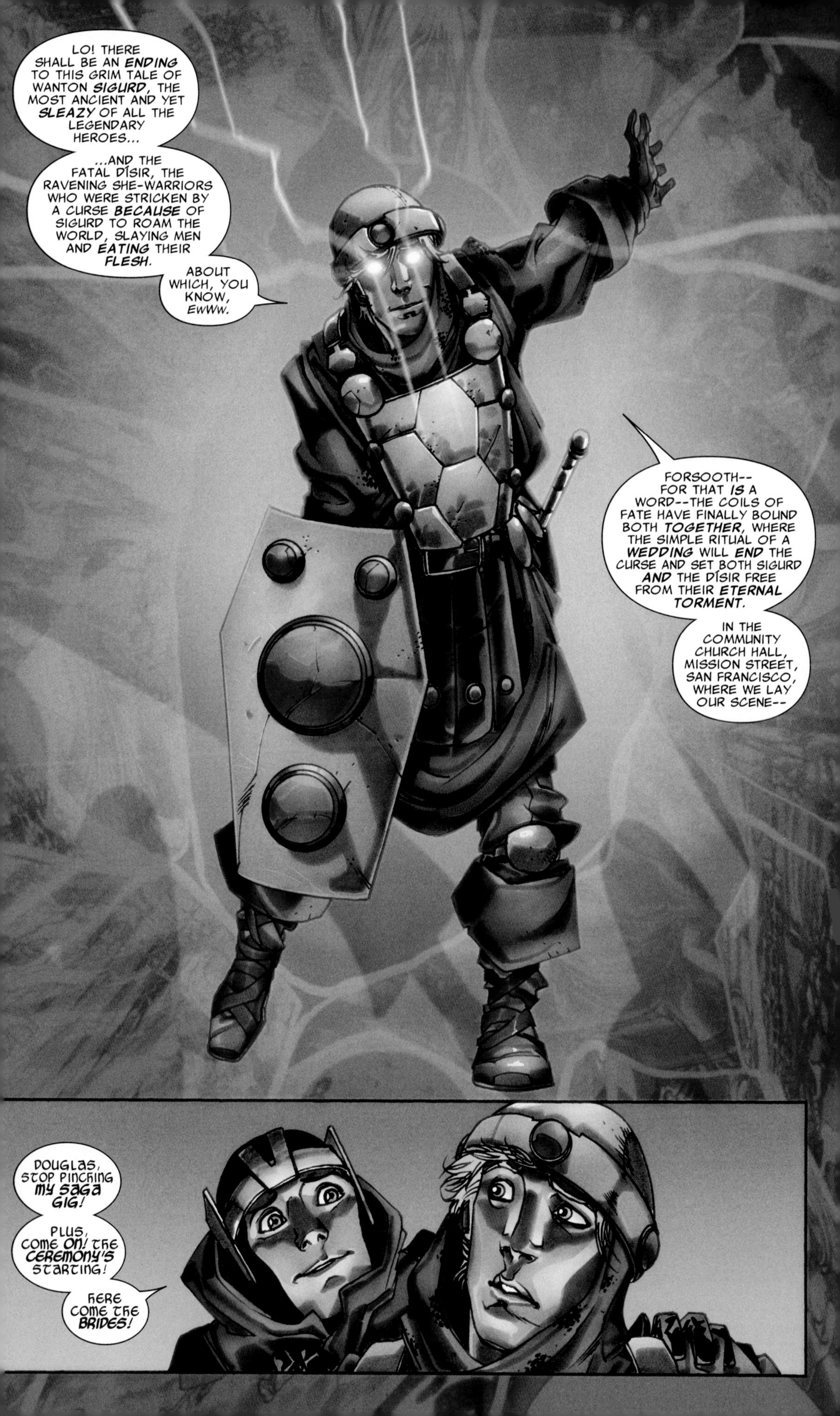
LO! THERE SHALL BE AN ENDING TO THIS GRIM TALE OF WANTON SIGURD, THE MOST ANCIENT AND YET SLEAZY OF ALL THE LEGENDARY HEROES...
...AND THE FATAL DÍSIR, THE RAVENING SHE-WARRIORS WHO WERE STRICKEN BY A CURSE BECAUSE OF SIGURD TO ROAM THE WORLD, SLAYING MEN AND EATING THEIR FLESH.
ABOUT WHICH, YOU KNOW, EWWW.
FORSOOTH-- FOR THAT IS A WORD--THE COILS OF FATE HAVE FINALLY BOUND BOTH TOGETHER, WHERE THE SIMPLE RITUAL OF A WEDDING WILL END THE CURSE AND SET BOTH SIGURD AND THE DÍSIR FREE FROM THEIR ETERNAL TORMENT.
IN THE COMMUNITY CHURCH HALL, MISSION STREET, SAN FRANCISCO, WHERE WE LAY OUR SCENE--
DOUGLAS, STOP PINCHING MY SAGA GIG!
PLUS, COME ON! THE CEREMONY'S STARTING!
HERE COME THE BRIDES!

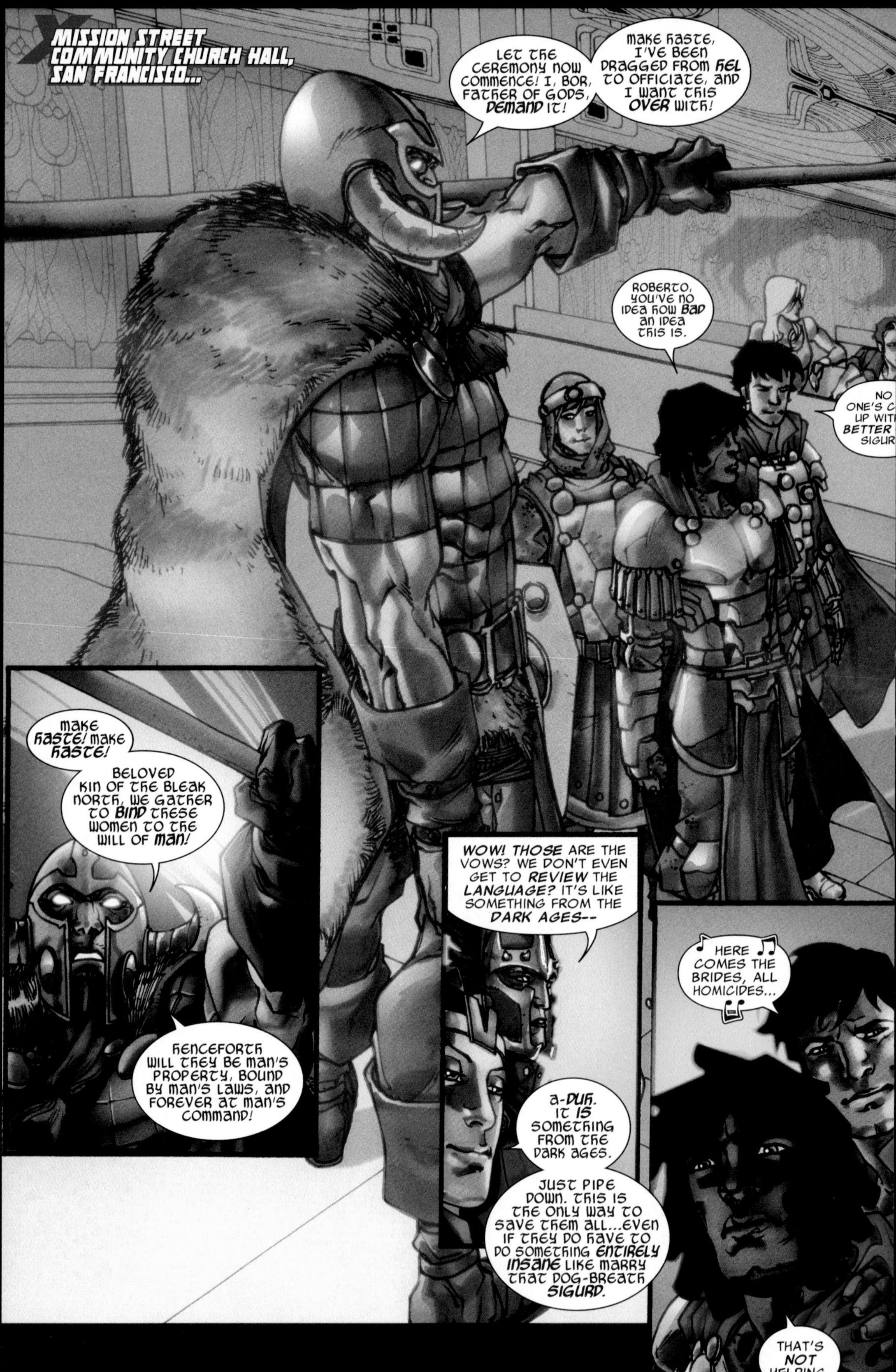
MISSION STREET COMMUNITY CHURCH HALL, SAN FRANCISCO...
LET THE CEREMONY NOW COMMENCE! I, BOR, FATHER OF GODS, DEMAND IT!
MAKE HASTE, I'VE BEEN DRAGGED FROM HEL TO OFFICIATE, AND I WANT THIS OVER WITH!
ROBERTO, YOU'VE NO IDEA HOW BAD AN IDEA THIS IS.
NO ONE'S C UP WITH BETTER SIGUR
MAKE HASTE! MAKE HASTE!
BELOVED KIN OF THE BLEAK NORTH, WE GATHER TO BIND THESE WOMEN TO THE WILL OF MAN!
HENCEFORTH WILL THEY BE MAN'S PROPERTY, BOUND BY MAN'S LAWS, AND FOREVER AT MAN'S COMMAND!
WOW! THOSE ARE THE VOWS? WE DON'T EVEN GET TO REVIEW THE LANGUAGE? IT'S LIKE SOMETHING FROM THE DARK AGES--
A-DUH. IT IS SOMETHING FROM THE DARK AGES.
JUST PIPE DOWN. THIS IS THE ONLY WAY TO SAVE THEM ALL...EVEN IF THEY DO HAVE TO DO SOMETHING ENTIRELY INSANE LIKE MARRY THAT DOG-BREATH SIGURD.
HERE COMES THE BRIDES, ALL HOMICIDES...
THAT'S NOT HELPING.

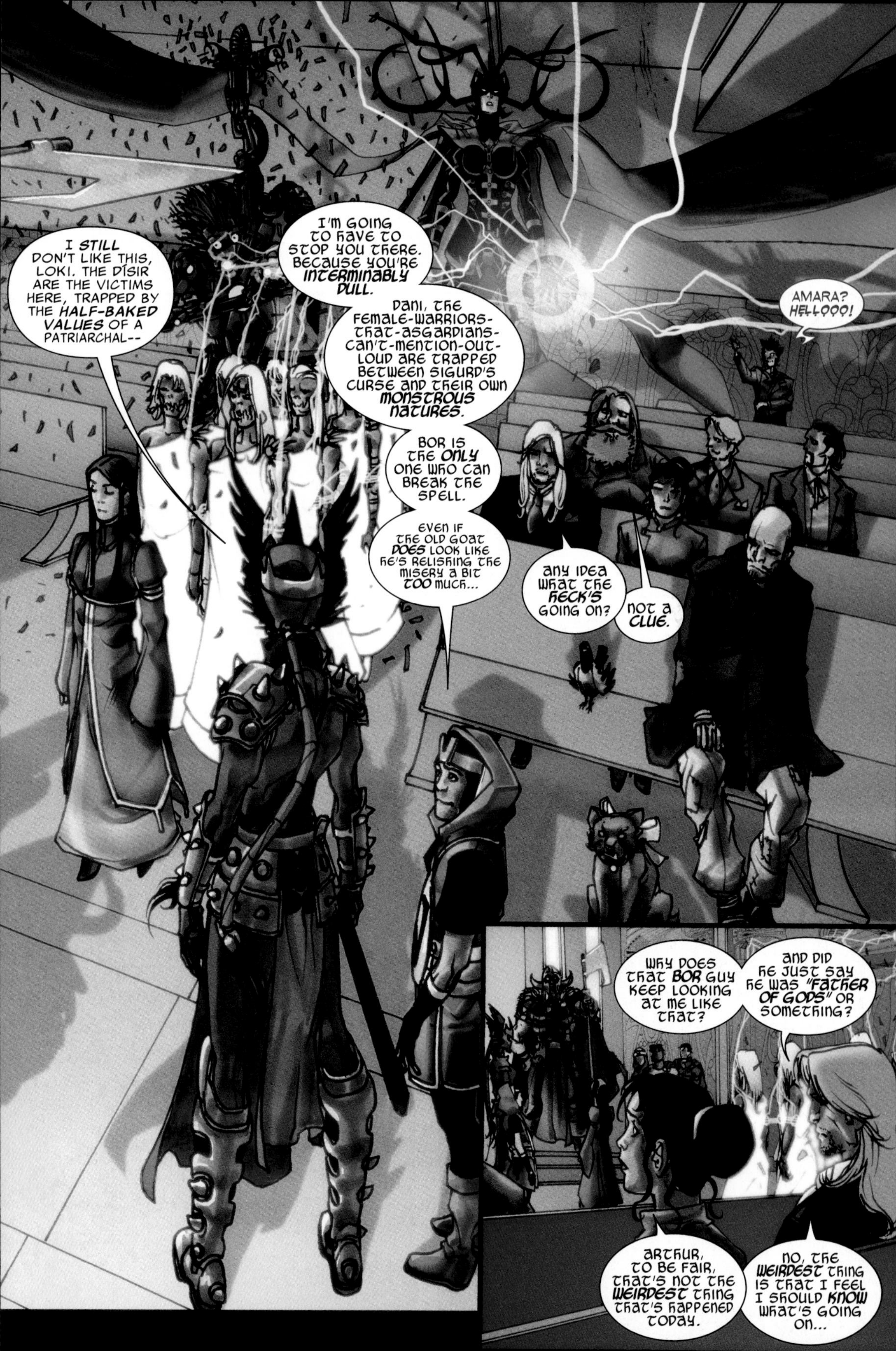
I STILL DON'T LIKE THIS, LOKI. THE DÍSIR ARE THE VICTIMS HERE, TRAPPED BY THE HALF-BAKED VALUES OF A PATRIARCHAL--
I'M GOING TO HAVE TO STOP YOU THERE. BECAUSE YOU'RE INTERMINABLY DULL.
DANI, THE FEMALE-WARRIORS-THAT-ASGARDIANS-CAN'T-MENTION-OUT-LOUD ARE TRAPPED BETWEEN SIGURD'S CURSE AND THEIR OWN MONSTROUS NATURES.
BOR IS THE ONLY ONE WHO CAN BREAK THE SPELL.
EVEN IF THE OLD GOAT DOES LOOK LIKE HE'S RELISHING THE MISERY A BIT TOO MUCH...
AMARA? HELLOOO!
ANY IDEA WHAT THE HECK'S GOING ON?
NOT A CLUE.
WHY DOES THAT BOR GUY KEEP LOOKING AT ME LIKE THAT?
AND DID HE JUST SAY HE WAS "FATHER OF GODS" OR SOMETHING?
ARTHUR, TO BE FAIR, THAT'S NOT THE WEIRDEST THING THAT'S HAPPENED TODAY.
NO, THE WEIRDEST THING IS THAT I FEEL I SHOULD KNOW WHAT'S GOING ON...

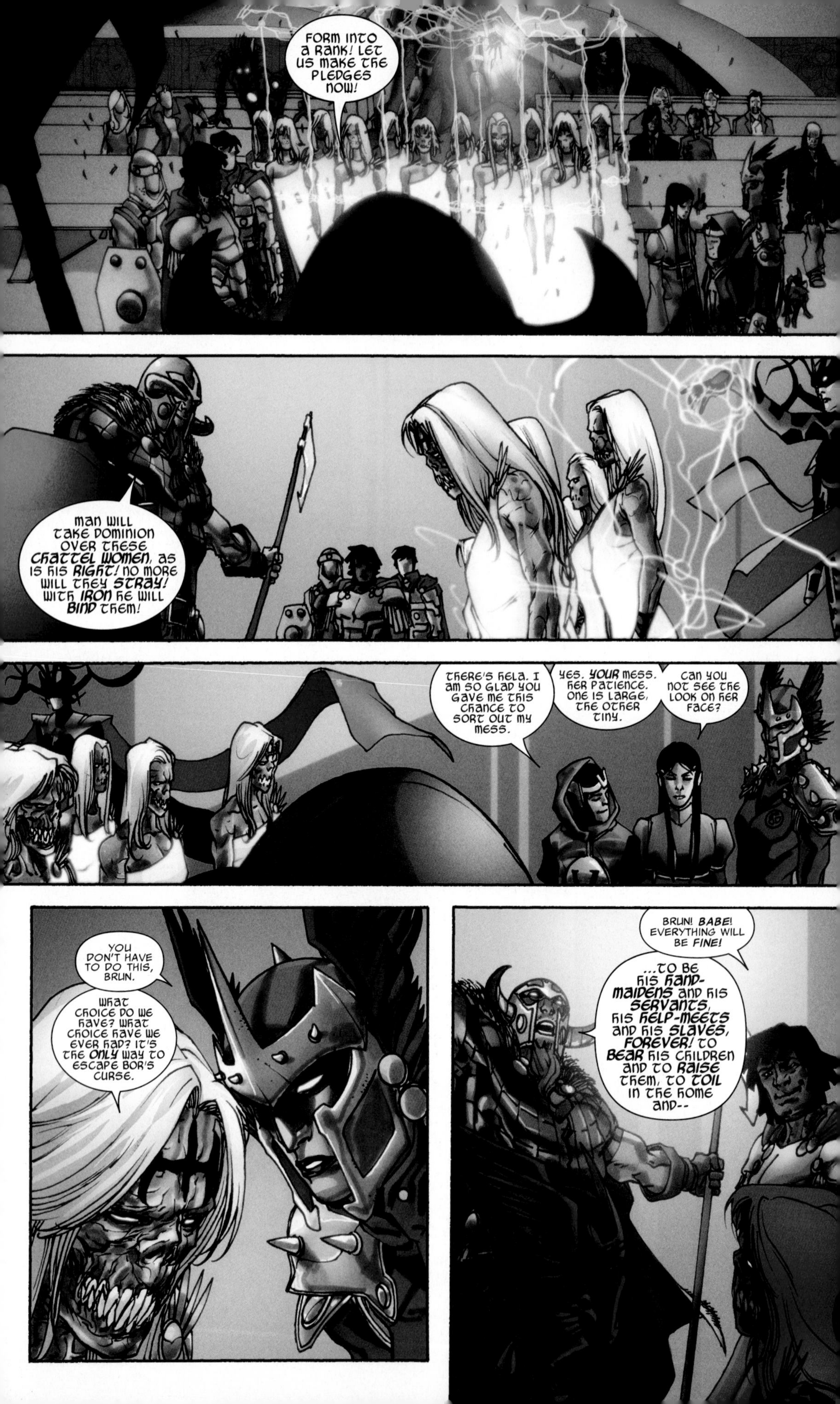
FORM INTO A RANK! LET US MAKE THE PLEDGES NOW!
MAN WILL TAKE DOMINION OVER THESE CHATTEL WOMEN, AS IS HIS RIGHT! NO MORE WILL THEY STRAY! WITH IRON HE WILL BIND THEM!
THERE'S HELA. I AM SO GLAD YOU GAVE ME THIS CHANCE TO SORT OUT MY MESS.
YES. YOUR MESS. HER PATIENCE. ONE IS LARGE, THE OTHER TINY.
CAN YOU NOT SEE THE LOOK ON HER FACE?
YOU DON'T HAVE TO DO THIS, BRUN.
WHAT CHOICE DO WE HAVE? WHAT CHOICE HAVE WE EVER HAD? IT'S THE ONLY WAY TO ESCAPE BOR'S CURSE.
BRUN! BABE! EVERYTHING WILL BE FINE!
...TO BE HIS HAND-MAIDENS AND HIS SERVANTS, HIS HELP-MEETS AND HIS SLAVES, FOREVER! TO BEAR HIS CHILDREN AND TO RAISE THEM, TO TOIL IN THE HOME AND--

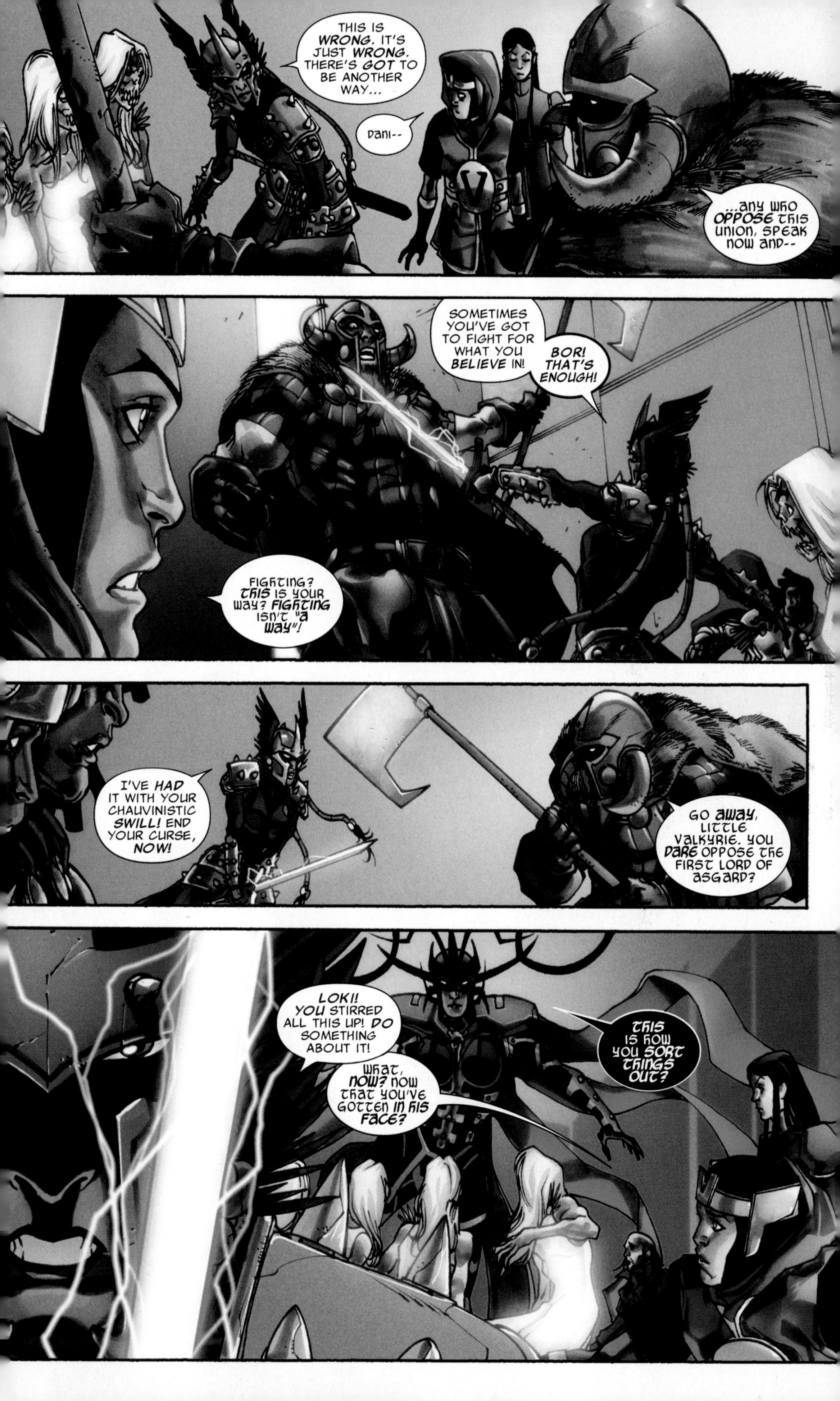
THIS IS WRONG. IT'S JUST WRONG. THERE'S GOT TO BE ANOTHER WAY...
DANI--
...ANY WHO OPPOSE THIS UNION, SPEAK NOW AND--
SOMETIMES YOU'VE GOT TO FIGHT FOR WHAT YOU BELIEVE IN!
BOR! THAT'S ENOUGH!
FIGHTING? THIS IS YOUR WAY? FIGHTING ISN'T "A WAY"!
I'VE HAD IT WITH YOUR CHAUVINISTIC SWILL! END YOUR CURSE, NOW!
GO AWAY, LITTLE VALKYRIE. YOU DARE OPPOSE THE FIRST LORD OF ASGARD?
LOKI! YOU STIRRED ALL THIS UP! DO SOMETHING ABOUT IT!
WHAT, NOW? NOW THAT YOU'VE GOTTEN IN HIS FACE?
THIS IS HOW YOU SORT THINGS OUT?

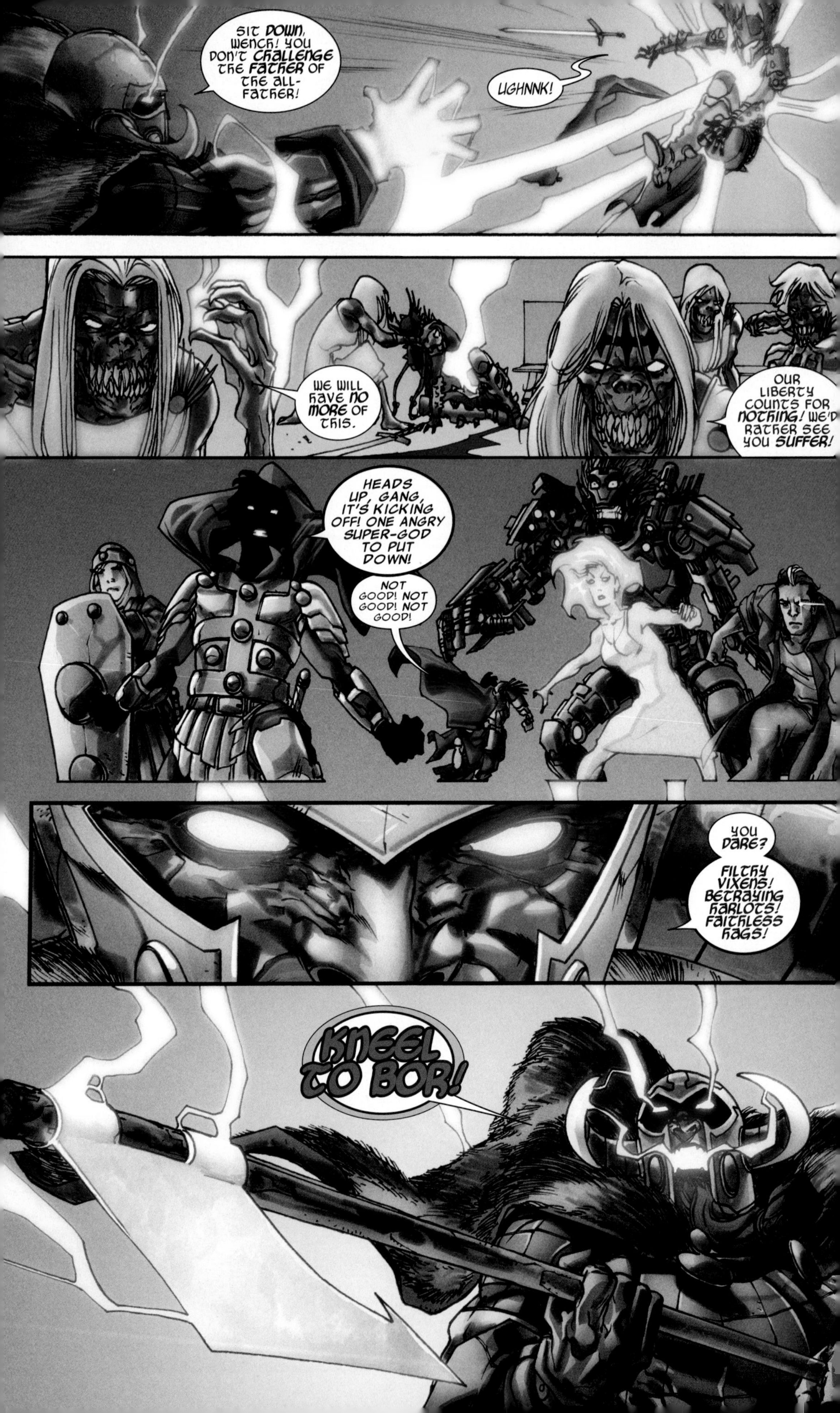
SIT DOWN, WENCH! YOU DON'T CHALLENGE THE FATHER OF THE ALL-FATHER!
UGHNNK!
WE WILL HAVE NO MORE OF THIS.
OUR LIBERTY COUNTS FOR NOTHING! WE'D RATHER SEE YOU SUFFER!
HEADS UP, GANG, IT'S KICKING OFF! ONE ANGRY SUPER-GOD TO PUT DOWN!
NOT GOOD! NOT GOOD! NOT GOOD!
YOU DARE?
FILTHY VIXENS! BETRAYING HARLOTS! FAITHLESS HAGS!
KNEEL TO BOR!

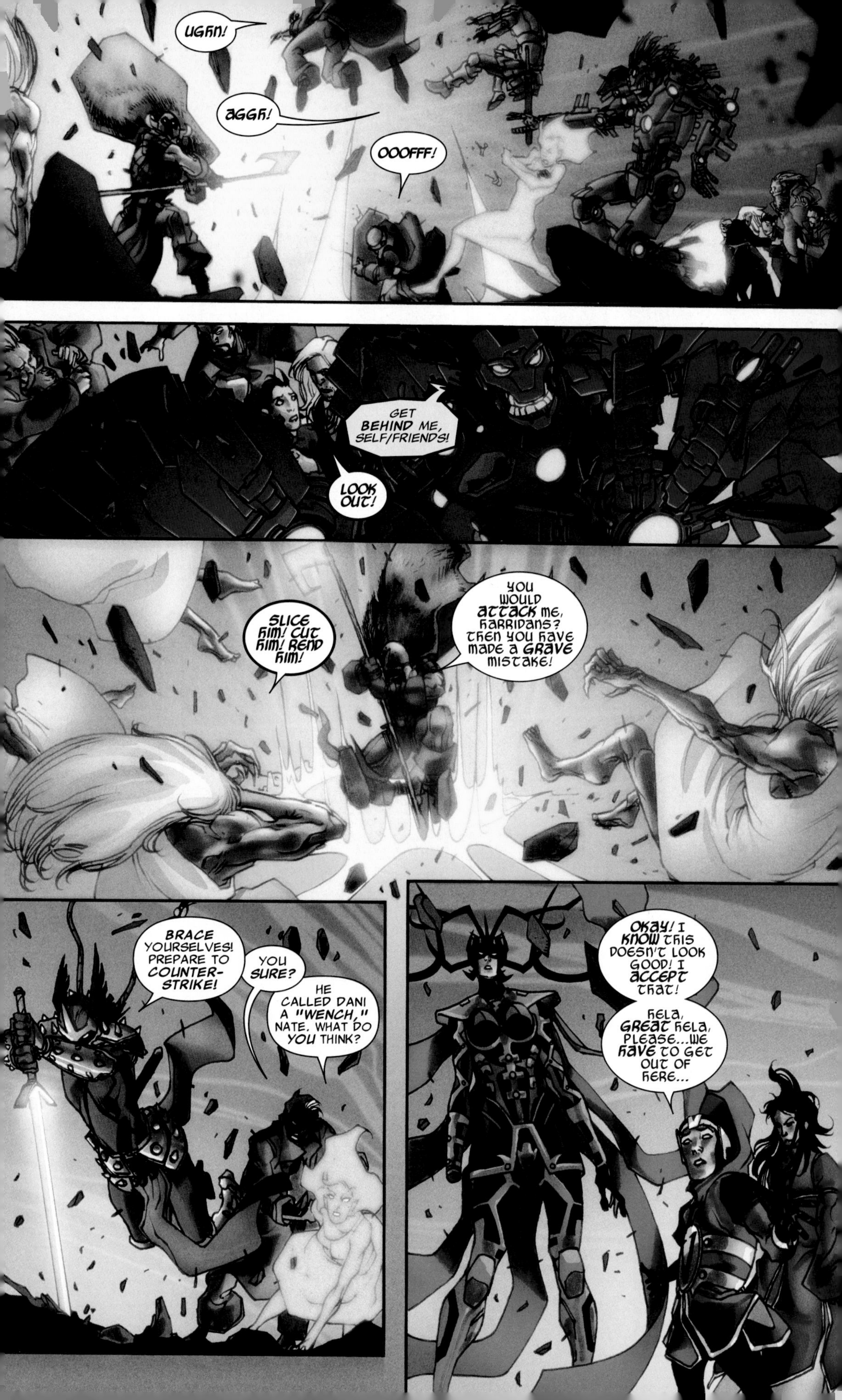
UGH!
AGGH!
OOOFFF!
GET BEHIND ME, SELF/FRIENDS!
LOOK OUT!
SLICE HIM! CUT HIM! REND HIM!
YOU WOULD ATTACK ME, HARRIDANS? THEN YOU HAVE MADE A GRAVE MISTAKE!
BRACE YOURSELVES! PREPARE TO COUNTER-STRIKE!
YOU SURE?
HE CALLED DANI A "WENCH," NATE. WHAT DO YOU THINK?
OKAY! I KNOW THIS DOESN'T LOOK GOOD! I ACCEPT THAT!
HELA, GREAT HELA, PLEASE...WE HAVE TO GET OUT OF HERE...

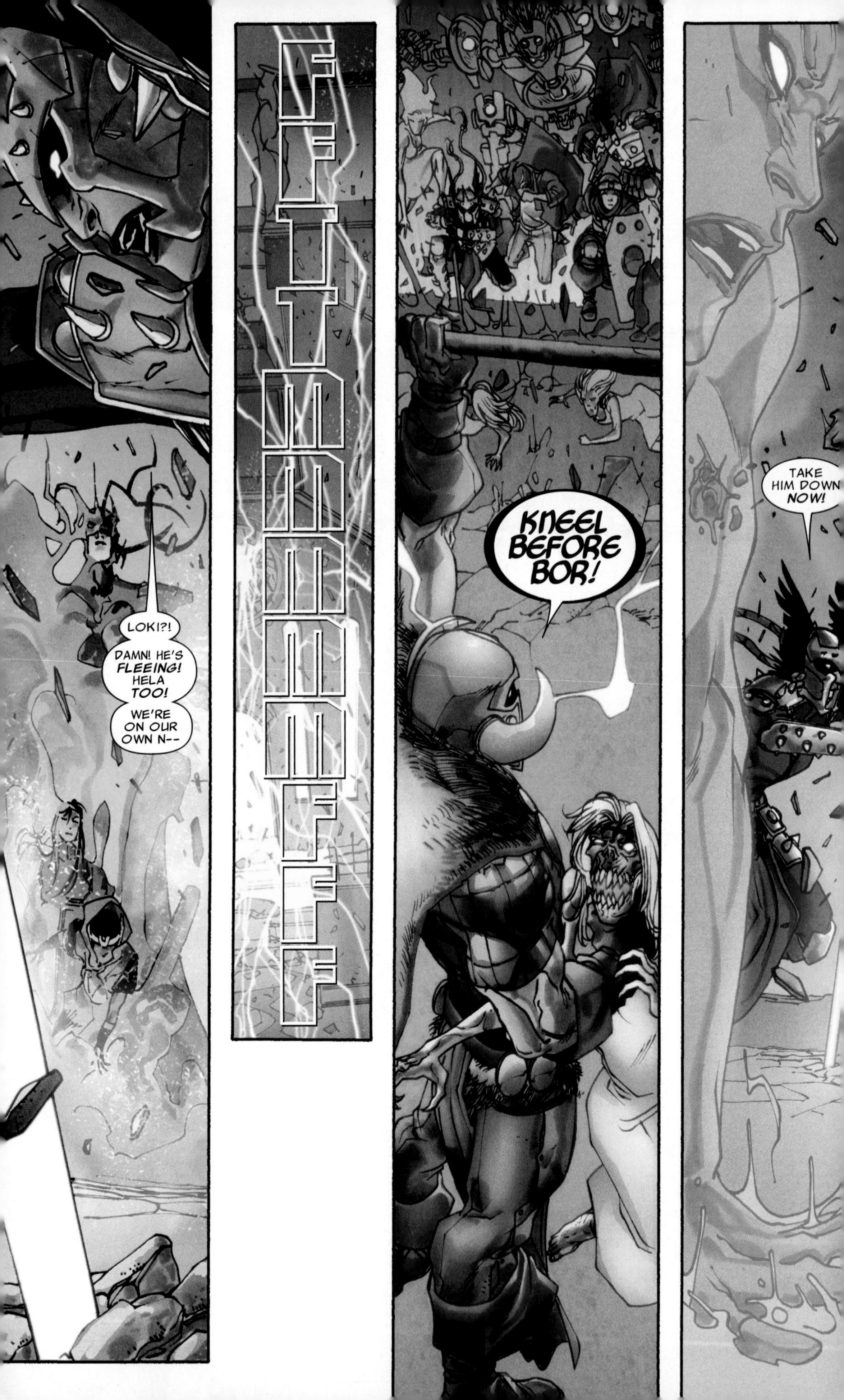
LOKI!?!
DAMN! HE'S FLEEING! HELA TOO!
WE'RE ON OUR OWN N--
FFTTHHMMMFFFF
KNEEL BEFORE BOR!
TAKE HIM DOWN NOW!

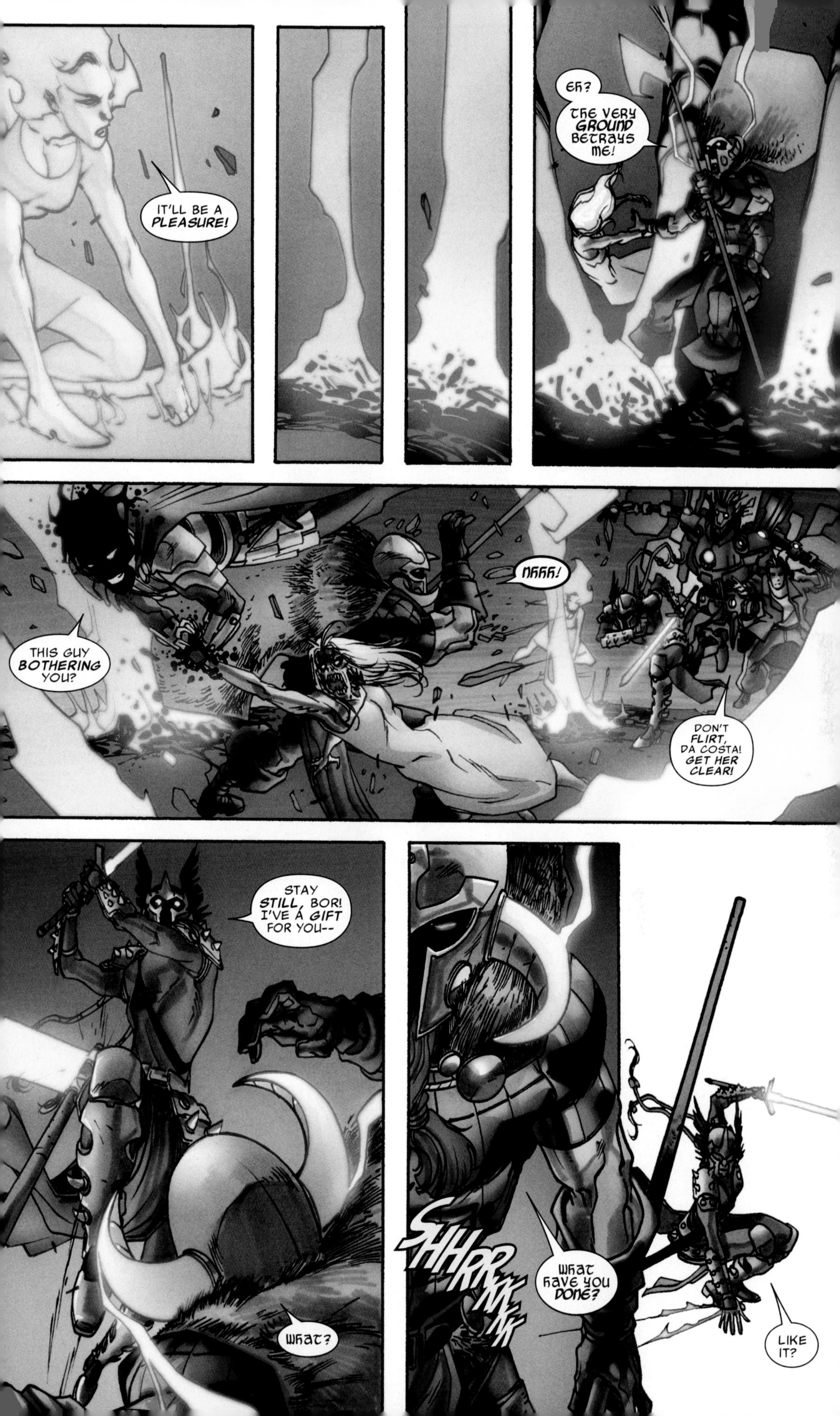
IT'LL BE A PLEASURE!
EH?
THE VERY GROUND BETRAYS ME!
THIS GUY BOTHERING YOU?
NHHH!
DON'T FLIRT, DA COSTA! GET HER CLEAR!
STAY STILL, BOR! I'VE A GIFT FOR YOU--
WHAT?
SHHRRKKK
WHAT HAVE YOU DONE?
LIKE IT?

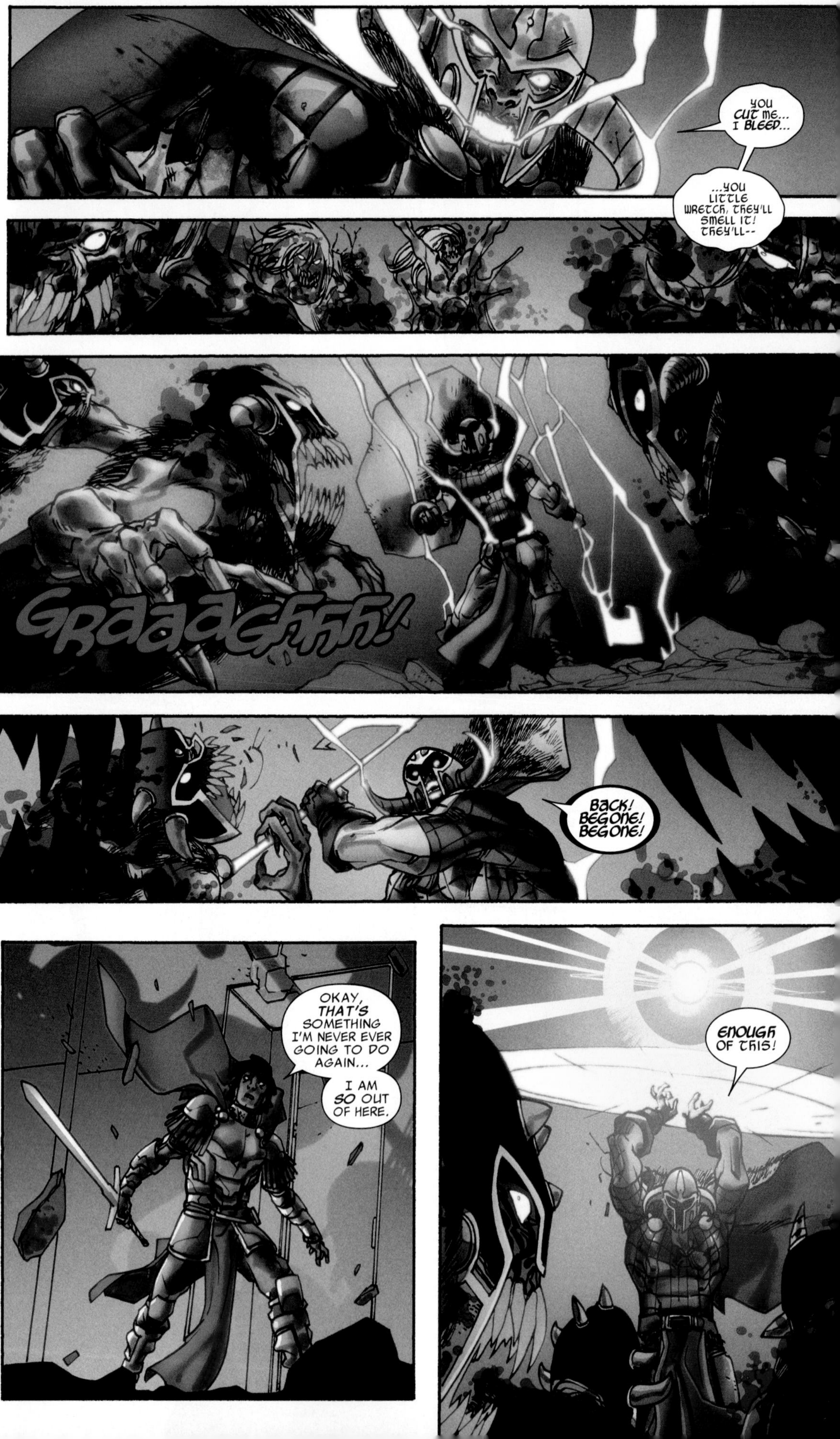

YOU CUT ME... I BLEED...
...YOU LITTLE WRETCH, THEY'LL SMELL IT! THEY'LL--
GRAAAGHHH!
BACK! BEGONE! BEGONE!
OKAY, THAT'S SOMETHING I'M NEVER EVER GOING TO DO AGAIN...
I AM SO OUT OF HERE.
ENOUGH OF THIS!

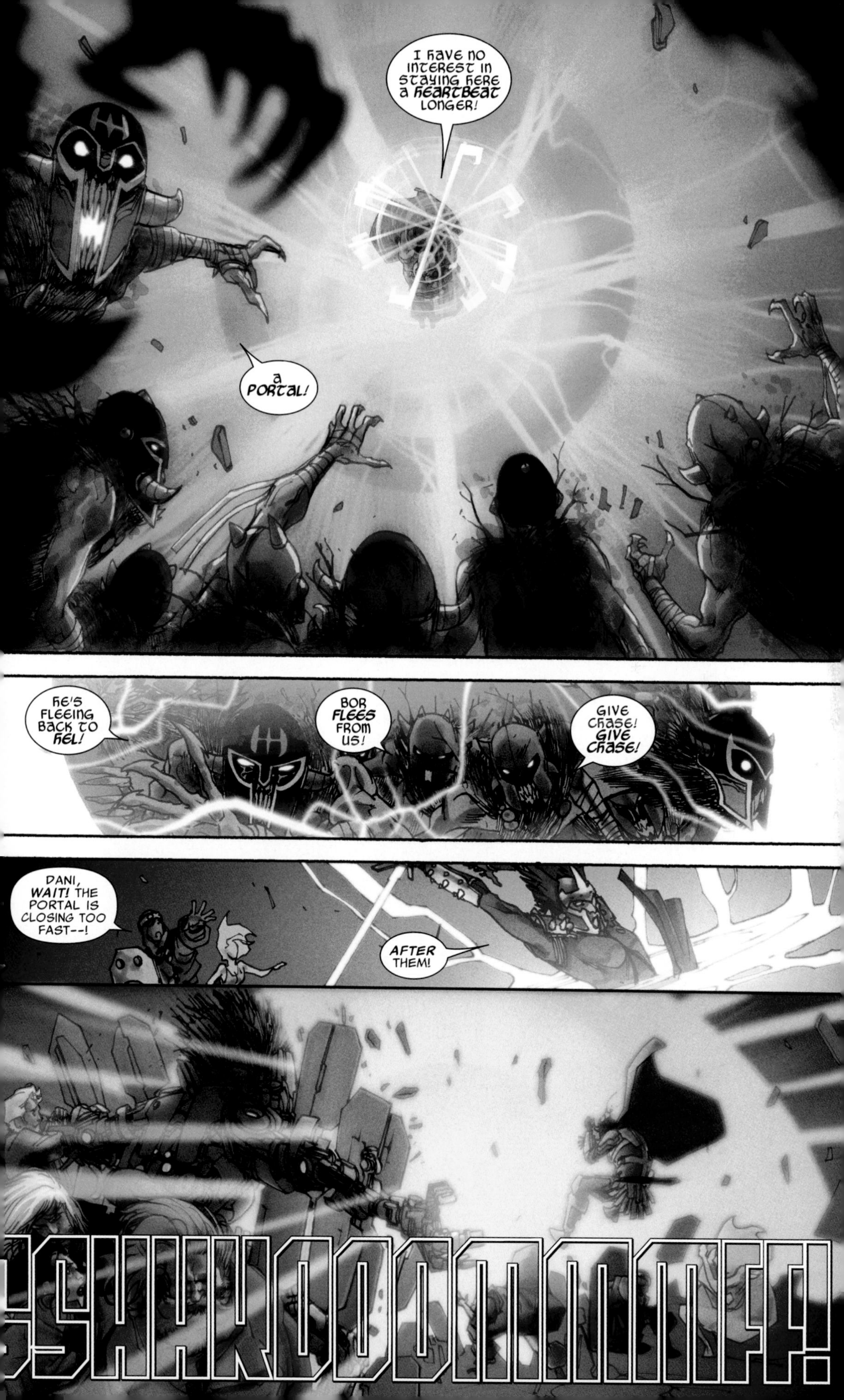
I HAVE NO INTEREST IN STAYING HERE A HEARTBEAT LONGER!
A PORTAL!
HE'S FLEEING BACK TO HEL!
BOR FLEES FROM US!
GIVE CHASE! GIVE CHASE!
DANI, WAIT! THE PORTAL IS CLOSING TOO FAST--!
AFTER THEM!
SHHKOOOMMMFF!

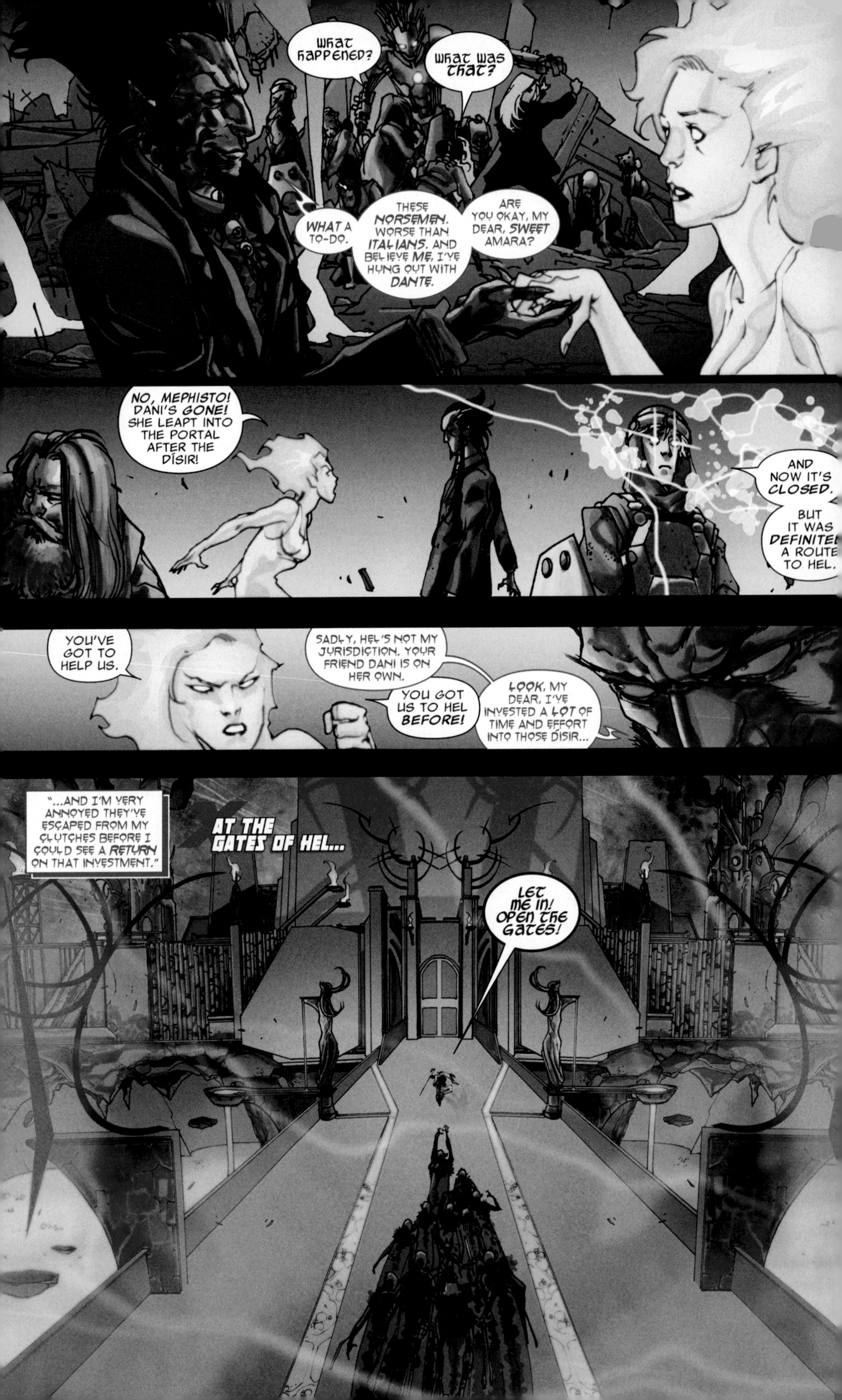
WHAT HAPPENED?
WHAT WAS THAT?
WHAT A TO-DO.
THESE NORSEMEN. WORSE THAN ITALIANS. AND BELIEVE ME, I'VE HUNG OUT WITH DANTE.
ARE YOU OKAY, MY DEAR, SWEET AMARA?
NO, MEPHISTO! DANI'S GONE! SHE LEAPT INTO THE PORTAL AFTER THE DÍSIR!
AND NOW IT'S CLOSED.
BUT IT WAS DEFINITE A ROUTE TO HEL.
YOU'VE GOT TO HELP US.
SADLY, HEL'S NOT MY JURISDICTION. YOUR FRIEND DANI IS ON HER OWN.
YOU GOT US TO HEL BEFORE!
LOOK, MY DEAR, I'VE INVESTED A LOT OF TIME AND EFFORT INTO THOSE DÍSIR...
"...AND I'M VERY ANNOYED THEY'VE ESCAPED FROM MY CLUTCHES BEFORE I COULD SEE A RETURN ON THAT INVESTMENT."
AT THE GATES OF HEL...
LET ME IN! OPEN THE GATES!

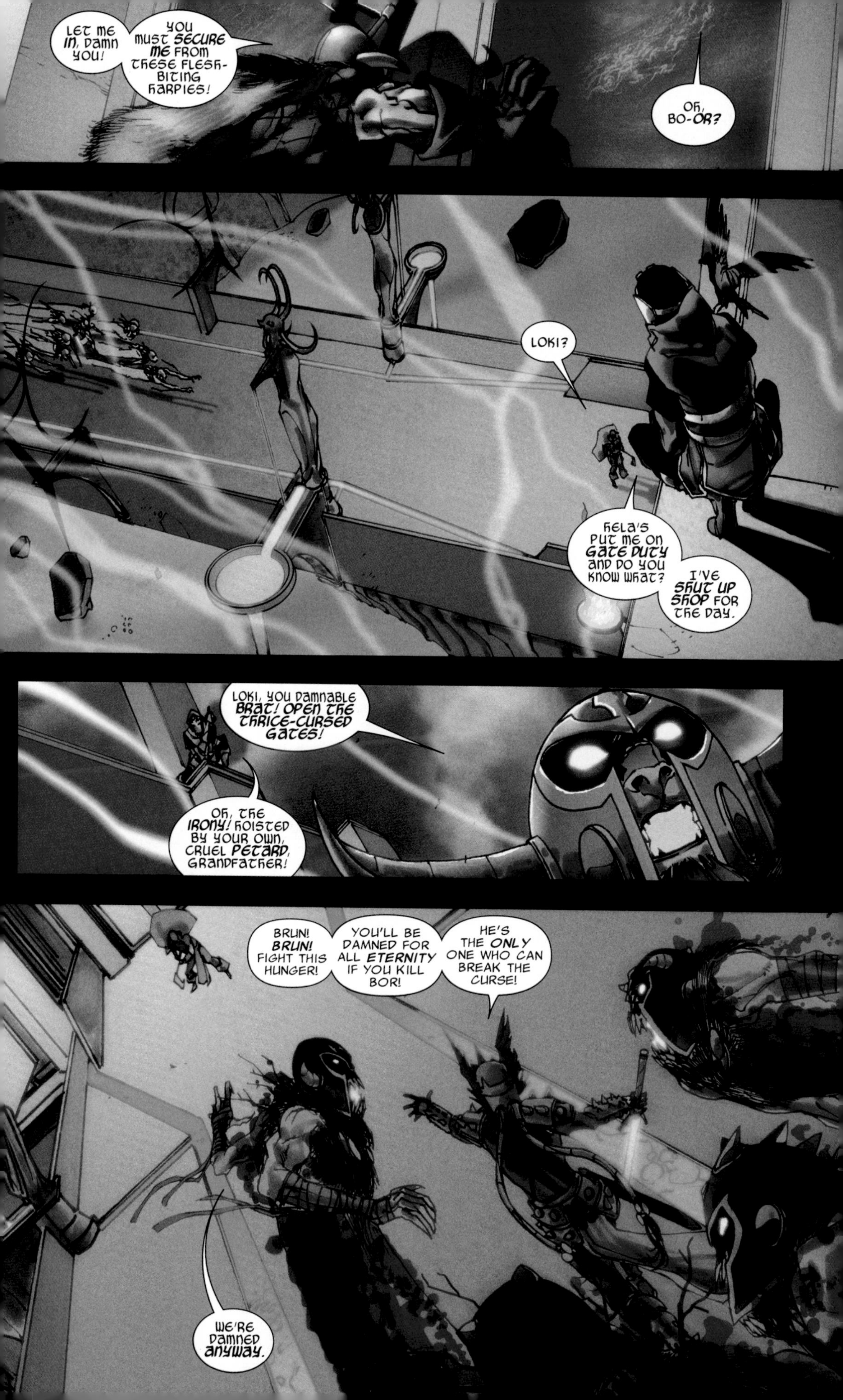
LET ME IN, DAMN YOU!
YOU MUST SECURE ME FROM THESE FLESH-BITING HARPIES!
OH, BO-OR?
LOKI?
HELA'S PUT ME ON GATE DUTY AND DO YOU KNOW WHAT?
I'VE SHUT UP SHOP FOR THE DAY.
LOKI, YOU DAMNABLE BRAT! OPEN THE THRICE-CURSED GATES!
OH, THE IRONY! HOISTED BY YOUR OWN, CRUEL PETARD, GRANDFATHER!
BRUN! BRUN! FIGHT THIS HUNGER!
YOU'LL BE DAMNED FOR ALL ETERNITY IF YOU KILL BOR!
HE'S THE ONLY ONE WHO CAN BREAK THE CURSE!
WE'RE DAMNED ANYWAY.

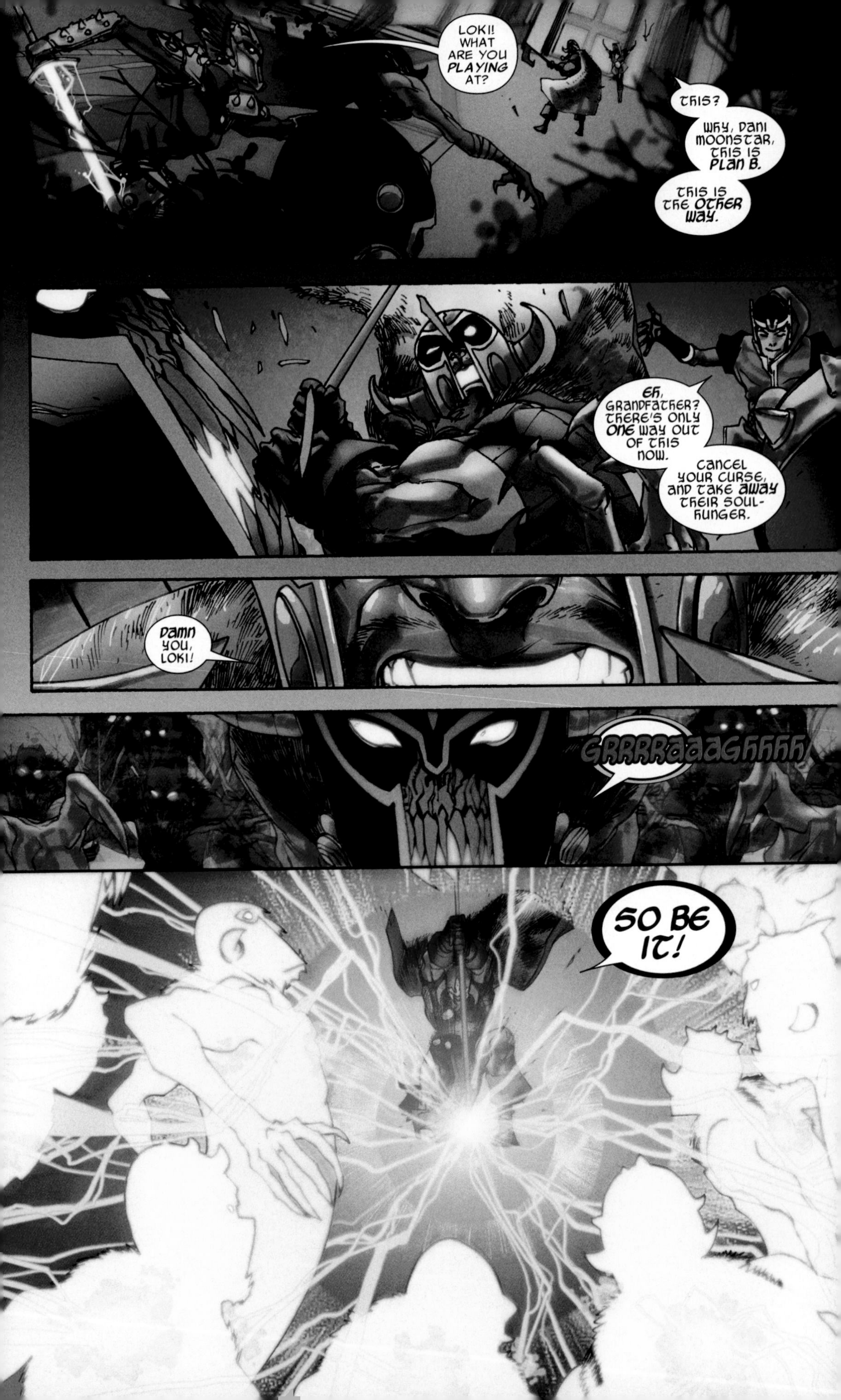
LOKI!! WHAT ARE YOU PLAYING AT?
THIS?
WHY, DANI MOONSTAR, THIS IS PLAN B.
THIS IS THE OTHER WAY.
EH, GRANDFATHER? THERE'S ONLY ONE WAY OUT OF THIS NOW.
CANCEL YOUR CURSE, AND TAKE AWAY THEIR SOUL-HUNGER.
DAMN YOU, LOKI!
GRRRRAAAAGHHHH
SO BE IT!

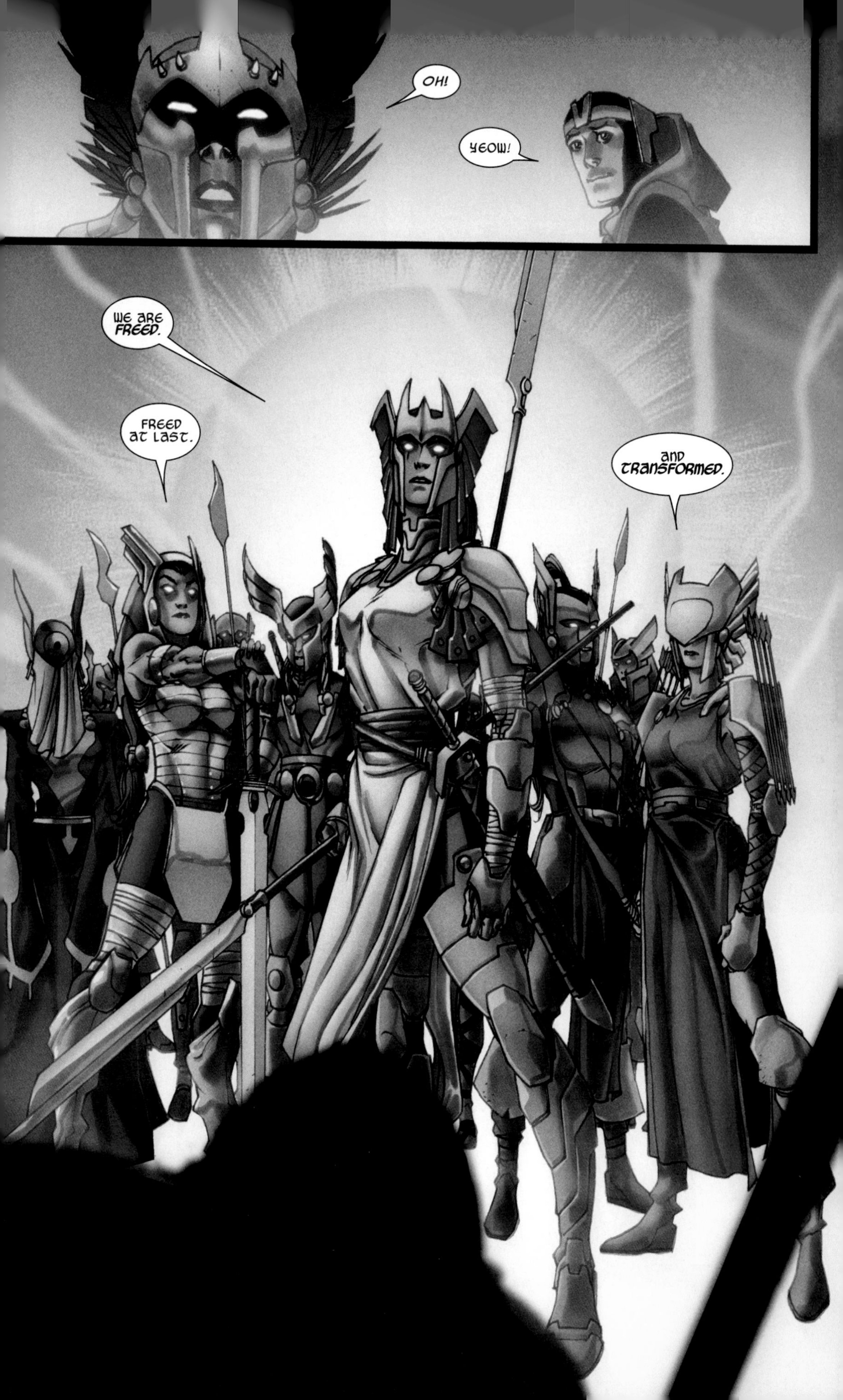
OH!
YEOW!
WE ARE FREED.
FREED AT LAST.
AND TRANSFORMED.

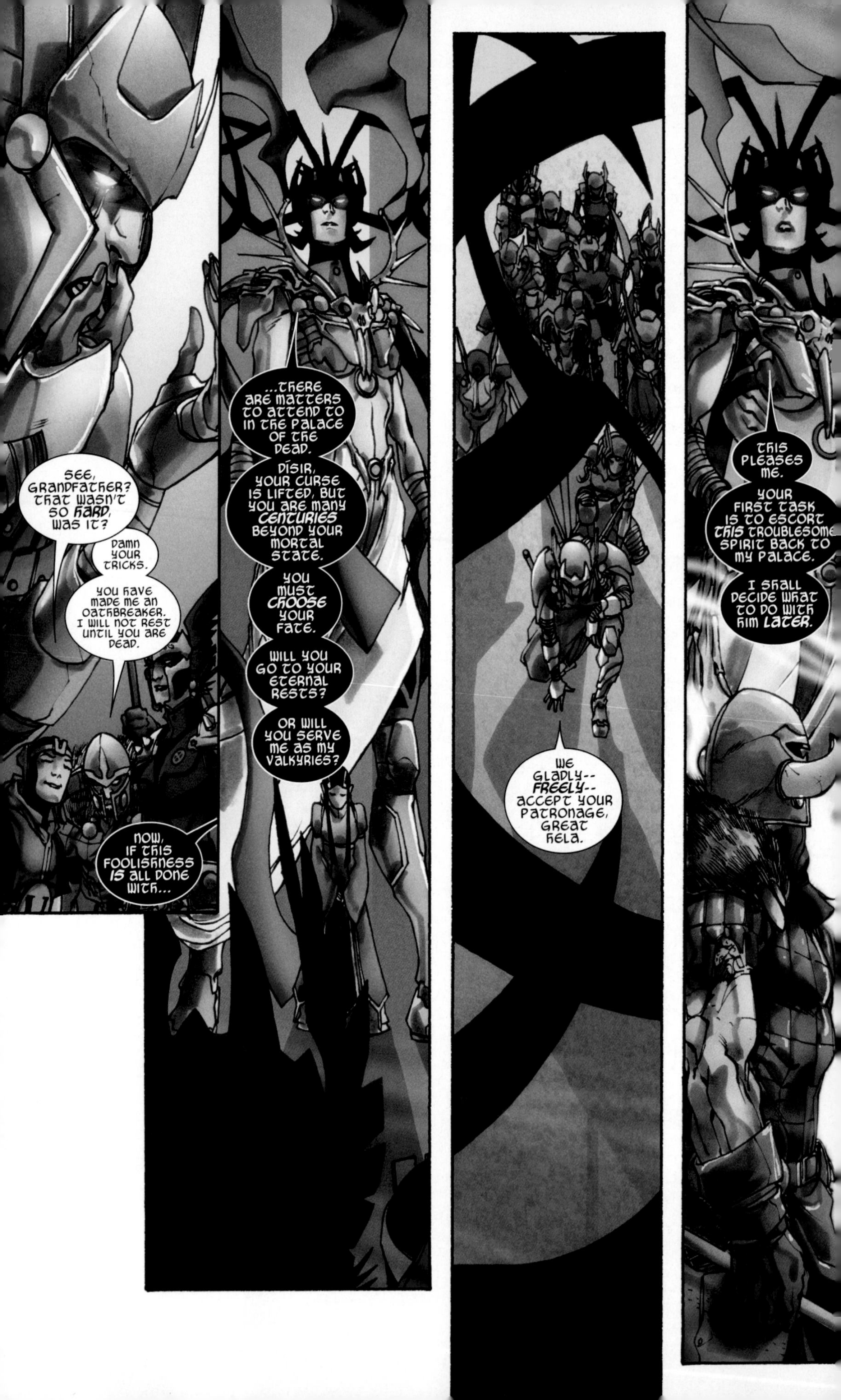

SEE, GRANDFATHER? THAT WASN'T SO HARD, WAS IT?
DAMN YOUR TRICKS.
YOU HAVE MADE ME AN OATHBREAKER. I WILL NOT REST UNTIL YOU ARE DEAD.
NOW, IF THIS FOOLISHNESS IS ALL DONE WITH...
...THERE ARE MATTERS TO ATTEND TO IN THE PALACE OF THE DEAD.
DÍSIR, YOUR CURSE IS LIFTED, BUT YOU ARE MANY CENTURIES BEYOND YOUR MORTAL STATE.
YOU MUST CHOOSE YOUR FATE.
WILL YOU GO TO YOUR ETERNAL RESTS?
OR WILL YOU SERVE ME AS MY VALKYRIES?
WE GLADLY-- FREELY-- ACCEPT YOUR PATRONAGE, GREAT HELA.
THIS PLEASES ME.
YOUR FIRST TASK IS TO ESCORT THIS TROUBLESOME SPIRIT BACK TO MY PALACE.
I SHALL DECIDE WHAT TO DO WITH HIM LATER.

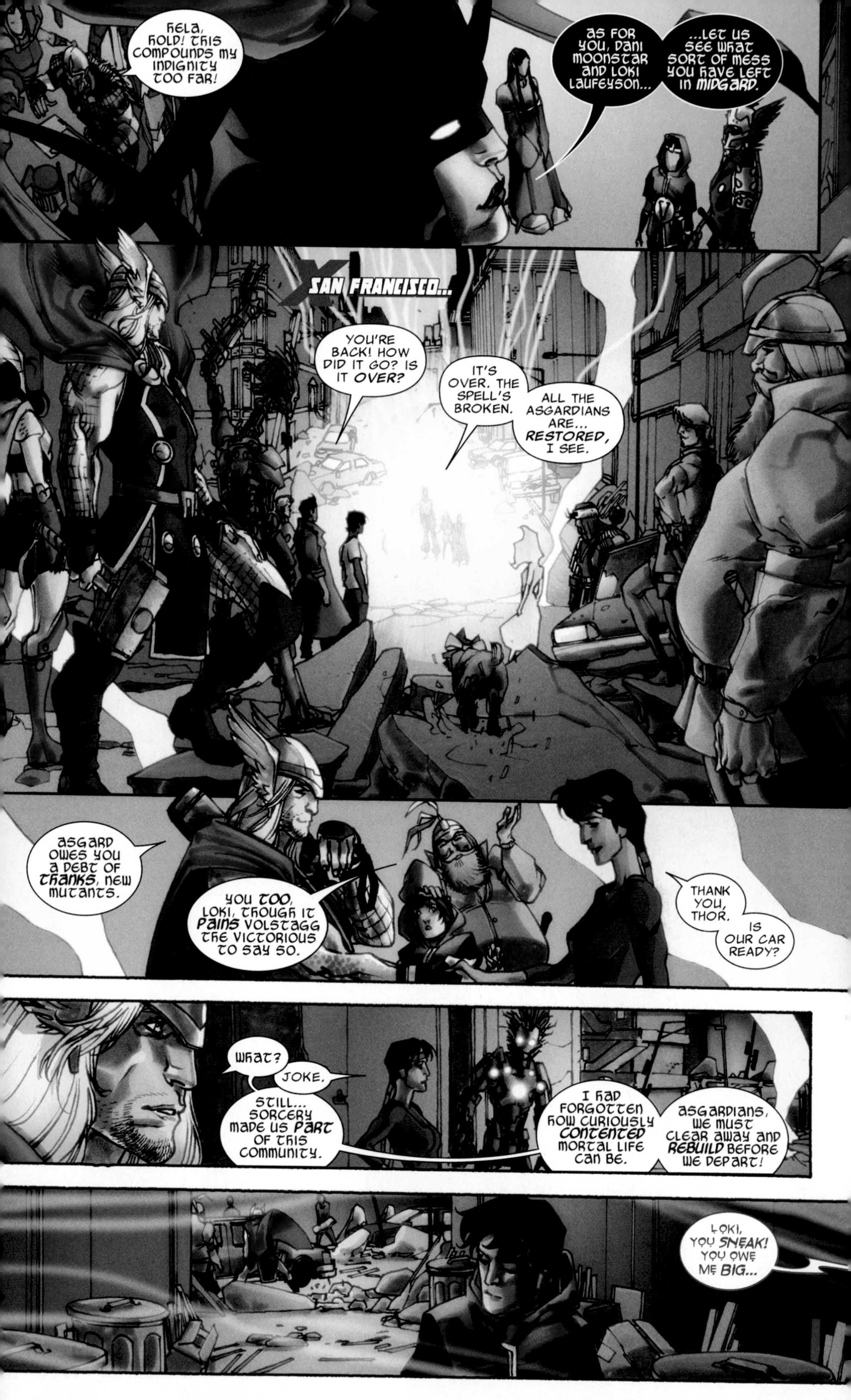

HELA, HOLD! THIS COMPOUNDS MY INDIGNITY TOO FAR!
AS FOR YOU, DANI MOONSTAR AND LOKI LAUFEYSON...
...LET US SEE WHAT SORT OF MESS YOU HAVE LEFT IN MIDGARD.
SAN FRANCISCO...
YOU'RE BACK! HOW DID IT GO? IS IT OVER?
IT'S OVER. THE SPELL'S BROKEN.
ALL THE ASGARDIANS ARE... RESTORED, I SEE.
ASGARD OWES YOU A DEBT OF THANKS, NEW MUTANTS.
YOU TOO, LOKI, THOUGH IT PAINS VOLSTAGG THE VICTORIOUS TO SAY SO.
THANK YOU, THOR.
IS OUR CAR READY?
WHAT?
JOKE.
STILL... SORCERY MADE US PART OF THIS COMMUNITY.
I HAD FORGOTTEN HOW CURIOUSLY CONTENTED MORTAL LIFE CAN BE.
ASGARDIANS, WE MUST CLEAR AWAY AND REBUILD BEFORE WE DEPART!
LOKI, YOU SNEAK! YOU OWE ME BIG...

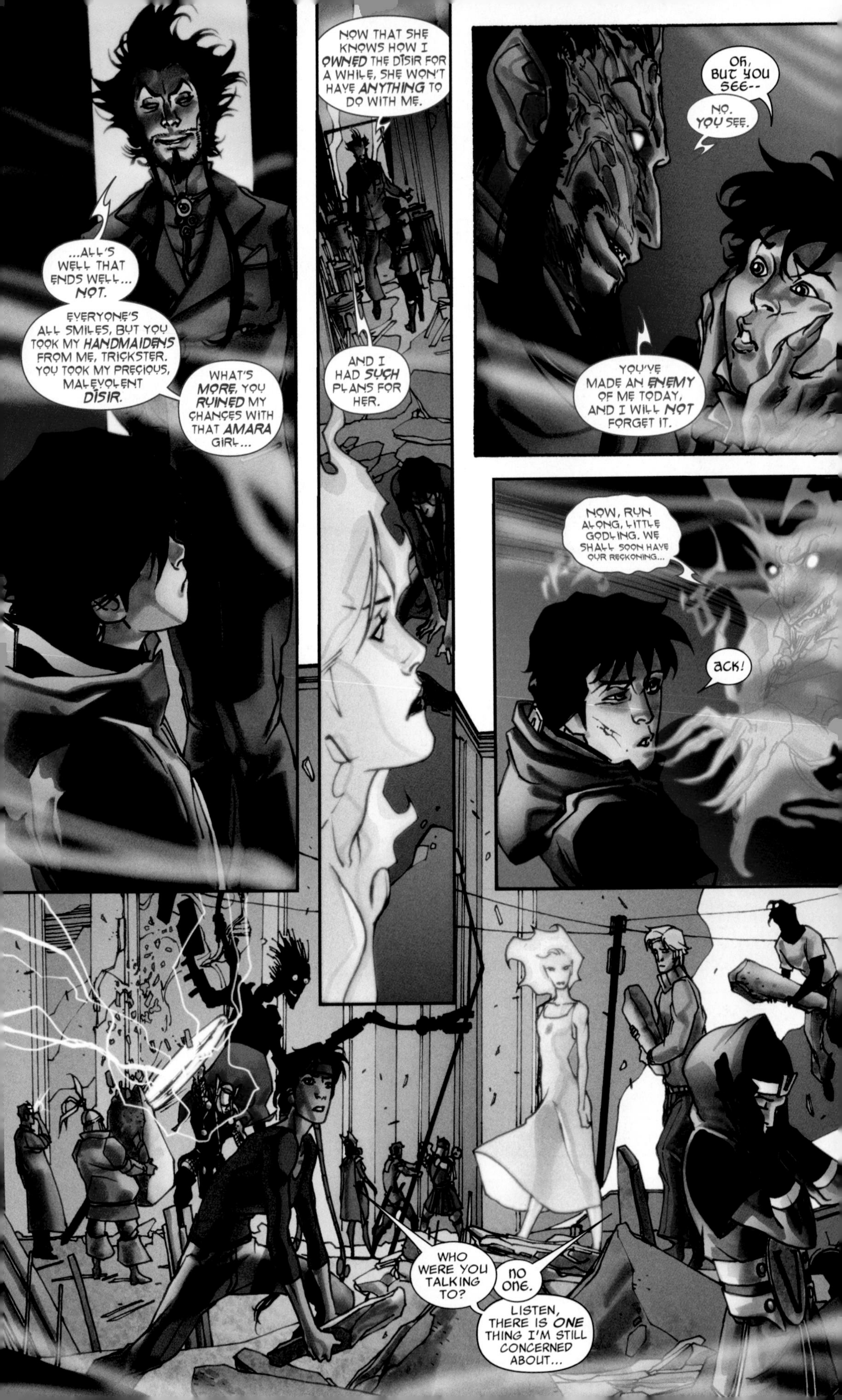
...ALL'S WELL THAT ENDS WELL... NOT.
EVERYONE'S ALL SMILES, BUT YOU TOOK MY HANDMAIDENS FROM ME, TRICKSTER. YOU TOOK MY PRECIOUS, MALEVOLENT DÍSIR.
WHAT'S MORE, YOU RUINED MY CHANCES WITH THAT AMARA GIRL...
NOW THAT SHE KNOWS HOW I OWNED THE DÍSIR FOR A WHILE, SHE WON'T HAVE ANYTHING TO DO WITH ME.
AND I HAD SUCH PLANS FOR HER.
OH, BUT YOU SEE--
NO. YOU SEE.
YOU'VE MADE AN ENEMY OF ME TODAY, AND I WILL NOT FORGET IT.
NOW, RUN ALONG, LITTLE GODLING. WE SHALL SOON HAVE OUR RECKONING...
ACK!
WHO WERE YOU TALKING TO?
NO ONE.
LISTEN, THERE IS ONE THING I'M STILL CONCERNED ABOUT...

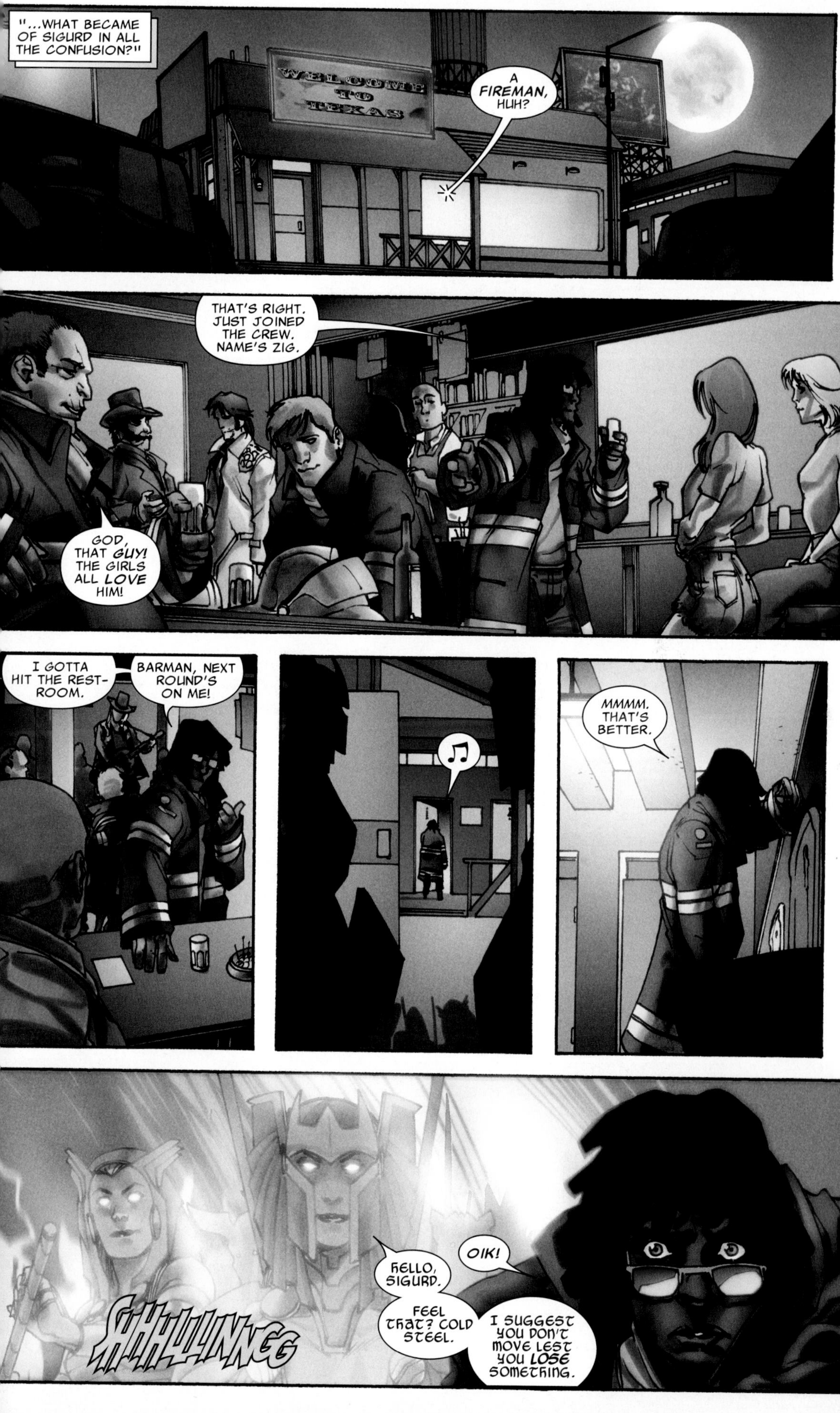
"...WHAT BECAME OF SIGURD IN ALL THE CONFUSION?"
WELCOME TO TEXAS
A FIREMAN, HUH?
THAT'S RIGHT. JUST JOINED THE CREW. NAME'S ZIG.
GOD, THAT GUY! THE GIRLS ALL LOVE HIM!
I GOTTA HIT THE REST-ROOM.
BARMAN, NEXT ROUND'S ON ME!
♫
MMMM. THAT'S BETTER.
HELLO, SIGURD.
OIK!
FEEL THAT? COLD STEEL.
I SUGGEST YOU DON'T MOVE LEST YOU LOSE SOMETHING.
SHHLLINNGG

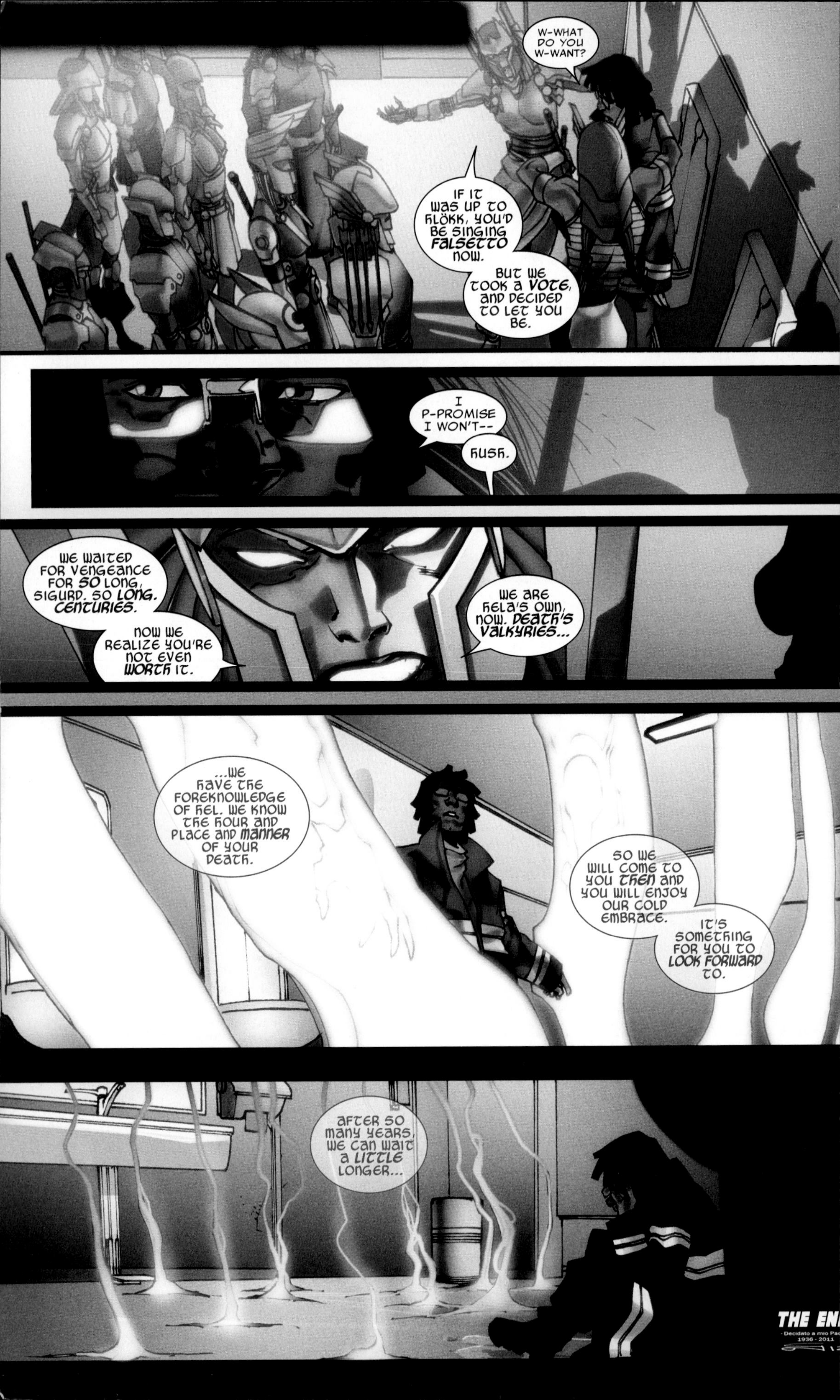
W-WHAT DO YOU W-WANT?
IF IT WAS UP TO FLÖKK, YOU'D BE SINGING FALSETTO NOW.
BUT WE TOOK A VOTE, AND DECIDED TO LET YOU BE.
I P-PROMISE I WON'T--
HUSH.
WE WAITED FOR VENGEANCE FOR SO LONG, SIGURD. SO LONG. CENTURIES.
NOW WE REALIZE YOU'RE NOT EVEN WORTH IT.
WE ARE HELA'S OWN, NOW. DEATH'S VALKYRIES...
...WE HAVE THE FOREKNOWLEDGE OF HEL. WE KNOW THE HOUR AND PLACE AND MANNER OF YOUR DEATH.
SO WE WILL COME TO YOU THEN AND YOU WILL ENJOY OUR COLD EMBRACE.
IT'S SOMETHING FOR YOU TO LOOK FORWARD TO.
AFTER SO MANY YEARS, WE CAN WAIT A LITTLE LONGER...
THE EN
1936 - 2011

CONNECTED COVER ART BY STEPHANIE HANS

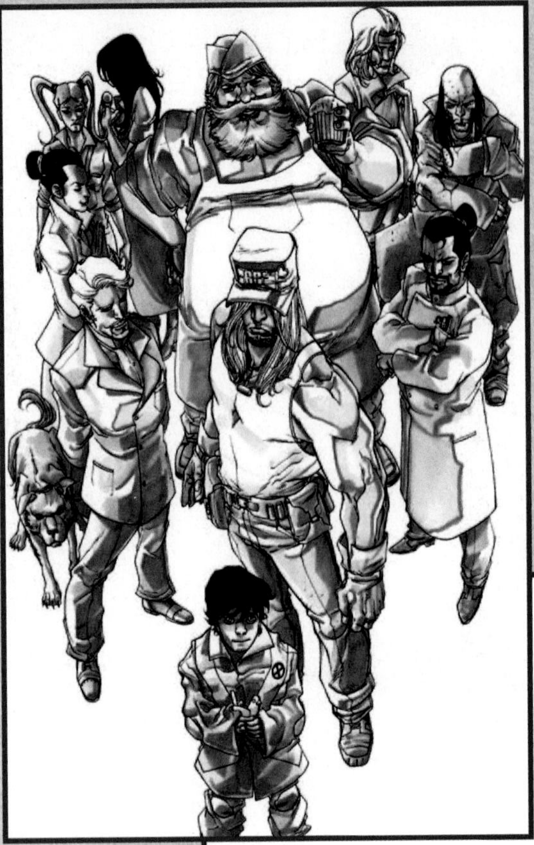

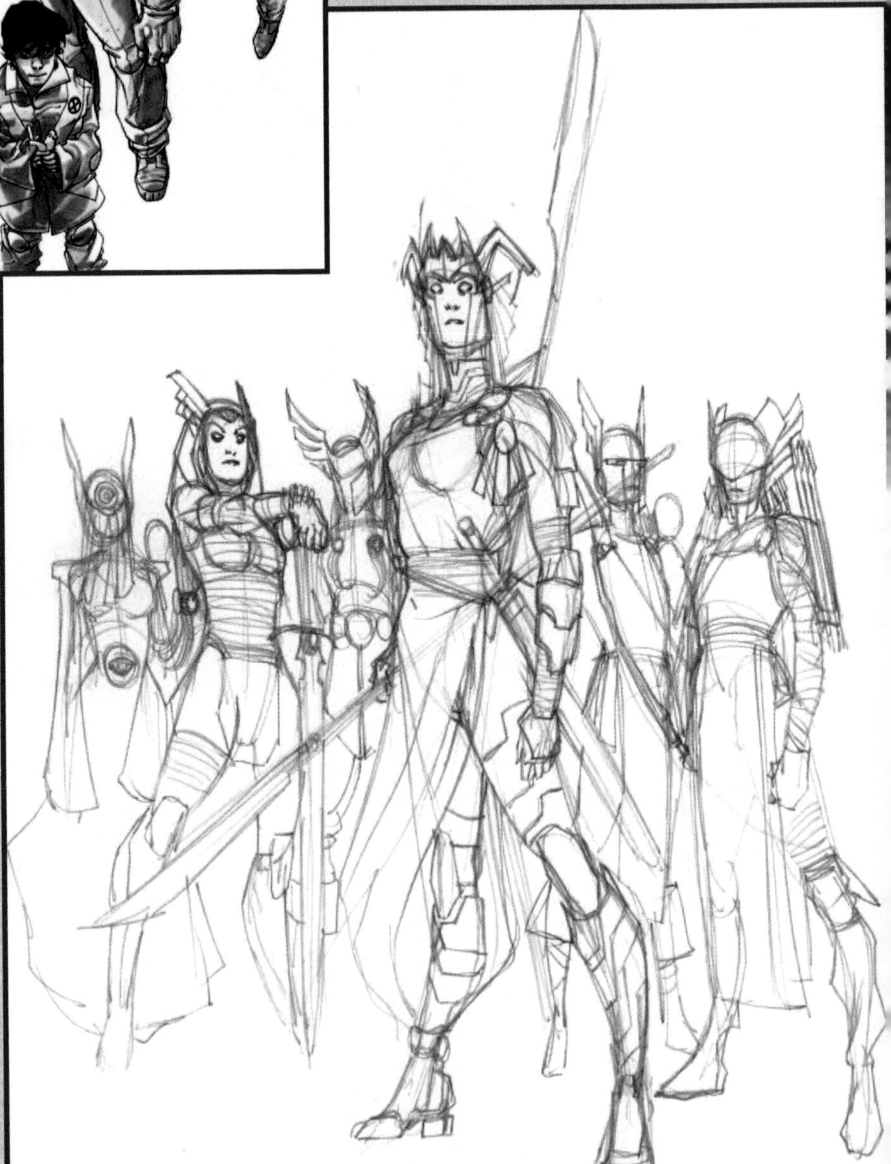

CHARACTER SKETCHES BY CARMINE DI GIANDOMENICO